BUSINESS STUDIES

A NEW APPROACH

STEVE ROBERTSON

Causeway Press Limited

Causeway Press Limited
PO Box 13, Ormskirk, Lancs, L39 5HP
©Steve Robertson
1st Impression 1988

British Library Cataloguing in Publication Data

Robertson, Steve
  Business Studies.
  1. Business studies – For schools
  I. Title
  658

  ISBN 0-946183-38-4

Typesetting by Chapterhouse, Formby, L37 3PX
Printed and bound by The Alden Press, Oxford.

Contents

Unit 1 Industry in the Economy   1
Part 1 How industry creates wealth   2
Part 2 Economic systems   4
Part 3 The development of business activity   6
Part 4 Stages of production   10

Unit 2 The Structure of Industry   13
Part 1 The private sector   14
Part 2 The public sector   20
Part 3 Internal organisation   22

Unit 3 The Firm and its Market   31
Part 1 The nature of marketing   32
Part 2 Market research   33
Part 3 The product   39
Part 4 Advertising and promotion   45
Part 5 Distribution   55
Part 6 Market pricing   63

Unit 4 Production Decisions   67
Part 1 The method of production   68
Part 2 The scale of production   74
Part 3 The location of production   79

Unit 5 People in Organisations   84
Part 1 Labour needs   85
Part 2 Recruitment   86
Part 3 Training   91
Part 4 Salaries and motivation   94
Part 5 Workplace communication   102
Part 6 Worker participation and trade unions   108

Unit 6 Finance and the Firm   117
Part 1 Sources of finance   118
Part 2 Uses of finance   127
Part 3 Published accounts   130
Part 4 Management accounting   137

Unit 7 External Influences on the Firm   143
Part 1 Economic considerations   144
Part 2 Political considerations   151
Part 3 Technological considerations   155
Part 4 Social considerations   158
Part 5 Legal considerations   164

Index   173

Acknowledgements

The author and publisher would like to thank the following for permission to reproduce copyright material, photographs and artwork.

Advisory, Conciliation and Arbitration Service
   pp. 87, 115
Advertising Association p. 47
Advertising Standards Authority pp. 49, 50, 53
Association of British Travel Agents p. 168

The Bank of England p. 137
Barclays Bank plc p. 60
Eve Barker/Artworkers p. 113
BBC Hulton Picture Library p. 111
Birds Eye/Wall's p. 44
British Coal p. 10
British Petroleum Oil Ltd p. 55
British Railways Board pp. 55, 61
British Standards Institute p. 72
British Telecom pp. 55, 131, 132
BTR plc p. 55
Business Statistics Office p. 59

Cadbury Ltd p. 31
Central Television p. 29
Colin/REA p. 157
Computerland Europe SA p. 61
Co-operative Union Ltd p. 19
Consumer news p. 165
Crown Copyright. Reproduced by permission of
   the Controller of Her Majesty's Stationery
   Office pp. 20, 33, 144, 146, 151, 160

Daily Mail p. 162
Department of Employment p. 151
Department of Trade and Industry p. 136

Eastleigh College of Further Education p. 88
The Economist p. 9
Employment News pp. 11, 84, 92, 149, 159

Ford Motor Company Ltd pp. 10, 67, 68, 134
Fotomas Index p. 110
Free Association Books p. 8

Mike Gibbons p. 57
The Guardian/Manchester Evening News p. 154

Ingrid Hamer p. 59
The Henley Centre for Forecasting Ltd p. 56
The History of Advertising p. 51

Inter-Bank Research Organisation p. 60
The Independent p. 121

Lloyds Bank plc p. 55

Malliac/REA p. 157
Marks and Spencer plc pp. 55, 57
Mercedes-Benz (United Kingdom) Ltd
   (Trademark property of Daimler-Benz, AG
   Stuttgart, Federal Republic of Germany.)
   p. 55
Merseyside and North Wales Electricity Board
   p. 10
Metal Box plc p. 94
Midland Bank plc pp. 25, 55, 124
Mirror Group Newspapers p. 52
Motor Agents Association p. 168

National Westminster Bank p. 163
NEC Business Systems (Europe) Ltd p. 108
New Society pp. 100, 109
Novamark International Ltd p. 42

Proctor and Gamble Ltd pp. 39, 102
Reproduced by permission of Punch p. 102

Rowntree plc pp. 25–3 photographs, 45, 156
RTH McCann GUS Transport p. 61

Malcolm Sanders Design and Photography
   p. 120
Shell UK Oil p. 55
Sunday Telegraph p. 88

The Tobacco Advisory Council p. 143
Today Newspaper p. 92 – photograph

Unilever plc p. 123

Warrington–Runcorn New Town p. 82
WH Smith Ltd p. 129

Cartoons drawn by John Taylor, Studio Mitre.

Graphics and cover by Windridge and Jane.

Every effort has been made to locate the copyright owners of material quoted or used in the text. Any omissions brought to the attention of the publisher are regretted and will be credited in subsequent printings.

Preface

This book has been written in such a way as to reflect the needs of the reader as well as the demands of the subject. Whilst providing a comprehensive coverage of the syllabus for all GCSE boards, therefore, it has also been organised in such a way as to follow a logical sequence and to allow easy reference to specific topics.

The layout of the book means that it will also be of use to students studying for examinations other than GCSE. It can be used as an introductory text for those studying at a higher level, and relevant sections of the book can be incorporated into other subjects.

Business studies is about the real world of work and, wherever possible, real world examples have been used in the text. To get the best out of this book, the reader should therefore continually attempt to relate the topics being covered to the world of industry and commerce. To do this, students should make full use of newspapers and magazines. They should also be prepared to talk to friends and relations about their experiences of business.

Another feature of this book is a wide range of **activities** contained within the text. These activities should not be ignored as they serve two important functions:

- Some of the activities act as a check on what has been learned and test the student's ability to apply what has been learned to a practical situation. This allows gaps in understanding to be pinpointed so that they can be revised.
- Other activities allow the student to 'learn by doing'. A number of topics are therefore introduced by means of an activity and students can identify for themselves the main points which need to be explored in more detail.

Although a variety of activities are provided, teachers will want to be flexible in the way in which they use these activities and may well want to make use of a GCSE workbook such as **Coursework in Business Studies and Commerce**, by Diane Wallace. They may also want to use material provided in this book in a rather different way – possibly by making up their own questions.

The independent student may also wish to take a flexible approach to using this text and not work slavishly from cover to cover. It is important, however, that the reader takes an active approach to studying and does something with the subject matter. This could involve completing the activities, marking the text, talking to other people and relating what you are learning to the real world.

Each unit of the book is introduced by means of a **case study**. These case studies are designed to introduce the main topics contained within the unit and to demonstrate how the various topics link together.

It is important to remember that business studies is not a series of separate topics such as marketing, finance and production; but that all of these elements are linked together in providing an understanding of the way in which business operates.

At the end of each unit is a **quick quiz**. This acts as a final check on your understanding of the key topics contained in the unit. It will help you to identity those topics which you need to refer to again and will be particularly valuable at revision time.

The list of questions is by no means comprehensive, and it would be useful if you could add further questions which you feel that you should be able to answer by the time you have reached the end of each unit.

Symbols have been used to identify the different types of actitity. These are:

 Group activities

 Research/investigation

 Individual exercises

 Role play

 Discussions/debates

Case Study: Alan and Judith

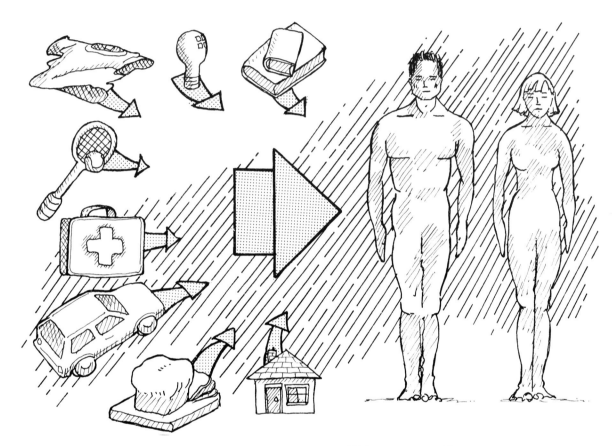

Alan and Judith live in Westbury. They work in the town's car manufacturing factory and live in a two bedroomed house near the town centre. They are both 26 years old; Alan earns £12,500 a year and Judith £9,000. They usually shop on a Saturday at the supermarket and go out once or twice a week. Next year they hope to move to a larger house, as they expect their salaries to increase.

Both Alan and Judith are involved in local community activities and they are also members of a political party.

Alan and Judith live in an industrial society. Industry provides them with employment and pays their wages. This allows them to share in the country's wealth (the goods and services produced by industry).

This example illustrates the different roles which individuals play in the economy:

● As consumers – they demand the goods and services produced by industry.
● As producers – they have a vital role to play in the production of these goods and services.
● As voters – they influence the decisions made by the government and local authorities.

1 What do you think are Alan and Judith's most important needs?
2 What is the difference between their most important needs and other wants they may have?
3 Why can't they satisfy all of their wants and needs?

Part 1 How industry creates wealth

Business studies is the study of how wealth is created and distributed. Wealth does not just mean money but anything which it is possible to sell. We can see this from the case study. An individual's wealth may include a car and a house. A community's wealth may include hospitals, roads, resources and even the skills of the population.

Wealth has a value and can be exchanged for money. Money allows the ownership of wealth to be transferred. When workers produce goods they are entitled to a share of what they produce. A car worker, for example, is entitled to a share of car production. It is more practical, however, to pay the worker a sum of money which represents the value of his or her output. The worker could then exchange this for cars, but it is more likely to be exchanged for a range of goods. A portion of his or her income will be taken by the government in taxes or rates and redistributed to others, or it may be spent on such things as defence and housing.

The nature of production

Production is the changing of resources into goods and services. It is individual firms that make decisions concerning what to produce, how to produce and where to produce.

All firms have inputs and outputs. The inputs are the raw materials and components which the firm uses and the outputs are the goods and services they produce. These are sold to consumers, the government and other firms. The resources available to firms are known as the factors of production. There are four main categories:

● **Land** – This term is used for all natural resources and includes mineral deposits, forests, building land and even the sea. Owners of land receive rent for their services.
● **Labour** – Labour refers to all human mental and physical effort and is rewarded with wages.
● **Capital** – This refers to man-made resources which are not wanted for their own sake but for their contribution to output, eg factories and machines. The owners of capital are rewarded with interest.
● **Enterprise** – Although carried out by people, enterprise is seen as a separate factor of production as it involves the organisation of all other factors of production. This requires making decisions such as how much of each factor should be employed and how much of a risk is to be taken. Entrepreneurs are rewarded with profit.

Place the following resources under the headings land, labour, capital and enterprise.

a A nurse.
b A lathe.
c The owner of a corner shop.
d A factory building.
e A pine forest.
f Coal deposits.
g A shop assistant.
h A factory worker.
i An electrician's screwdriver.
j A shareholder in ICI.

Figure 1: The nature of production

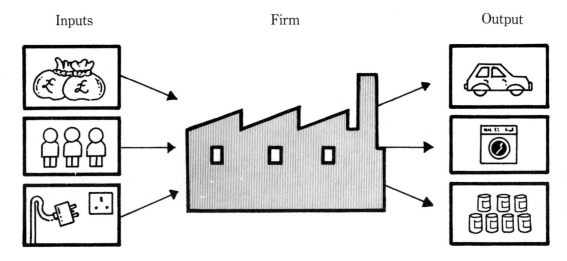

Inputs   Firm   Output

When a firm takes resources and converts them into final goods and services they add value to these resources. A carpenter, for example, may take wood which he buys for £10 and convert it into a table which he sells for £16. He has added £6 to the value of this wood. This does not all represent profit. Most if it will go to pay the factors of production which are used by the carpenter. There is the cost of his own labour and that of any assistants he may employ, together with his overheads such as power and the rent of his buildings. This value added is the wealth that the carpenter has created.

Figure 2: Value added

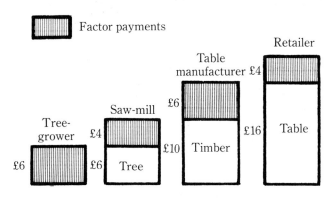

Figure 3: The creation and distribution of wealth

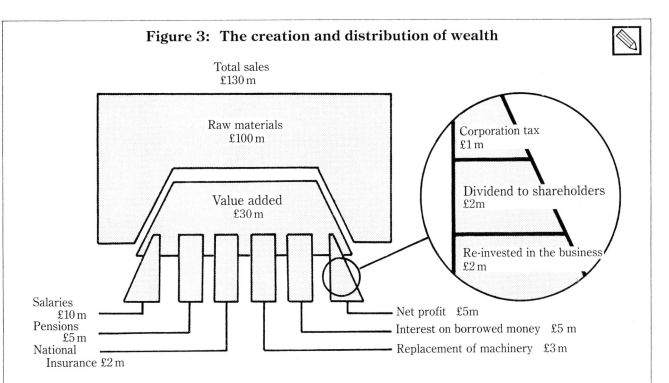

Figure 3 shows how a firm creates and distributes wealth. The firm has bought raw materials and services costing £100m and its finished products are sold for £130m. The difference between the costs and the sales revenue is the value added of £30m.

Some of this is used to pay wages, pensions, interest on borrowed money and for the replacement of equipment. This leaves a profit of £5m. Some of this goes in taxation, some goes to shareholders and the remainder is reinvested in the business.

1 What is meant by the terms:

   a value added?
   b net profit?

2 What proportion of the firm's value added goes to:

   a its workers?
   b its shareholders?

3 A school shop buys Mars bars at £7 for a box of 50. These are sold at 20p each. Over a week the shop sells two boxes. Half of the profit is placed in school funds. The other half is used to increase the stocks held in the shop. Draw a simple diagram to illustrate:

   a the value added over the week
   b the distribution of value added.

The firm and its markets

As we saw earlier, firms act as a link between consumers and resources. They make decisions about what goods people want to buy and they then obtain the resources they need to produce these goods. The goods are then sold to the customers.

It must be remembered that many firms do not serve the public directly but produce goods and provide services to other business organisations.

Whenever buyers and sellers come together we say that a **market** exists and there are three main types of market in which a firm operates:

● **Factor markets** – where resources such as labour, raw materials and capital are bought and sold.
● **Product markets** – where goods and services are sold to consumers.
● **Financial markets** – where money is provided to help firms to grow.

Part 2   Economic systems

All communities face the same problem. The resources necessary to produce goods are limited, but the wants of the individuals who make up that community are infinite. Choices therefore have to be made as to what these scarce resources are to be used to produce, how they are to be combined in producing these goods and how this output is to be distributed.

In considering the problem of scarcity and choice we meet with the idea of **opportunity costs**. Each individual has a limited income which represents his or her claim on the nation's wealth. By spending income on one particular good, however, the individual is giving up the opportunity to buy other goods. You may be able to use your pocket money to buy more records, for example, but in doing so you will have less money to buy magazines or clothes.

The true cost of deciding to buy more records is the satisfaction which you have given up by not buying the alternative goods. This is known as the opportunity cost.

Opportunity cost is also important for a firm to consider. If it decides to use its reinvested profits to purchase a new machine, for example, it needs to consider the other uses that could have been made of that money such as investing outside the company.

The free enterprise economy

This is an economy in which firms are free to respond to the needs of consumers. Consumers express their preferences from amongst the goods on offer by buying those that they want most in the product markets. Firms producing these goods will spend the revenue they receive

Put yourself in the position of a 15 year old student earning £20 per month from a Saturday job on a fruit and vegetable stall in the local market. Decide how you would spend this income and draw up a table similar to Figure 4.

Figure 4: Monthly income and expenditure

Expenditure	(£)	Income	(£)
Records/tapes	2	Saturday job	20
Food/drink	3		
Clothes	5		
Entertainment	6		
Savings	4		
	20		20

Answer the following:

1 a What would be the opportunity cost of saving an extra two pounds?
   b What are the benefits of increased savings?

2 a What would be the opportunity cost to your employer of increasing your wage to £24 per month?
   b What might be the benefits to your employer of paying you a higher wage?

3 a What is the opportunity cost of staying on at school after the age of 16?
   b What are the benefits to you and to the community which would result from you staying on at school?

in the factor markets. Producers of popular goods will be able to buy more and more resources and so increase output. Producers of goods which are declining in popularity will be able to purchase fewer resources and will contract or go out of business completely. Hence it is only the goods that people want to buy that will be produced.

Decisions as to how to produce and where to produce will also be taken by the firm. These decisions will be based on the profit motive. Firms seeking to maximise their profits will produce in the most efficient way to keep down costs. Hence if it is profitable to use more machines and less labour then they will do so, and if it is more profitable to locate in the South-East

rather than the North-West then that is where they will go.

The quantity of goods and services that an individual can buy will be determined mainly by their income. Those with a high income will be able to buy more goods and those with a low income will obviously be able to buy far less. Many feel that this is unfair.

Another important feature of a completely free enterprise economy is that the government plays no part in economic activity. This means that goods and services which we normally associate with the state, such as health, law and order, and defence, would either only be provided to those who could pay for them or would not be provided at all.

A tale of two economies

Freeland

Planitaria

In the Freeland economy the state makes no economic decisions. The citizens earn their living by selling their factor services. Those unable to earn a living, such as the young, the old, the sick and those unable to find work, rely on support from their families or charity.

The owners of those factors in short supply, such as capital and skilled labour, earn a much larger income than those who can only offer unskilled labour. The pattern of production constantly changes to reflect changes in the tastes of consumers.

Health and education must be paid for by those who make use of them. There is no national defence as no one is prepared to pay for a service that benefits other people. Firms aim to make as much profit as possible and as a result pollution is a problem as firms will not pay for its control.

Working conditions are poor but those in work have seen the amount of goods that they can buy with their income growing each year. Shortages are rare and those who have the money can usually find what they want to buy in the shops.

Planitaria used to be similar to Freeland but the poor workers rebelled against the rich owners of land and capital. To avoid the same situation arising again, they set up a government of their own to make economic decisions, deciding what goods and services are to be produced and providing free health and education.

All resources, including labour, are fully employed but there are shortages. This is because resources are limited and also because the government sometimes makes mistakes when estimating people's wants.

Despite this, the population are reasonably content. Everyone enjoys more or less the same standard of living and everyone has the basic necessities. Those who cannot work are looked after by the state and people do not fear unemployment, sickness or old age.

1 From the stories above, pick out the main advantages and disadvantages of the two economies described.
2 How might it be possible to obtain the best of both worlds?

The planned economy

An alternative to a free enterprise economy is one where the state plays a far greater role. In a planned economy it is the state that makes the major economic decisions. It estimates how much of each good and service is required and then sets quotas for firms to make sure that the necessary quantity is produced.

This system involves complete state control over how resources are used. Goods are distributed on a first come, first served basis and incomes tend to be fairly equal. This is seen as a fairer system for organising production and distribution.

The mixed economy

In practice, all economies are a mixture of free enterprise and state control. They attempt to obtain the benefits of both systems, ie the efficiency of the free enterprise system with the social benefits and fairness of a planned economy.

In a mixed economy firms make decisions on what, how and where to produce, but the government intervenes in the market to try to influence these decisions.

The government may also control resources more directly. Some industries, notably in areas such as energy and transport, may be under direct state control. These are the so-called **nationalised industries**. The government may also take responsibility for a range of services which, it is felt, are better provided collectively, rather than being left to the market. These include health, education, law and order and defence.

Part 3   The development of business activity

Industry as we know it today is not very old. Our great grandparents would have difficulty recognising the highly automated world with its massive multinational companies, rapid communications and sophisticated welfare system which we now take for granted.

Primitive man was a hunter/gatherer who had to work from dawn to dusk hunting animals and gathering plants and berries to provide the minimum food and shelter necessary to survive. This was known as a subsistence economy and individuals or families attempted to satisfy their own needs without the assistance of others.

Later men and women set about meeting their needs in a more productive way. They began to farm the land and use primitive tools to increase their output. Individuals began to specialise. Some would farm the land, some would continue to hunt for meat, whilst others would remain in the village to make tools or pots.

Individuals no longer attempted to be self-sufficient because they realised that by specialising they could produce far more than they needed and could exchange their surplus with other people. This exchange of goods is known as **barter**.

The origins of money

Imagine you are a farmer who wants to exchange one of your pigs for a quantity of corn. Firstly you would have to tramp around the village to find one of your neighbours who not only had corn to spare but who also happened to be looking for a pig.

Deciding on a rate of exchange would also be a problem. How many kilograms (kg) of corn is a pig worth? Even if you agree that a pig is worth 20 kg of corn, what happens if you only want 5 kg? The answer might seem easy; a quarter of a pig is worth 5 kg of corn but which quarter, and what do you do with the other three-quarters? Here you are faced with the additional problem of storing wealth in the form of goods rather than money.

In societies making use of barter it soon became apparent that certain commodities, such as salt, ivory and precious metals like gold and silver, were acceptable to everyone. These goods acted as mediums of exchange between buyers and sellers. The owner of the pig could exchange it for salt and this could then be used to exchange for corn.

Functions of money

Money evolved as an attempt to overcome the problems of barter. Unlike barter it can act as:

a a medium of exchange
b a measure of value
c a store of value.

Attributes of money

To carry out these functions, money needs to be:

a acceptable
b scarce
c durable
d portable
e divisible
f stable in value.

With reference to the functions and attributes of money, discuss how well the following items could be used as money:

    a Iron.   **c** Chickens.
    b Sand.   **d** Gold.

Metals soon became the most common medium of exchange because of their scarcity, durability and divisibility. Gold and silver were the most popular. This was how our modern system of coins developed.

"I invented the penny yesterday but I'm having trouble with the 50p piece!"

Bank notes evolved from the practice of medieval goldsmiths issuing receipts for valuables and gold deposited with them for safe keeping. Instead of withdrawing valuables in order to buy goods, it was possible to exchange these receipts and in so doing transfer the ownership of the valuables. To aid this form of exchange, receipts were issued in round sums such as £5 and £10 which could easily be transferred from one person to another.

Similarly the cheque system developed from the practice of depositors giving written instructions to the goldsmiths asking them to transfer money from one account to another. A modern cheque is simply a standard letter requesting the transfer of funds.

Division of labour

The development of a monetary system encouraged specialisation. Specialisation in turn increased output and was the first step towards the division of labour. It was this which led to the development of the factory system and mass production, eg the Yorkshire and Lancashire textile industry.

Division of labour

Advantages

- Each person does the job to which they are best suited.
- Skill is gained with constant repetition.
- Time is not wasted changing from one tool to another.
- Specialised machinery can be used.
- Little training is required as individual processes are simple.

Disadvantages

- Work is monotonous.
- Skills are lost as the need for craftsmen declines.
- Training is narrow and specific to one employer.
- Each worker is dependent on others on the production line.
- A strike by a small group can affect the whole factory.
- There is little job satisfaction.

In his book '*The Wealth of Nations*', written in 1776, Adam Smith made these observations about a local pin factory.

'A man not educated to this business could scarcely perhaps with his utmost industry make one pin a day, and certainly could not make twenty ... But in the way this trade is carried on it is divided into a number of branches, of which the greater part are likewise peculiar trades. One man draws out the wire, another straights it, a third cuts it, a fourth points it, a fifth grinds it at the top (for receiving of the head). To make the head requires two or three distinct operations. To put it on is a peculiar business, to whiten the pins is another. It is even a trade by itself to put them into the paper, and the important business of making a pin is divided in this way into eighteen different processes, which in some manufactories are all performed by distinct hands.

'I have seen a small manufactory of this kind where ten men only were employed, and where some of them consequently performed two or three distinct operations. But although they were very poor, and therefore but indifferently accommodated with the necessary machinery they could, when they exerted themselves, make among them twelve pounds of pins a day. There are in a pound upwards of 4,000 pins of a middling size. Each person, therefore, could make one-tenth of 48,000 pins a day.'

1 Suggest reasons why the division of labour allowed production to increase from less than 20 pins per day to 4,800 pins.
2 List some of the disadvantages which could result from splitting jobs up into simple tasks in this way.
3 Try an experiment. Design and manufacture a paper doll similar to that in Figure 5. This will involve a series of tasks – folding the paper, drawing the design, cutting it out and pasting in onto the card.
   Time how long it takes to carry out all of these tasks. Next, set up a production line using the principle of division of labour. Compare the time that it now takes to produce a doll.

Figure 5:

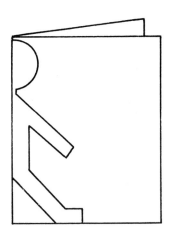

Equipment

Coin (for drawing head)
Ruler
Scissors
Glue
Paper
Card

The division of labour.

Decline of traditional industries

Specialisation brought further technological advances. New products, such as televisions and new materials such as plastics, meant the decline of some of the older industries. For example, man-made fibres replaced traditional textiles. As a result, prosperity was not evenly spread with some regions benefiting more than others. There was growing unemployment amongst workers in the traditional industries such as shipbuilding, iron and steel and textiles.

A further change was that, with rising living standards, demand began to shift towards services rather than goods. People wanted to spend their extra income on services such as hairdressing, insurance and leisure. At the same time there was an expansion in employment in the Civil Service and in local government.

This shift in employment from manufacturing into the service sector is known as **de-industrialisation** and has been a marked feature of the past decade. This process has been speeded up by a growing demand for imported manufactured goods at the expense of home produced goods.

With increased prosperity has come a desire for more welfare services. In a society where only half of the population works there is a need to provide for those who do not, including the old, sick, young and the unemployed.

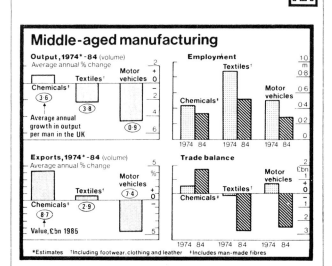

Source: *The Economist* November 16 1985

With the aid of Figure 6, describe the changing fortunes of the chemical, textile and motor vehicle industries over the period 1974 to 1984.

The Welfare State

With improved living standards has come a demand for better standards of education, health, housing, pensions etc. The demand for minimum standards of welfare to be provided by the state was first met in the second half of the nineteenth century. Since then there have been significant improvements, notably by the Liberal government after 1906 and by post-war governments following the Beveridge Report on Social Insurance in 1942. Before 1908, for example, there

was no old age pension, but by 1985 the government was spending over £15½ bn on this service.

By providing minimum standards of health and education, the wealth of the country is increased. Workers are better educated, healthier and do not have to worry about the future. If they are ill, lose their jobs or become too old to work, the state will provide for them to ensure that they can maintain at least a minimum standard of living.

All this has to be paid for, however, and this involves redistributing some of the income of those in work to those in need. This is done through taxation and National Insurance contributions.

Using leaflets available from the Post Office and other sources, find the following:

1 What the current retirement pension is for:
   a a single person
   b a married couple.

2 What the present unemployment benefit is for a single person?

3 Compile a list of other state benefits which are available and produce a booklet giving brief details of each of these benefits.

4 Organise a class debate to argue the case for and against an increase in the size of unemployment benefits.

The future

Britain has few natural resources. Its strength lies in its skills and its capital. The future, therefore, depends on new technology. The silicon chip has brought new products such as digital watches and home computers. It has also led to new techniques of production, such as robot production lines, and major improvements in communications and information storage and retrieval.

Growth will continue to be rapid with other new technologies such as fibre optics, nuclear technology and bio-technology making a great impact. The future will therefore be one of change and uncertainty in the business world. There will be further new products and new techniques with existing products and equipment becoming obsolete very quickly.

Part 4   Stages of production

The production of goods and services can be broken down into three stages.

Primary production

This is concerned with the use of resources found on or beneath the land and in the sea. The primary industries are important in that they supply both the raw materials needed by other industries and food to feed the population. The main industries involved in primary production are fishing, agriculture, mining and quarrying, ie the **extractive** industries. As an economy develops so the proportion of the working population employed in the primary sector declines.

Secondary production

This involves the use of raw materials obtained from primary industries, together with men and machines, to produce a finished good which can either be used by other firms or can be sold to a final customer.

Goods which are bought by firms to produce further goods and services are known as **capital goods**. They include fixed capital such as building and machines, and working capital such as raw materials and components. Capital can

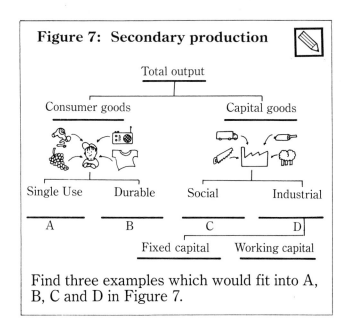

Figure 7: Secondary production

Total output
- Consumer goods
  - Single Use (A)
  - Durable (B)
- Capital goods
  - Social (C)
  - Industrial (D)

Fixed capital   Working capital

Find three examples which would fit into A, B, C and D in Figure 7.

also belong to the community. This is known as social capital and includes roads, schools and hospitals. It is referred to as **infrastructure**.

Goods which are bought by consumers are known as **consumer goods**. They include single use goods such as food and drink, and durable goods which give satisfaction to the consumer over a period of time. These include cars, radios and washing machines.

Figure 8: Stages of production

Primary   Secondary   Tertiary

Extractive industries   Construction   Manufacturing   Commerce   Direct services
                                                                        Public services

As we saw earlier, there has been a decline in employment in the manufacturing sector in recent years (de-industrialisation). A number of reasons have been put forward for this trend:

- Job losses due to new technology.
- Increased demand for cheap foreign imports.
- A lack of investment in new machines, causing a loss of exports.
- High labour costs compared without overseas competitors.
- A shift in employment to the service sector due to changing tastes.

Tertiary production

This refers to the production of services rather than physical goods. These services can be divided into three types:

- Services to industry including banking and insurance (commercial services).
- Services provided to the public such as hairdressing and leisure services (direct services).
- Services provided by the state such as health and education (public services).

We have seen that as an economy expands it tends to expand the size of the tertiary sector.

Study the extract below and answer the questions that follow.

Types of jobs

OF the 26½ million people in the labour force, over 23 million are in work. This is not very different from the total in work 30 years ago; but the similarity masks big changes in the nature and location of jobs.

In 1955 manufacturing accounted for 40 per cent of employees in employment; in 1984, 26 per cent. But the service sector has grown from 45 to 65 per cent.

The sectoral shift has been matched by an occupational shift: even within manufacturing industry a much higher proportion of people are in non-manual occupations, particularly scientific, technological and professional ones.

The number of self-employed has grown markedly too—from 1.7 million in the 1950s to 2.4 million now.

With the change in the industrial balance, there has been a change in the geographical balance, hitting hard those regions most dependent on the older industries. But other regions meanwhile have profited from the growth of new services and high-technology manufacturing.

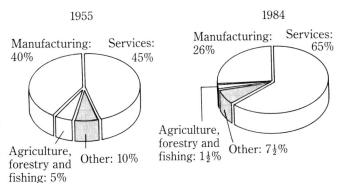

Figures for 1955 on estimated standard industrial classification 1980.

1 Define primary, secondary and tertiary production. Give two examples of each.
2 Describe the employment trends that have taken place over the period 1955 to 1984.
3 Give possible reasons for the trends outlined in your answer to question 2.
4 What are the major implications for the nature of future employment if these trends continue?

Source: *Employment News* March 1985

QUICK QUIZ

1. What do we mean by the term 'wealth'?
2. How is wealth created?
3. List the four factors of production and give two examples of each.
4. What is meant by the term 'value added'?
5. Give three advantages and three disadvantages of a free enterprise economy.
6. What is meant by the term 'opportunity cost'?
7. Give three problems associated with the use of barter as a method of exchanging goods.
8. What are the three main functions of money?
9. Briefly explain what is meant by 'division of labour'.
10. List three welfare services provided by the state.
11. What is meant by 'de-industrialisation'?
12. What are the main differences between 'capital' goods and 'consumer' goods?

Case Study: Britain, an economic profile

Production in the UK can be broadly split as follows:

Primary	13%
Secondary	30%
Tertiary	57%

Figure 1: Economic profile

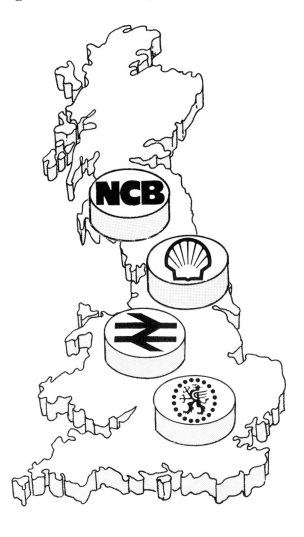

Energy has been the most rapidly expanding sector, mainly because of the North Sea oil production. The UK manufacturing sector has been in decline for many years. In the service sector, communications and finance are the main growth areas.

Of the eleven largest UK enterprises shown in Figure 2 the majority are now in the private sector. Some have been recently transferred from the state or public sector into the private sector as the government pursues a policy of privatisation, eg British Telecom and British Gas.

Figure 2: The largest UK enterprises (1985)

	Turnover £bn	Employees at home and abroad (000s)
British Petroleum	38.0	132
Shell Transport and Trading	24.4	n/a
BAT Industries	11.7	187
Imperial Chemical Industries	9.3	118
Electricity Council	9.1	141
British National Oil Corporation	7.9	n/a
Shell UK	7.8	18
Esso UK	7.6	7
British Telecom	6.4	249
British Gas Corporation	5.9	103
Unilever plc	5.4	127

We can see that the UK has a mixed economy with goods and services being provided by firms operating in both the private and the public sector.

In addition there are some organisations which, although they are within the private sector, do not operate to make profits in the same way as other private sector organisations. These include clubs and charities.

Source: Adapted from 'Britain, an economic profile' Lloyds Bank

1 Of the companies listed in Figure 2, which ones are in the public sector?
2 Can you name four organisations which provide goods and services but which do not attempt to make a profit?

Part 1   The private sector

There are many different ways in which businesses in the private sector can be organised, from small one man businesses to large multinational corporations with multi-million pound turnovers. There are, however, only three different legal forms which a business in the private sector can take. These are the sole trader, the partnership, and the limited company.

The main factors distinguishing these forms of businesses from each other are the number of owners, the 'legal personality' of the business and the financial liability of the owners. We will need to consider these last two differences in a bit more detail.

Legal personality

In the case of the sole trader or partnership there is no distinction in law between the business and the owners of that business. When the firm agrees to buy from a supplier, the individuals who own the business are responsible for paying for these goods. It is, in fact, the owners themselves who have entered into a contract with the supplier.

As a firm expands, however, it is possible to split the business itself from the owners. This is known as **incorporation**. The result of incorporation is that the business now has legal rights and responsibilities which are separate from its owners. It is said to have a legal personality. The business can enter into agreements in its own right.

This has a number of advantages. The business can continue to exist beyond the lifetime of those who manage it. The business can also sue and be sued in the courts which allows the interests of the business to be protected.

Limited liability

Because a sole trader's business is not separate in law, the owner of the business is personally liable for any debts which arise from the firm's activities. This could require the sale of the owner's personal assets such as his house or car to pay off a debt. The owner could be declared a bankrupt until any unpaid debts have been settled.

The sole trader has direct control over his

business and so the risk of losing large sums of money are usually small. As firms grow, however, the risks increase. This made it very difficult for new firms developing in the eighteenth and nineteenth centuries to raise money. People were reluctant to invest in new businesses when the result could be the loss, not only of their investment, but also their personal property. As a result, the principle of **limited liability** was established by the Joint-Stock Companies Acts (1856–1862).

Limited liability means that the most that anyone providing capital for a business can lose is the amount that they have invested or have agreed to invest. If a company is unable to pay its debts then one of two things can happen:

● It may be possible to borrow the money to pay off the debts or alternatively creditors may be prepared to wait for payment.
● The company can go into liquidation. This may be voluntary or enforced by the creditors. The company's assets will be sold off and used to meet its debts. If the assets are insufficient then creditors will lose out, as there is no obligation on the owners of the business to pay off the debts themselves.

Suppliers dealing with companies with limited liability obviously take a risk that any debts may not be paid. To act as a warning to suppliers a company which has limited liability must have, after its name, the word limited (Ltd) or public limited company (plc).

The sole trader

This is the simplest and oldest form of business and also the most common. There are many areas of business where sole traders dominate. You only have to look through the advertisements in the local newspapers to see how many independent tradesmen such as joiners, plumbers and electricians there are, or walk along the local high street to see how many retailers are sole traders.

The sole trader owns his or her own business. Although we sometimes refer to them as one man businesses, this does not mean there are no employees, it simply means that only one person owns the business. This individual directs the business and is personally responsible for all decisions. If the business is unsuccessful then he or she is personally liable for any debts. There are no formalities in setting up as a sole trader although a trading licence may be required to trade in certain goods such as alcohol.

Advantages of the sole trader

- The owner maintains personal control of the business. Decisions can be taken quickly.
- All profits go to the owner.
- Direct contact with customers is maintained. This is particularly important if credit is to be given.
- Labour relations tend to be good since the fortunes of employees are linked to those of the business.
- The sole trader's accounts are not published so financial affairs remain confidential.
- It is easy to start in business with no complicated legal formalities.

Disadvantages of the sole trader

- The owner is fully liable for all the debts of the business.
- It may be difficult to raise capital for the expansion of the business.
- Long hours and business worries cannot be shared.
- Ill health may force the closure of the business as will the death of the owner.
- The owner is expected to deal with all the management tasks such as marketing, finance and personnel matters.

1   Design a questionnaire to be used to survey local small businesses.
The information you may want to obtain could include:

a the type of business and the activity it is involved in
b how the business was started
c who owns the business
d how many employees it has
e how the business raises capital
f what the owner feels are the advantages and disadvantages of being a small business.

You may be able to think of other questions you would like to ask, but remember that business people are very busy so keep your questionnaire fairly short.

2   Split up into groups and use your questionnaires to carry out a survey of businesses in your area. Each group should produce a report of its findings to be presented to the class.

The partnership

To overcome the problem of shortage of capital, a partnership may be formed. This is where between two and twenty people set up in business together, although there are exceptions.

Each partner contributes some capital and any profits or losses are shared between the partners.

The control of the business is the responsibility of all the partners. Decisions taken by any one partner are binding on the others and, in most partnerships, all partners have unlimited liability.

People can enter into partnership with one another without any formal written agreement. In practice, however, it is advisable to draw up a **partnership agreement**. This is a book of rules which will hopefully help to avoid disagreements. The agreement usually includes the following:

- The capital to be contributed by each partner.
- The ratio in which profits and losses are to be shared.
- The salaries, if any, that are to be paid to specific partners.

Although we have stated that, in most cases, all partners have limited liability, it is possible to distinguish two types of partnership.

Ordinary partnerships

This is where all partners play an active role in the running of the business, ie the partners work in the business and consult each other when decisions have to be made. In the event of losses being made, each partner has unlimited liability. It is therefore crucial that all the partners are capable, trustworthy and honest since the mistakes of one partner may affect the others financially.

Ordinary partnerships are commonly found in the accounting and legal professions where, for example, a firm of solicitors may have one partner who specialises in tax law while another specialises in family law.

Limited partnership

This kind of partnership is not very common. Limited partnerships have some **sleeping partners** who take no part whatsoever in the decision making process. Should the business fail, they lose no more than their original investment in the business. Sleeping partners therefore face limited liability, ie it is limited to their original stake in the business. In contrast, the remaining or **general partners** still face unlimited liability. There must be at least one partner with unlimited liability.

Advantages of the partnership

- It permits greater specialisation.
- Additional capital can be raised by admitting new partners.
- The ill health or death of one partner does not mean an end to the business.
- Holidays become possible as the work of the business can be shared.
- Partners can consult one another and make more informed decisions.
- The financial affairs of a partnership are private.

Disadvantages of a partnership

- All partners (except sleeping partners) face unlimited liability.
- Decision making may be slow since partners must be consulted.
- There are many opportunities for the partners to disagree.
- The death or retirement of one member brings the partnership to an end.
- Profits must be shared.

Jim, Dave, John and Gill have decided to go into partnership to produce a new pop magazine that will be sold nationally. Having done a Business Studies course at a local college, Gill was aware of the importance of a partnership agreement and arranged a meeting to discuss the matter further.

You are given the following information relating to the business and the partners:

a   The first year's profits are expected to be £50,000.

b   Jim has put £20,000 into the business but, because of other business commitments, he will not take an active part in the running of the business.

c   Dave spends three afternoons a week in the business. He is responsible for the book keeping and has agreed to allow the business to operate for the first year from his house.

d   John works six days a week in the business but has not contributed any capital. He is responsible for writing many of the articles used and is in charge of advertising.

e   Gill has not contributed any capital to the business. She spends five days a week going to newsagents and persuading them to stock the magazine. She also provides her own transport.

In groups of four, take on the roles of the four partners and decide upon the contents of the partnership's written agreement.

You should clearly state the percentage of profits each partner should receive, any salaries to be paid and the action to be taken should one of the partners choose to leave during the first year.

The limited company

We saw earlier how a business could obtain the benefits of limited liability by forming a company (incorporation). This is not difficult, which explains why there are so few limited partnerships. By forming a company, limited liability can be obtained for all members.

As with a partnership, individuals provide capital to the business. They are known as **shareholders** and they own a part of the business and will share in any profits which are earned. They elect a number of **directors** who will run the business on their behalf.

The law requires a meeting of shareholders once a year and other meetings may be called if required. Shareholders generally play little part in the running of the business, however, unless they are also directors.

Various Companies Acts have been passed over the years to protect the interests of shareholders and creditors of limited companies.

In order to set up a company two documents must be drawn up. The first is called the **memorandum of association**.

Companies must also draw up **articles of association** (the company's rule book).

The next step is to send the above documents to Companies House in Cardiff. If all is in order, the Registrar of Companies will issue a **certificate of incorporation** which is the company's birth certificate.

It is relatively cheap and easy to set up a company in this way. A company may be based on an existing business or it could be a completely new business. About 50,000 companies are started in Britain each year, although it is interesting to note that about 10,000 of these are wound up within a year.

Private and public limited companies

There are two types of limited company, each having a minimum of two shareholders. The first is known as a private limited company and is identified by the word limited (Ltd) after the company name. Shares in a private limited company are not freely available and the transfer of shares must be agreed by the directors.

This is the form of organisation often chosen when a sole trader wants to expand but at the same time wishes to maintain personal control. 95% of limited companies are private but most are small. 85% of private limited companies employ less than ten people.

The second type of limited company is a public limited company. These are normally larger companies and they must have an (authorised) share capital of at least £50,000. This is dealt with in more detail in Unit 6. Most employ over 500 people. A public limited company must have the letters plc after its name.

Unlike a private company, shares in a public company are offered to the general public and there is no restriction on the transfer of shares. Around half of the shares in these companies are in the hands of financial institutions such as pension funds and insurance companies.

Many public companies consist of more than one firm. In many cases each firm will have its own **board of directors**. There will, however, be a main board with responsibility for major investment and planning decisions within the group. The original company is often known as the **parent company**, and where this company does not itself trade but simply manages the subsiduary firms it is known as a **holding company**.

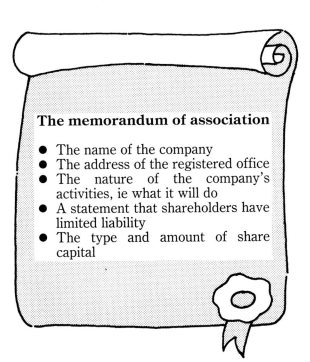

The memorandum of association

- The name of the company
- The address of the registered office
- The nature of the company's activities, ie what it will do
- A statement that shareholders have limited liability
- The type and amount of share capital

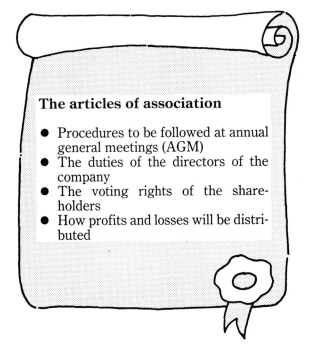

The articles of association

- Procedures to be followed at annual general meetings (AGM)
- The duties of the directors of the company
- The voting rights of the shareholders
- How profits and losses will be distributed

Advantages of the limited company

- The shareholders benefit from limited liability.
- Large-scale production is possible.
- The ill health of shareholders does not affect the running of the business.
- In the case of a public limited company, shareholders can easily sell their shares.

Disadvantages of the limited company

- Conflicts of interest can arise between the owners and the managers.
- There is a danger of poor communications between the various departments within the company.
- Large companies are often accused of being impersonal to work for and to deal with.
- Limited companies are required by law to produce annual reports and public companies are required to publish these at great expense.
- Rates of tax on profits are higher than for sole traders and partnerships.

Consider the following case studies and answer the questions which follow:

Case 1

Smith, Taylor, Hoskins and Mitchell are a well-known and much respected firm of solicitors. The firm has been established for more than seventy years.

Case 2

Alf Thomas owns and manages a small grocery business. He runs the shop with the help of a part-time assistant who helps out on a Saturday.

Case 3

Britcar (UK) plc manufacture a popular family saloon car. They employ 67,000 full-time workers and have six production sites located throughout the United Kingdom.

Case 4

Ace Products Ltd produce windscreen wipers for the Leyland Range Rover. They produce their product in a small factory unit and currently employ fifty full-time workers.

1   What types of business organisations are described above?
2   Compile a list of 20 firms in your locality and organise them under the following headings:

a   Public limited companies.
b   Private limited companies.
c   Partnerships (more than one owner).
d   Sole traders.

3   Use the words and phrases below to complete the following:

A sole trader has the advantage of independence but also has the problem of _____. In order to grow, the sole trader may form a partnership with all partners signing a _____. There must be at least two partners, one of which must be a _____ partner with unlimited liability.

When a company is formed it must have a _____ of association and _____ of association. _____ limited companies may sell shares to family and friends and have _____ after their names. Public limited companies can sell shares on the _____ and have _____ after their names. A large number of shares in public limited companies are in the hands of _____.

memorandum   plc
general   unlimited liability
financial institutions   Ltd.
articles   partnership agreement
private
Stock Exchange

Multinational companies

The activities of many of the larger public companies extend beyond their country of origin. Where a company has overseas branches it is known as a multinational company.

Multinationals have become increasingly important and in Britain around 20% of manufacturing industry is foreign owned. Major multinationals include almost all car manufacturers and oil companies.

Figure 3: The world's leading multinationals

Company	Country of origin	Main activity
Exxon	USA	Petroleum products, gas, chemicals
General Motors	USA	Automobiles
Royal Dutch Shell	UK/Neth.	Petroleum products, gas, chemicals
Texaco	USA	Petroleum products, gas, chemicals
Ford Motor Company	USA	Automobiles
Mobil Oil	USA	Petroleum products, gas
Standard Oil of California	USA	Petroleum products, gas, chemicals
National Iranian Oil	Iran	Petroleum products, gas, chemicals
British Petroleum	UK	Petroleum products, gas, chemicals
International Business Machines	USA	Office equipment, computers
Gulf Oil	USA	Petroleum products, gas, chemicals
Unilever	UK	Food, detergents

"Want to do business?"

The largest multinational company in the United Kingdom is British Petroleum, which operates in over 70 countries and has over 600 subsidiary companies.

It is estimated that within the next decade, the world's largest 250 multinational companies will account for around 50% of world output.

Co-operatives

A co-operative is a voluntary organisation of individuals or businesses who join together to achieve certain benefits such as bulk buying. Any profits are shared between the members of the co-operative.

Retail co-operatives

These are the most familiar form of co-operative and the first one was founded in Britain in 1844. This was the Society of Equitable Pioneers, which started when a number of Rochdale flannel weavers opened a shop which bought goods at wholesale prices and sold them at a higher price. After expenses had been taken out of income, the profits were shared between the customers according to the value of the purchases they had made.

The Society of Equitable Pioneers' shop

The co-operative movement has expanded nationally since these early days and has become a major force in retailing. As with a registered company, the owners of a retail co-operative have limited liability. Membership is open to anyone who buys at least one £1 share. Unlike a public limited company, however, these shares cannot be sold and the co-operative can reclaim them if it wishes. Another difference is that members have only one vote each, however many shares they own.

Profits can be shared out in three ways. Through interest payments on shares, through the issue of dividend stamps to customers which can be exchanged for money or gifts and through reduced prices.

Employee co-operatives

This is a type of organisation where the employees are also the owners of the business.

There are many small-scale co-operatives run by groups of skilled workers and the numbers have grown with increasing unemployment and a lack of employment opportunities in larger organisations.

Large-scale co-operatives have not been successful in this country, but many examples can be found abroad. A notable example is in Northern Spain around the town of Mondragon, where 100 co-operative firms employ around 19,000 people.

Part 2   The public sector

So far we have studied business organisations that are found in the private sector of the economy. Now we must turn our attention to those organisations that belong to the public sector. These public sector organisations are owned and directed by either local or central government.

Figure 4: Jobs in privately and publicly-owned business

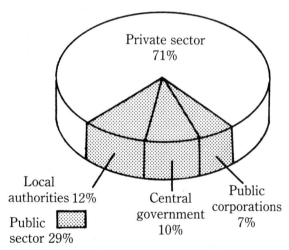

Source: *Economic Trends* CSO March 1984

Some areas, such as defence and law and order, are clearly the responsibility of the state. Other activities have been taken over by the state because they are essentially non-profit making, eg health and education. These services are provided by central or local government departments. The government also takes responsibility for providing certain goods and services which are sold to industry or the public.

Nationalised industries

Industries which are under state control are normally referred to as **nationalised indus-**

tries and they include, coal, steel and rail transport. These nationalised industries are run as **public corporations** which are not in the private sector, but are also not under such close ministerial control as government departments. Each corporation is established by an Act of Parliament which lays down its duties and structure. Boards are appointed by the government and these boards are accountable to Parliament rather than shareholders. Major policy decisions for the corporations are taken by the appropriate minister but the day-to-day running of the industry is left to the board.

There has been a great deal of controversy in recent years about which industries should be in the private sector and which in the public sector.

The 1970s saw a marked increase in the number of businesses that were nationalised. This means that they were taken into public ownership by the government buying up shares held by private citizens, companies and other institutions.

Most, but not all, nationalisation has been undertaken by Labour governments. Indeed, even today, the Labour Party is arguing in favour of more rather than less public ownership.

In contrast, since 1979, when a Conservative government was elected, a number of previously nationalised industries have been returned to the private sector through a policy of privatisation. Recently privatised companies include British Aerospace, the British National Oil Corporation, British Telecom, Jaguar and British Airways. In addition, the government is looking at ways of introducing private enterprise into the hospital and transport services.

The policy of privatisation, which involves the selling back of shares held by the government to the general public, is hotly debated. In order to be able to form a personal view on the matter, we must first look at the arguments for and against state ownership.

Arguments for state ownership

- The public sector provides services which should be available according to need rather than the ability to pay, eg health care, education and sanitation.
- There are many industries where competition would be wasteful and lead to higher prices due to the duplication of expensive equipment, eg electricity. Nationalisation provides a means of ensuring that these natural monopolies cannot exploit their position.
- The commanding heights argument. It is sometimes argued that an industry which is vital to the effective running of the economy should be under public rather than private control, eg steel and coal.
- Where an industry is vital to national security it is frequently in public hands, eg atomic energy.
- In addition to the large sums of money required for capital investment, certain industries with a low level of profitability would find it difficult to obtain finance from private sources for development.
- In order to achieve its economic objectives the government may wish to control certain sectors of the economy. Control over the money supply, for example, would be easier to achieve if the government controlled the banks.
- Nationalised industries are able to take account of the costs and benefits to society of their actions. The policy of the nationalised industries can take account of such factors as regional unemployment and pollution.
- Political arguments. Support for public ownership can be found in Socialist theory and the Constitution of the Labour Party.

Arguments against state ownership

- Public corporations are very large and are difficult to manage owing to their size.
- The management of nationalised industries are not free to manage the industry as they see fit owing to government interference.
- Nationalised industries have no incentive to perform well since there is no reward for taking risks and innovation may therefore be discouraged.
- They are costly to the taxpayer since the losses that some nationalised industries make must be paid for by taxing people on their income or their expenditure.

Privatisation

Since 1979, there has been a trend towards privatisation. This involves either the selling of publicly owned assets, the opposite of nationalisation, or the opening up of the public sector to competition. The first stage in the privatisation of British Telecom, for example, was the removal of the company's monopoly on the supply of telephones. The next stage was to sell shares in BT to the general public.

Figure 5 shows the revenue received by the government from the sale of public sector assets up to 1986. The sale of British Gas and British Airways in 1987 continued this upward trend and, at the time of writing, further sales are planned including British Steel and the Water Authorities.

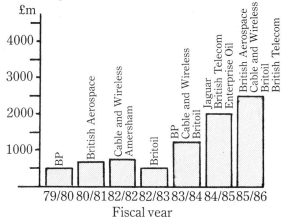

Figure 5: Privatisation

1 Describe the view of the privatisation of transport illustrated in the cartoon above.
2 Organise a class debate with speakers for and against the motion:
   'The privatisation of refuse disposal will benefit ratepayers.'

Arguments in favour of privatisation	Arguments against privatisation
• Managers will be able to make decisions without government 'meddling'. • The managers and owners of the business will be rewarded for successful risk-taking. • The public will benefit from the increased choice which will result from more competition. • Wider share ownership is encouraged with millions of people now owning shares in British industry. • The government receives income from the sale of shares which helps to reduce borrowing.	• The government loses the revenue from the profits earned by some nationalised industries. • The loss of state control over certain industries may lead to the exploitation of the consumer with higher prices and falling standards. • There may be social costs as the subsidies offered by certain nationalised industries are lost.

ALL CLEAR FOR THE GREAT TRAFFIC LIGHTS SELL-OFF

'For sale: 2,576 traffic lights. Good condition, one previous owner'

The government is preparing plans to save public money by handing over all London's traffic lights to the private sector. Bids have been invited from companies willing to maintain the lights, but so far there has been only one bidder, British Telecom.

Given the condition of London's telephone boxes, the prospect of BT taking over traffic lights is believed to have caused some alarm in government circles.

Nine London boroughs have formed a committee to block the move and to take control of the lights themselves. They have proposed radical changes in the system, introducing new measures to favour pedestrians and public transport users and to slow down motorists by making the 'red phase' longer.

A spokesman for the AA said that they were unhappy with this prospect and that if the scheme were to go ahead it would cause chaos.

1 Produce a report on the privatisation of traffic lights setting out the likely views of:

  a British Telecom
  b the London borough councils
  c motorists.

2 Over a period of two or three weeks, collect all the newspaper articles you can which mention either nationalised industries or privatisation.

Pick out information under the following headings:

  a Criticisms of nationalised industries.
  b Benefits of nationalised industries.
  c Motives for privatisation.

Part 3 Internal organisation

In this part we will consider the way in which a company is organised. By this we mean the relationships which exist between individuals. For example:

• Who are the bosses and who are the subordinates?
• Who makes the decisions and who carries them out?
• How does information flow from person to person?

Organisation can vary from one company to another and often changes take place in a rather haphazard way over many years. There are some similarities, however, which enable us to illustrate a typical organisational structure.

At the base of the organisation are the majority of the workforce. At each higher level there are fewer people and this gives us the traditional 'pyramid' organisation. Shareholders and directors can also play a part in the running of the business even though they may not work for the organisation.

As you move up through the organisation, the more important become the skills of leadership and management. Responsibility increases and is concentrated on a smaller number of people. It is at the higher levels within the organisation that planning, co-ordination and other managerial and administrative tasks take place.

Organisation charts

Many firms, particularly larger ones, produce organisation charts. These show how the various jobs within an organisation relate to each other. A typical chart would look similar to Figure 6.

Figure 6 also illustrates how an organisation can be split up into departments. Each department has a department head and a number of staff. In a large organisation, a department might be split into sections. The finance department might be split into financial accounting and management accounting, for example.

The production of a organisation chart can benefit a firm in a number of ways. The management will be able to carefully consider the way in which the firm is organised and may be able to spot communication problems. The chart will also prove useful when training employees, to show them where they fit into the overall organisation. However, charts quickly become out of date as jobs change and employees may look no further than their own department when applying for jobs. This can cause inflexibility within the firm.

Organisation charts illustrate the two dimensions of the organisational structure of the firm. These are known as the vertical and the horizontal dimensions.

The vertical dimension

This illustrates the levels of responsibility within the organisation. Employees at lower levels have less **responsibility** and also less **authority**. However, these terms do not mean the same thing. Although a task may be delegated (or passed down) from a superior to a subordinate, eg a manager to an office worker, the manager still has the responsibility for making sure the job is done.

Authority, on the other hand, is the ability to carry out the task. For example, it would make no sense asking the office worker to pay company debts if he or she did not have the authority to sign cheques.

Delegation

No one individual is capable of doing everything. Although responsibility may rest with one person, tasks must be delegated to others. To be effective, delegated tasks must be clearly defined so that employees can carry them out with confidence.

The sort of tasks which should be delegated are those where similar decisions are made on a regular basis. An employee could, for example, be given the task of supervising a group of staff or dealing with an aspect of finance. This will allow the employee to develop a skill in that area. However, tasks which are vital for the success of the company, such as the selection of senior staff, should not be delegated. Senior management should also decide on such things as production and sales targets, although information and advice from subordinates may be helpful.

It is often the case that too little delegation takes place within an organisation rather than too much. Employees often hold on to work simply because they are familiar with it and they find it

Figure 6: A simple organisation chart

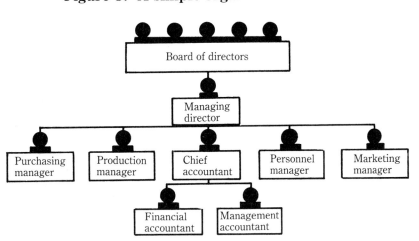

easy. It is also common for employers not to trust their subordinates to do a job as well as they can themselves. If they do trust their subordinates they may be worried that the job will be done too well and their position might be threatened.

Jean Thomas is the personnel manager of a firm with 500 employees. The firm has grown rapidly over the past five years and Jean's job has become too much for her to handle on her own.

An assistant has now been appointed and Jean must decide which of her duties she will delegate. The list below sets out some of Jean's duties.

Suggest which duties should be delegated and which should be retained. Give reasons for your answers.

a Inviting shortlisted candidates for interview.
b Negotiating with unions over pay.
c Updating employee record cards.
d Reporting to the managing director on personnel matters.
e Interviewing new staff.

Span of control

This term refers to the number of people for whom a manager or supervisor is responsible. There is no one correct figure for the most desirable span of control. It will depend very much on the tasks being undertaken and the personality and competence of both supervisors and subordinates. For small and medium size companies with up to 1,500 employees, each supervisor tends to be in control of five people, on average.

The span of control in a particular organisation can be too large. Subordinates in this situation will often be poorly controlled. There will be little training and employees will not have the information they need to carry out their work efficiently.

For their part, managers will be overworked and will have too little time for making decisions. Bottlenecks may develop as managers are not able to do anything but the most urgent tasks.

Too small a span of control, on the other hand, will result in waste and inefficiency. There will be too many levels in the hierarchy resulting in poor communications and slow decision making. Superiors are likely to interfere too much in the work of subordinates and will not delegate in such a way as to make the best use of the staff under them.

Figure 7: Wide span of control

Managing director

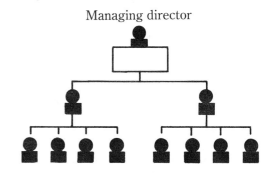

Figure 8: Narrow span of control

Managing director

The horizontal dimension

This deals with the grouping of people and tasks within the organisation. The most common groupings are based on **functions** such as marketing, finance, production and personnel. This is usually termed the **departmental system**.

Although departments are usually based on functions, they can also be based on locations or products. A sales department, for example, may be split between export and domestic sales or between areas within the UK. Similarly production may be split between different products. In the case of motor manufacturers, for example, there may be separate divisions producing engines, car bodies and parts.

It is not unusual to find that when there is a split within the organisation based on location or product, there is a certain amount of independence given to each section. In some cases there may even be a separate board of directors, although one board will have ultimate control over all companies in the group. Where regions or branches have a certain amount of independence, this is known as **decentralisation**. This is one way of coping with the organisational problems which result as a company grows in size.

Companies which have grown naturally over the years tend to keep a fairly centralised organisation which enables the senior executives to maintain control.

When a company has grown through a series of mergers and takeovers, it is more likely that its structure will be decentralised.

Figure 9: The departmental system

Personnel

Finance

Marketing

Production

Formal and informal organisation

Any organisation will have a formal and an informal structure. By structure we mean the relationships which exist between the people in an organisation and between the positions they hold. Where these relationships are the result of management decisions we refer to them as being part of the formal structure. Where the relationships develop naturally without being planned, we refer to them as part of the informal organisation.

> Split up into small groups and, using the example of your school, draw a diagram to illustrate the relationship between members of staff.
>
> You will need to consider both the formal and the informal relationships.
>
> Compare your diagrams.

Formal relationships

As we have seen, production is very much a group activity. People must work together to achieve the firm's objectives. This results in a series of relationships between individual employees and the people they work with.

Line relationships

This relationship involves the passing of instructions from superior to subordinates and the feedback of information from subordinates to superiors.

These types of relationship are usually linked with a departmental structure. The advantage of line relationships is that an individual knows who he or she is responsible to and delegation is straightforward.

There are problems however. A departmental structure tends to result in individual departments becoming isolated and co-operation is reduced. The strength of the department also depends, to a great extent, on the personality and skills of the department head. A weak individual at the head of the department will often result in an ineffective department.

Functional or staff relationships

This is where **experts** are in charge of a particular function within the organisation and their authority overrides that of line managers. An example would be a personnel officer who has responsibility for personnel matters within all departments.

This allows specialists to be used more effectively in the organisation and may help to co-ordinate the work of the departments. There is the problem, however, that there are no clear lines of authority and workers may be confused as to who they should be dealing with on a particular issue. Disagreements may arise when, for example, a personnel manager wants an employee to attend a course but this would present problems to the line manager because of the employee's absence from normal duties.

Informal relationships

Research by social scientists has highlighted the importance of informal groups within the organisation. Despite the existence of the formal organisation, workers still tend to form themselves into informal groups based on skills or interests.

New employees may have to undergo certain 'initiation rites' before being allowed entry into a work group. These include false errands such as being sent to the stores for a 'long weight' (wait!). Work groups may also operate on a social level outside work.

It is important for managers to understand how these groups work as it can have an effect on communications and morale. We will see in a later unit how a great deal of communication within an organisation is based on the informal channels often known as the 'grapevine'.

Managers should be aware of how people 'get on' with each other when organising the work.

This is particularly important when employees work in a team. The work group also has a role to play in helping new employees to settle in, in exercising discipline over members and in determining work practices. Factors such as how individuals should dress and the language they should use will be determined by the informal organisation.

The role of management

It is difficult to define exactly what we mean by the term 'management'. It would be generally agreed, however, that a manager is responsible for the effective planning and running of a business.

Who manages?

It is not always clear who the managers are as there are a number of individuals and groups who help to plan and run the business.

The owners of the business

At first sight it might seem that the owners of the business should be the ones who manage it. This may well be the case in a small organisation but we saw earlier how, in larger firms, ownership and control are split. Shareholders have the right to elect directors who make decisions on their

---

S and S Car Sales Ltd is a private joint-stock company selling cars and vans. It has three showrooms located in the north of England, in Manchester, Rochdale and Wigan. The head office is based at the Manchester branch.

Each showroom has a manager responsible to the sales director at head office. In addition, there are a number of salesmen. Manchester has ten salesmen and the other two branches each have six.

The head office has sections dealing with finance, personnel and sales, each headed by a director:

- Managing director – Roy Hawkes
- Finance director – Jean Baker
- Sales director – Ray Winter
- Personnel director – Ken Sharp

There are ten head office clerical and secretarial staff. Two are in the personnel section, four in the finance section and four in the sales section.

Split up into groups to carry out the following tasks:

1 Prepare an organisation chart to show the structure of the company.
2 List the main tasks which you think are likely to be undertaken by each of the head office sections.
3 Prepare a brief presentation for the class distinguishing between 'line' and 'staff' relationships.

Illustrate your answer from the case study.

behalf and have a further right to a share in the profits of the organisation. They will play no part in the day to day running or management of the organisation, however.

The board of directors

The **board of directors** are the representatives of the shareholders. Their role is to deal with major policy matters such as decisions on capital investment. The directors have a responsibility to act in the interests of the company. They are normally shareholders in the company but not always major shareholders.

Directors can be either **executive directors**, who work as managers in the business or **non-executive directors**, who may attend board meetings but do not exercise day to day control. Non-executive directors are often appointed because of their expertise or because they represent an important interest. Occasionally they are appointed because of the prestige which their name gives to the company.

The **chairman** of a company is often a non-executive director. He will chair the board meetings and will have a significant influence in the appointment of the **managing director**. It is the managing director, as the name suggests, who takes the leading role in the day to day running of the company. He will be supported by a number of other specialist managers, some of whom may themselves be executive directors.

The process of management

A manager can be defined as someone with a supervisory role. That is to say, someone who is responsible for more than his own work.

There will, therefore, be different levels of management within the organisation from the managing director to shop-floor supervisors. There are, however, some common features of the manager's work, whatever the level at which he or she operates.

What does a manager do when he or she is managing? We can look at the work of managers under five main headings.

Setting objectives

Modern organisations consist of a number of groups all trying to influence the actions of the firm. Take, for example, a car manufacturer. The aim of the firm is presumably to make cars profitably, but different groups within the firm may have their own objectives:

● The workforce will want good pay and working conditions.

● Shareholders will be primarily concerned with profits.
● Managers may be aiming to maximise growth to improve their own status.
● Society as a whole will be concerned with such issues as job creation and protection of the environment.

Because of these differing views as to what the organisation is trying to achieve, management must decide on the direction the firm is to take. It is impossible to manage a business if you don't know what that business is trying to achieve.

The setting of objectives gives direction to the organisation. It helps to bring together the various interest groups in pursuing a common aim and helps to motivate those who work in the organisation by providing them with a goal to aim for. Objectives also allow managers to assess how well the business is doing by comparing the progress the business is making with the objectives that have been set.

The objectives set by a particular organisation will depend to a great extent on the nature of their business. A firm in the private sector, for example, will place a higher priority on profit than a firm in the public sector which may be more concerned with providing a service to the public.

The area of activity that a firm is involved in will also influence its objectives. A transport firm, for example, will be concerned with safety whilst a banking firm will be interested in security.

Nature of business

1 Building society.
2 Restaurant.
3 Public transport firm.
4 Discount store.
5 Motor manufacturer.
6 Department store.

Objective

a High standards of hygiene.
b Good service to customers.
c Security.
d Quality products.
e Safety.
f High turnover.

Match the businesses listed above with possible objectives that they might adopt. Each business may have more than one objective. Choose only those which you consider would be the most important in each case.

Planning

A plan can be defined as 'a way of proceeding' and planning is therefore that part of the manager's task which involves deciding how to achieve the objectives of the firm.

It is a difficult task because of the problem of attempting to predict the future. There will always be uncertainty and the information available to the manager will always be incomplete. It is nonetheless an important task given the complexity of the modern business world.

The main steps in the planning process are as follows:

- Collect information to help in making decisions.
- Examine the alternative ways available to achieve objectives.
- Select the best course of action.

Organising

The next step is to organise the firm's resources in order to follow the course of action decided upon. This will involve organising the work, the people and the situation:

- The work – What tasks need to be performed in order to achieve the objectives which have been set?
- The people – What actions are required by individuals and groups of employees? Tasks will have to be allocated and responsibilities defined.

- The situation – How is the work to be organised? What technology is required? What outside agencies will be involved?

Controlling

This is the function of management which is designed to ensure that the company's objectives are being achieved.

This involves the following:

- Setting standards.
- Measuring actual performance.
- Comparing actual performance with the standards set.
- Taking action to correct any deviation.

Standards can be set for the organisation as a whole and also for individual parts of the organisation. The production department, for example, can set standards for quality or costs, the finance department can set standards for profitability, the personnel department may set standards for recruiting new staff and the marketing department may set standards for market share or total sales.

Discipline is another part of the manager's role in controlling the organisation. This involves setting standards for behaviour such as time keeping and imposing penalties if these standards are not met.

Leadership

A leader is a person who makes decisions which help the organisation to achieve its objectives.

The following activity gives you the opportunity to plan the location of an old people's home in Exton village. There are three possible locations which can be chosen.

Using the information available in the map below, examine the alternative sites and consider the advantage and disadvantages of each.

Decide on the best location and produce a brief report to be presented to the class outlining the reasons for your choice.

What other information would have been useful in helping you to make your decision?

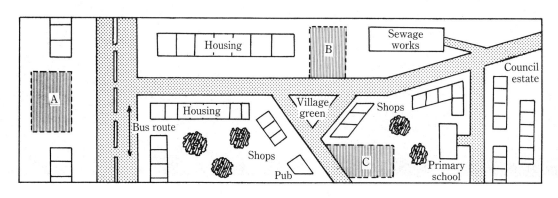

Leadership can be exercised in a number of ways but will be influenced by three main factors. These are the personality of the leader, the staff that he or she has to lead and the particular task that is being undertaken.

A leader is the best person to solve a particular problem. Discuss in groups the qualities that a leader would require to deal with each of the following situations:

1 A large group of students are protesting about grants. There is a confrontation with the police and tempers are strained. Who should lead the students to avoid violence?
2 The country is in a poor position economically. Inflation and unemployment are at the highest levels ever and there is no sign of recovery. Who should lead the nation?
3 A group of workers are unhappy about their pay and conditions and want to choose a leader to put their case to the management. Who should they choose?

We can identify four basic leadership styles. the first is the **autocratic** style. This is where the leader takes decisions alone and expects the other members of the group to carry these decisions out without question. This is the most appropriate style in emergencies where decisions have to be made and acted upon quickly. If this style is adopted on all occasions, however, then it can create a number of problems. The group becomes too dependent on the leader and work ceases when he is not present to make decisions. It can also lead to dissatisfaction within the group who are rarely enthusiastic about the decisions made.

The second style of leadership is the **persuasive** style. Here the leader still takes decisions alone but he or she then spends time persuading others that these decisions were correct. This produces more commitment and enthusiasm on the part of the group members, although there may still be some resentment that they have not been consulted before the decisions were made.

The third leadership style does involve conferring with workers prior to making decisions and this is known as **consultative** leadership. The advice of the group is taken into account before decisions are made, although it is still the leader's decision. The main advantage of this style of leadership is that group members will be better motivated because they feel that they have shared in the decision making process. The leader can make a more informed decision because useful information can be obtained from the group members.

The final leadership style is the **democratic** style. In this case a leader will allow a decision to emerge from the group through discussion. The leader will not attempt to enforce his or her own views. This helps to create a high degree of commitment from the group, but it can be a slow process and the decisions that emerge may often be compromises, attempting to please everybody but not in the best interests of the organisation.

Who should lead the nation?

QUICK QUIZ

1. What is meant by saying that a company has a separate legal personality?
2. What is meant by 'limited liability'?
3. What are the advantages of a partnership as a form of business organisation?
4. What should be included in a 'partnership agreement'?
5. Why might a sole trader consider turning his business into a private limited company?
6. What would be the disadvantages of a sole trader forming a private limited company?
7. What are the main differences between a retail co-operative and a public limited company?
8. What is an employee co-operative?
9. Distinguish between a public company and a public corporation.
10. List five motives for nationalisation.
11. What is meant by privatisation? Give two recent examples.
12. What is meant by delegation?
13. What is meant by span of control?
14. What are the problems which can arise when the span of control is too large?
15. What are the advantages to a large organisation of decentralisation?
16. Distinguish between line and staff relationships within an organisation.
17. What do you understand by the informal organisation?
18. What is the role of a manager in a business?
19. Briefly describe the four basic styles of leadership.
20. Under what circumstances is autocratic leadership most appropriate?

Case Study: The launch of Wispa

Despite the continued success of Cadbury's Dairy Milk, first introduced in 1905 and Flake, introduced in 1920, the company realised that there was still a need to develop new products.

Double Decker, launched in 1976 had been a success, but Cadbury wanted a new, all milk chocolate product which would be different from its existing products. Their product development team came up with a new textured chocolate. There were a number of factors which the company had to take into account before the new product could be launched onto the national market.

● **Product design** – Cadbury experimented with 20–30 shapes before deciding on the final one.

● **Packaging** – They chose a dark blue and red wrapper to look expensive and appeal to all age groups.

●**Price** – A price of 17p was decided on, 1p less than a Mars bar and 1p more than Aero, both strong rivals.

● **Distribution** – Eighty extra salesmen were taken on to ensure that the product was available in all shops that sold confectionery goods.

● **Consumer research** – The product was tested on a group of consumers to make sure they liked it before it was manufactured in large quantities.

● **Test marketing** – The product was launched in Newcastle upon Tyne in September 1981. Despite the fact that no advertising had taken place, three month's production was sold in one day. Production was halted so a new plant could be built to meet demand.

● **Name** – Before coming up with the name Wispa, Cadbury researched a number of names but, in the words of their commercial director, 'they were too like the names of cars'.

● **Advertising** – A major advertising campaign costing £6m was launched to promote the product. Within weeks Wispa was fourth in the confectionery league table.

We can see from this case study that there are a number of important points to remember about the nature of marketing.

● It starts before production with market research and product research.

● There are implications for other departments, such as ensuring that enough can be produced to meet expected demand.

● It involves 'promoting' the product to create a demand for it.

● It includes 'distribution' of the product. This involves both transport to the buyer and choice of outlet.

● Pricing is part of marketing activity.

We refer to these various elements of marketing as the **marketing mix** or the four Ps.

● **Product**, ie research, packaging.

● **Promotion**, ie advertising, sales promotion.

● **Price**, ie price levels, discounts.

● **Place**, ie distribution.

1   Suggest reasons why Cadbury decided on:

   a   the package design shown in the photograph

   b   the name 'Wispa'

   c   a price of 17p.

2   What do you think were the most important reasons for the success of Wispa?

Part 1   The nature of marketing

All the activities linking the producer with the consumer come under the heading of **marketing**. As the name suggests, marketing is concerned with 'the market' and a market exists when buyers and sellers exchange goods for money.

A possible definition of marketing offered by the Institute of Marketing is:

> 'Marketing is the management process responsible for identifying, anticipating and satisfying customer requirements profitably.'

The history of marketing

Before the Industrial Revolution there were close links between producers and consumers. The needs of the consumer were clear and craftsmen produced goods to order within small communities. As a result, there was little need for a great deal of marketing activity. Some craftsmen did, however, put their names on their goods as a guarantee of quality and this was the start of **branding**. Some of the craftsmen are still famous and their goods are bought and sold for large sums in antique markets. These craftsmen included Wedgwood and Chippendale. Can you name any others?

The Industrial Revolution brought with it mass production and hence the need for mass distribution. The close link between producer and consumer was broken and producers now had to advertise their products. Demand was growing rapidly, however, and firms were mainly production led, ie they produced products and then persuaded people to buy them rather than trying to find out what consumers required.

Soon after the Second World War the supply of goods began to exceed demand and producers were under pressure to keep up their sales if they were not to be left with expensive machinery lying idle. This has made producers increasingly aware of the importance of studying the market.

The marketing department

We have seen that marketing is vital for the success of a modern firm. The organisation of marketing activities will, however, vary a great deal between firms. At one extreme, a small firm will not be able to employ specialist managers and there may therefore be no individual with sole responsibility for marketing. At the other extreme, a large firm may have a team of managers specialising in the various marketing functions. This department may be further divided up to deal with different products or to specialise in different markets. You should be able to pick out some of these specialist personnel from the job advertisements in Figure 1.

Figure 1: Marketing personnel

Figure 2: The marketing team

Marketing
Director

Market Research Manager

Product Development Manager

Advertising and Promotions Manager

Sales Manager

Distribution Manager

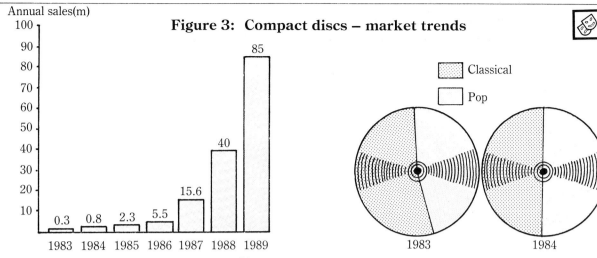

Figure 3: Compact discs – market trends

Source: *Trade Estimates* HMSO

The marketing of compact discs

By 1986 the market for compact discs was growing rapidly. The small, grooveless discs, making use of laser technology, give much better reproduction than traditional records and were first introduced into the UK in 1983. Originally compact discs were used mainly by lovers of classical music, but increasingly pop music has been available in this form.

Imagine that it is 1986 and you are the marketing director for a large consumer electrical goods firm. Your product development section have designed a new compact disc player and you have been asked for your views on whether you should enter this new market.

1 What does the information in Figure 3 tell you about the market for compact discs?

2 **a** Does this information suggest that entry into this new market could be worthwhile? Explain your answer.

   b What other information would you require in order to help you to make your recommendations?

3 Assuming that the company has decided to launch the new product, list the factors which would need to be considered before a national launch can take place (use the Wispa case study to help you).

Hint

Remember that success depends on getting the right product, in the right quantity, to the right place, at the right price, at the right time and also letting the customer know about it.

Part 2   Market research

A successful business depends on managers making the right decisions. Decision making involves considering alternatives and making choices based on a combination of information and guesswork. There is always an element of risk involved in business, but accurate information allows businessmen to identify opportunities and to reduce the uncertainty of decision making. Making the wrong choices can be extremely costly and information helps to reduce the chances of making mistakes.

A definition of market research from the American Marketing Association is:

'The systematic gathering, recording and analysing of data about problems relating to the marketing of goods and services.'

Research helps bridge the gap between producers and consumers and has developed alongside marketing as this gap has widened. In addition, rising costs have made it even more important that a firm's marketing activities are as effective as possible.

The first specialist research agency can be traced back to 1911 in the United States, but the biggest growth in research activity took place in the 1950s. Market research is now seen as essential by most successful companies.

Stages of market research

The first stage of market research is to decide on the questions to ask. The manufacturer will need to know how many people are likely to buy the product, what sort of people they are and where they live, where they buy the product and what they use it for, what they are prepared to pay for the product and what competitors are charging.

Having decided on the questions, the next step is to decide on the information which is needed in order to answer these questions and how this information is to be collected. This is known as the method of research.

The final step is to collect the information, draw conclusions and make recommendations based on the results.

Figure 4: The stages of market research

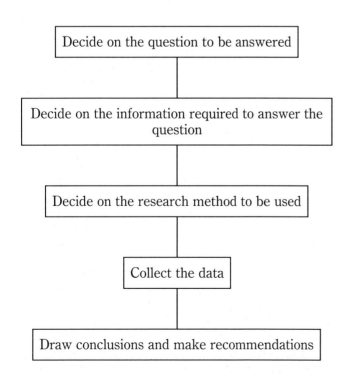

We saw earlier how the launch of Wispa could have been a costly mistake. To avoid this, Cadbury collected a great deal of information.

1   What information did the company need to know before launching the product on the national market?
2   How might they have obtained this information?

Splitting the market

Whilst historically firms often attempted to sell to the mass market, increased competition has made this more difficult. It is therefore likely that they will try to break down the market into sections or **segments** and to aim their product at one or more of these smaller markets. This recognises that there is no such thing as a single market composed of identical consumers, but that there are a number of well defined groups within the market with differing characteristics and preferences.

What groups of people are the following magazines aimed at?

a   *Smash Hits.*
b   *Woman's Own.*
c   *The Economist.*
d   *New Scientist.*
e   *Cosmopolitan.*
f   *Autocar.*

Market segments can be defined in a number of different ways.

These include the following:

- Demographic, eg age, sex, social class.
- Personality, eg extrovert, introvert.
- Geographic, eg urban, rural.
- Behavioural, eg occasional users, regular users.

One of the tasks of the market researcher will therefore be to find out what sector of the market a product is most likely to appeal to. Such things as product design and advertising can then be 'targeted' to achieve the best results.

Figure 5: Socio-economic groups

Social grade	Social status	Head of houshold's occupation
A	Upper middle class	Higher managerial, administrative or professional
B	Middle	Intermediate managerial, administrative or professional
C₁	Lower middle class	Supervisory or clerical and junior managerial, administrative or professional
C₂	Skilled working class	Skilled manual workers
D	Working class	Semi-skilled and un-skilled manual workers
E	Those at lowest levels of sub-sistence	State pensioners or widows (no other earner), casual or lower grade workers

Figure 6: Magazine readership

Publication	Sex		Class profile	
	Men %	Women %	ABC₁ %	C₂DE %
Cosmopolitan	30	70	59	41
Economist	75	25	84	16
Exchange & Mart	74	26	41	59
Practical Householder	66	34	46	54
Punch	69	31	72	28
Radio Times	47	53	50	50
TV Times	45	55	41	59
Vogue	20	80	59	41
Woman's Own	19	81	41	59

1 In the light of the information in Figures 5 and 6, in which publications would you choose to advertise:

a a luxury car **d** a new perfume
b beer **e** a range of DIY products
c microwave ovens **f** a luxury cruise.

Explain your answers.

2 As a class collect one copy of each of the magazines in Figure 6. Compare the advertising found in each paper and suggest reasons for any differences you find.

Collecting information

It would be far too time consuming and costly for a firm to obtain enough information to make decisions with certainty. Risks can be reduced but not removed entirely. To reduce costs, information is usually collected from a sample of the population.

The term population is used for all items about which information is wanted. A sample is a selected number of items which are actually investigated. For a survey of voting intentions, for example, the 'population' would be all those over the age of 18 who are able to vote. An opinion poll, however, might involve interviewing a sample of as few as 200 people.

If accurate results are to be obtained the sample must be carefully chosen. Sampling methods include:

● **Random sampling** – This is where every member of the population has an equal chance of being chosen. A number of addresses may be chosen at random from the electoral register and if there is no reply an interviewer may have to call back rather than call at another address.

● **Purposive samples** – Here there is a deliberate bias to allow a particular aspect of the market to be investigated, eg when investigating the use of supermarkets, the sample could contain more women than men.

● **Quota samples** – These are often used for street interviews where the interviewer has a choice of who to approach but they must interview a certain number of people in each of a number of groups, eg different age groups.

● **Stratified samples** – These are chosen to provide a representative cross section of the population. The main elements of the population such as age distribution, occupation, social class etc, are reflected accurately in the sample.

● **Cluster sampling** – This involves choosing a 'random group' rather than choosing individuals at random. The group chosen could be a street or sales district and this forms the sample. This reduces the cost of interviewing as those being interviewed will be concentrated in a small number of areas.

Split up into five groups. Each group has been given the task of finding out how students at your school feel about school dinners. Each group should choose one of the five sampling methods discussed earlier, such as random sampling, purposive sampling etc.

1   Decide on how you will choose a sample of 20 students to interview.
2   Carry out these interviews and prepare a report to be presented to the class.

Sources of information

Firms have access to a great deal of information to help them make decisions. There are basically two types of data which can be obtained from market research:

● **Primary data** – This is obtained from research such as questionnaires and interviews, and is intended to answer a specific question such as how large the market is for a particular product.
● **Secondary data** – This is information which has not been collected for a specific purpose but may help to answer a number of questions. It includes such sources as government statistics and trade publications.

Research methods

Desk research

This mostly takes the form of using the firm's own records and published statistics and is used to provide background information. A company's invoices, for example, may provide information on the type of retail outlet which is handling most of the company's goods. Government statistics may help to calculate the overall size of the market. To obtain more detailed information, however, the company may have to carry out field research.

Field research

Postal questionnaires

This is probably one of the cheapest research methods in that it does not require an interviewer. It can allow those who reply to remain anonymous and gives them time to consider their replies. The response rates, ie the number of questionnaires returned is low, however, and returns may not come from a representative sample of the population, as some groups are more likely to return questionnaires than others. In addition, the absence of an interviewer means that respondants cannot seek help if they do not understand a question.

Telephone surveys

This is also a relatively inexpensive method and has the added advantages that the response is immediate and results can be obtained quickly. Political parties have made use of telephone surveys to find out what electors think are the important issues in the run up to an election.

There is a possible bias, however, in that not all consumers have telephones and others may be reluctant to give full answers to strangers on the 'phone. The number of questions which can be included is usually limited.

"... AND QUESTION NUMBER 73 IS..."

Personal interviews

Because of the cost of this type of survey (one estimate puts it at £8 per interview), it is important that the sample is chosen carefully and that interviewers are well trained to prevent bias. In addition, as with all questionnaires, the questions must be very carefully thought out.

"I'm looking for a female pensioner to complete my quota!"

A great deal of information can be obtained, however, and the presence of a skilled interviewer has a number of advantages. Resistance on the part of the respondent may be overcome and products or advertisements can be shown. Unclear questions can also be explained.

Consumer panels

These provide a direct link with the consumer. Those taking part will usually be co-operative as they have volunteered their services. Consumer panels can take a number of forms. Informal 'coffee mornings' can be organised where a trained interviewer will move the conversation towards a discussion of such things as the group's reaction to the biscuits and coffee. More formal tech-

niques include consumer diaries, where a consumer will write down information on all major purchases over a period of time, with details of where the products were bought and how payment was made. In some cases special waste bins are provided so that an analysis of refuse can be used to support diary entries.

Retail audit

This technique allows researchers to obtain a great deal of valuable information by checking the stocks in shops. The information obtained may include the sales in each type of retail outlet, the average sales each week and which competitors brands are stocked.

"Joe came in here three weeks ago to sort out last months invoices."

Test marketing

As we saw with the example of Wispa, information about a new product can be obtained by introducing it into one region before launching it nationally. Local TV and press can be used to promote the product. Although the region might not be typical of the total market and there might be more advertising than usual during a test launch, valuable information can be obtained.

Observation

This technique is most commonly used to observe how consumers behave in shops. The information obtained is limited, but it is still valuable as it provides data about how retailers design store layouts and how manufacturers obtain the best shelf space for their products.

The questions contained in a questionnaire must be carefully thought out. The following questions 1–5 have been badly worded. Match each question with one of the criticisms (a) to (e).

Questions

1 When do you serve soup?
2 Do you agree that wholemeal bread is healthier than white bread?
3 How many cups of tea do you drink in a week?
4 What is the cubic capacity of your refrigerator?
5 Was the fitted wardrobe quick and easy to assemble?

Criticisms

a A loaded question which will normally be answered 'yes' whatever the respondant's real view.
b Too technical for most people.
c Too vague and imprecise.
d Two questions in one.
e This is asking too much of the respondant's memory.

Motivational research

This is used to try to find out about consumers' preferences where even the consumers themselves may not be clear as to why they are (or are not) buying a particular product. To do this a number of psychological techniques are used including in-depth interviews. These are informal and therefore better able to measure attitudes.

As well as in-depth interviews, other psychological techniques such as word association tests and role playing may be used to determine consumers' views.

Specialist research agencies

Whilst large companies may have their own research department, smaller firms may find research too costly. A number of specialist agencies have, however, grown up offering a range of services. Some of the better known names include:

● A. C. Nielsen – specialists in retail audit.
● Gallup – offering a range of services to business in addition to their well known political polls and weekly pop charts.
● Audit Bureau of Circulation – providing printed media circulation statistics, eg newspapers.
● Joint Industrial Committee for Television Audience Research (JICTAR) – providing weekly TV audience figures.
● Audits of Great Britain – making extensive use of consumer diaries to provide information on household expenditure.

A firm manufacturing fishing tackle is considering the introduction of a fishing rod using a new material giving it significant advantages over existing products, but at a slightly higher price. Match up the information required by the firm to any possible sources.

Information may be obtained from more than one source, and sources can be used to provide more than one piece of information.

Information required

1 The size of the market.
2 Trends in sales.
3 Consumer profile (who might buy the product?)
4 Strengths and weaknesses of existing products.
5 Price sensitivity (what effect will price have on demand?)

Sources of information

a A survey of leisure trends.
b Test marketing.
c Consumer panels.
d Questionnaires.
e The *Angling Times*.
f A '*Which?*' report on fishing rods.
g Trade statistics.

Part 3   The product

To be successful, it is important that a firm's products meet the consumer's needs. The product must serve the purpose for which it is intended and must also appeal to the customer.

Very few firms produce only a single product. The advantages of offering a number of products are considerable. Risks can be spread so that if one product is unsuccessful others will hopefully still be able to contribute to profits. It is likely that a number of products will share the same method of production, giving scope for economies of scale.

In addition, the costs of selling and advertising can be spread over a number of products, with one salesman dealing with a number of lines and the possibility of advertising being used to promote a variety of products rather than a single item. Distribution costs can also be kept down when a firm is dealing in larger quantities.

Finding new uses for products.

New product development

A successful company must continue to introduce new products to cater for changing markets as consumers demand new and better quality products. The company also needs to keep ahead of its competitors. We can see from Figure 7 how Proctor and Gamble have had to continuously introduce new fabric washing products over the years.

Figure 7: Proctor and Gamble Ltd: New products

Fabric Washing Products

Dreft	(1937)
Tide	(1950)
Daz	(1953)
Fairy Snow	(1957)
Ariel	(1969)
Bold	(1972)
Daz Automatic	(1979)
Ariel Automatic	(1981)
Dreft Automatic	(1984)
Ariel Automatic Liquid	(1986)

Source: Proctor and Gamble Ltd

In some firms the task of developing new products and changing existing products is the responsibility of the marketing department. In larger firms there may even be a separate **research and development** department to undertake this work, using market research information gathered by the company.

The sales department may be able to suggest changes to existing products based on comments made by customers, or a firm may simply copy ideas introduced by competitors. The Japanese company Matsushita, for example, has a team of engineers and a number of laboratories specialising in making improvements to products currently produced by other companies.

The need for new product development is increased as a result of **obsolescence**. This is the term used to describe the products which become out of date because of technological change or scientific advance. The vast majority of the products we purchase today have been developed over the past decade as older products become obsolete and changing technology has allowed new products to be produced, possibly using cheaper materials.

The product life cycle

As well as needing to develop new products, a firm must consider its existing products to see if any are unprofitable and need to be dropped. In some cases it may be possible to modify them. This modification can take the form of improved quality, new features or a new design.

All goods and services have a 'lifetime' over which their popularity changes. The overall pattern is of expanding sales at first followed by decline, although it is possible to identify a number of different stages of the so-called **product life cycle**.

The length of a product's life will vary. Extreme examples are the Volkswagon 'Beetle' which was popular for over 40 years and fashion items which may be in demand for only a matter of months. The aim of the marketing department must be to extend the life of a product where possible and to anticipate the need for new products to replace those with declining sales.

Stages of the product life cycle

A graph can be drawn to illustrate the typical pattern of sales for a consumer good and we can use this graph to identify the main stages of the product life cycle.

Figure 8: The product life cycle

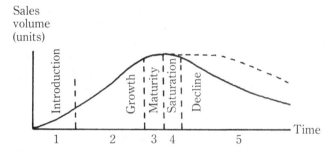

The dotted line shows what happens when improvements either to the product or to its marketing take place. Decline and obsolescence are delayed and the product's life cycle extended.

There comes a time, however, when changing the product and increased marketing activity can no longer prevent decline. Well before this point, the well-managed company will have started the development of new products to replace the old ones.

Stage one: Introduction

At this stage the product may still be changed or even withdrawn from sale. The reaction of customers to the product should be carefully researched to make sure that it will sell enough to contribute to profit.

The number of items produced is likely to be relatively small at this stage and the costs of launching the product, such as advertising costs, will be high. Profits will therefore be small or even non-existent. When a brand new product is being introduced onto the market the costs of the launch will be even higher, as it is necessary to overcome the resistance of both consumers and retailers to new products and new technology. The introduction of compact discs onto the market, for example, did not revolutionise the record industry overnight.

Stage two: Growth

At this stage consumers who have been waiting and gathering information from advertising, early buyers of the product and other sources, such as newspaper articles, will buy the product. This will be particularly true of goods which are quite expensive as many consumers are reluctant to buy them at first. Home video was a good example of this where the market expanded rapidly after a period of fairly modest sales.

The manufacturer is able to get wider distribution for his product once customers start to ask for it. Retailers who had previously been reluctant to stock the new product will now order it and possibly display it prominently because it is new. The manufacturers may help by providing display materials for retailers to use.

At first, prices will be high if the product is in some way unique and there is little competition. Firms which enter the market first with a new product will be keen to get back the money which they have used for research and development. The high profits earned by early entrants into the market will soon attract competitors, however, and the price will fall as similar, often improved products enter the market, eg pocket calculators and video recorders.

Stage three: Maturity

As competition increases, so the rate at which sales are growing starts to level off. Firms must fight harder to keep their share of the market with increased advertising and possibly increased incentives to retailers to take their products. Some of the weaker firms in the market could go out of business at this stage as they are no longer able to make a profit due to increased competition.

Stage four: Saturation

As sales begin to level off, stocks may eventually start to build up in wholesale and retail outlets causing new orders to fall even further. The market is said to be 'saturated' with sales, matching or even falling short of the amount industry can produce, ie its capacity.

Stage five: Decline

After a period of stability where sales are no longer growing, there will almost certainly be a decline in sales as consumers begin to lose interest in the product. This decline could be slow or extremely quick. Technological change could lead to a product becoming obsolete very quickly with manufacturers having to sell off stocks very cheaply or stopping production altogether.

The data given in the diagram below illustrate the pattern of revenue and profit earned over a product's life cycle. Study the diagram and answer the questions that follow.

Figure 9: Pattern of sales and profits

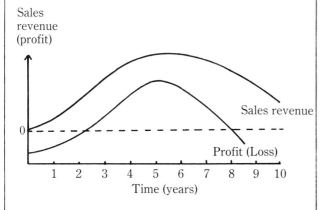

1 What is meant by the term 'product life cycle'?
2 Explain briefly the pattern of product sales and profit shown in the diagram.
3 What phase of the cycle is this product in once it has been on the market for 6 years?

Extension strategies

Extension strategies are methods which can be used by firms to attempt to delay the decline in sales which must eventually take place. The effect was illustrated in Figure 8 where the dotted line showed how the saturation stage could be extended.

There are five main types of strategy which can be used:

● New markets for existing products, eg selling Scotch whisky abroad.

● Finding new uses for the product, eg Rail Rover tickets which promote rail travel as a holiday.
● More frequent use of the product, eg the development of new turkey products – turkey is now no longer only eaten at Christmas.
● Wider product range, eg family size tins of Heinz baked beans.
● Styling changes, eg modifications to existing models of cars, such as more luxurious interiors.

Brand names

Despite the existence of a product life cycle, many products have been with us for a long time and their brand names have become well known. The brand name of a successful product is a valuable asset to a company. The product is easily recognised and is distinguished from competitive brands. Consumers feel more confident in buying goods when they recognise the name. In the United Kingdom well known brands such as Brooke Bond, Hoover and Gillette date back many years and in some cases, as with Hoover and Biro, the leading brand name is used to describe all brands of the product.

A product's name helps to give it an identity – that is it tells consumers something about the product or creates an image for the product.

---

1 What is the image created by the following brand names?

   a Care Bears.
   b Wispa.
   c Night Nurse cold remedy.
   d Kwik-Fit exhausts.
   e Aquafresh toothpaste.

2 Think up some good brand names for these products:

   a Goldfish food.
   b A new lipstick range.
   c Low fat crisps.
   d Instant coffee.

Brand names can take three main forms:

● Descriptive – telling you something about the product such as 'Yoghurt Juice'.
● Associative – creating an image for the product such as Wispa.
● Abstract – meaningless names which are sometimes produced by a computer. Examples include 'Xerox' and 'Quatro'.

YOU NAME IT...

WE PROBABLY NAMED IT.

Examples of brand names.

As with most areas of marketing, there are specialist companies which can be used to suggest brand names for a product. Once a name has been created it can be registered as a trademark to prevent anyone else using it. There are over a million trademarks registered although they are not all used. One of the oldest registered trademarks is 'Bass'.

A further development of branding has been the growth of **retail branding**. This is where retailers have their own brands on sale. One of the most successful 'own brands' has been St. Michael, the brand name used for products sold at Marks and Spencer. Other examples include Boots, Tesco and Sainsbury.

By having their own brands, retailers are able to sell more cheaply because advertising costs are reduced. They are also able to influence the look of the store by their choice of packaging and they can build up greater customer loyalty. If you like Tesco baked beans you can only buy them from Tesco.

Packaging

Branding does not stop with the brand name but is also continued into package design and colour, logos, slogans etc.

Originally goods were packaged to help protect them, but now packaging is an important part of the marketing mix. The design of a product, its packaging and the materials used can have a significant effect on sales.

A package can link together products produced by a particular manufacturer to create an identity. It can also attract the attention of the customer and help create an image for the product. The package may be an important part of the product being sold, such as the sleeve of a record or an aerosol spray or it can help a product to stand out from its competitors, such as a liqueur bottle. In many cases the cost of packaging is a significant proportion of the cost of the product.

You are the marketing manager for a firm of wine importers who have decided to launch a fairly inexpensive range of Californian wines onto the British market. Write a report to the managing director recommending the form that your packaging should take.

You will need to consider such things as:

a what material will the container be made of?

b what should it say on the label?

c will the container be re-useable?

d what quantity will the container hold?

e how can it be made to stand out on a supermarket shelf?

f will the product be easy to transport and store?

The next time you are in a supermarket which sells wine, take careful note of the many different ways in which wine can be packaged.

Pack design has had an increasingly important role to play since self-service shopping began. A good pack design can encourage impulse purchases, show how the product should be used and help to distinguish the product from its rivals.

An example of the effectiveness of good package design is the case of Johnson Wax. When they repackaged Glade air freshener they achieved increased sales of 300%. Another example of good package design, used to overcome customer resistance to a product, is St. Ivel Five Pints. By putting their dried skimmed milk powder in milk bottle shaped containers they associate their product with the 'real thing' in the minds of the customer. A similar principle applies to Jif lemon juice.

The colour of packaging used can also have a remarkable effect on consumers. Research has shown that consumers' attitudes are influenced by the colour of the container that goods are packaged in. Colours convey different images, some of which are set out below:

Black	– strong	Gold	– rich
Blue	– cool	Green	– fresh
Brown	– practical	Orange	– warm
Purple	– expensive	Red	– hot

Quality control

Quality is an important factor to be considered when consumers are deciding between the alternative products available to them and therefore it is a concern of the marketing department. The success of many companies is based on quality and reliability. Examples include Marks and Spencer for clothes and Volkswagon for cars. Top quality will not always be an objective however. Many goods sell because they are cheap and disposable rather than being durable and expensive. An example would be cheap ballpoint pens. The aim of the company must be to decide on a combination of price and quality which is acceptable to the consumer. Many products are available in a range of different qualities which aim at different sections of the market.

Quality will be influenced by a number of factors. These include the type of materials used in production, the design of the product, the methods of production and how well goods are checked before they go on sale.

Wall's Viennetta

Designed as an up-market desert, Viennetta became a best-selling ice cream brand within 2 years of its launch.

The ice cream market has been fairly static at around 290 m to 300 m litres annually. Within this total 'hand held' ice cream sales are declining whereas sales of take-home packs, helped by the spread of home freezer ownership, are increasing.

Take-home ice cream represents 70% of the market by volume, but only 48% by value. There was therefore a need for a high value take-home product and in 1979 the Wall's marketing department asked their product development colleagues to look into the possibility of producing an 'up-market' product. The result was an idea based on layers of ice cream interleaved with thin layers of crisp chocolate.

The product was designed to have year-round sales and to appeal mainly to adults. It took Wall's 18 months to work out how to produce the product commercially but by Spring 1982 it was ready for launch. The choice of name 'Viennetta' was meant to bring to mind the coffee and cake shops of Vienna and to identify the product with continental ice cream.

Wall's put in a patent application for the production process which was technically difficult, and also registered the name. The price was set at around £1 per half litre pack which was about twice the average price of take-home ice cream.

Initially advertising was in women's magazines featuring a large colour photograph of Viennetta on a silver salver. The response was so strong that Wall's soon moved to regional TV advertising.

Source: Adapted from *Marketing* May 31 1984

Read the Viennetta study carefully and answer the following questions.

1 How has the market for ice cream changed in recent years?
2 Explain the statement 'Take-home ice cream represents 70% of the market by volume, but only 48% by value'.
3 Why did Wall's choose the name 'Viennetta' for their new product?
4 Why did they register the name?
5 Explain the choice of colour advertisements for the early advertising of the product in women's magazines.

Part 4   Advertising and promotion

Promotion is the activity of bringing a firm's products to the attention of the public and persuading them to buy. It can take a number of forms including advertising, sales promotion and public relations.

Advertising

The form of promotion that we are most familiar with is advertising. The Advertising Association defines advertising as follows:

> 'An advertisement is an announcement paid for by those who send it and intended to inform or influence those who receive it.'

This definition gives some clue as to the wide range of activities which come under the heading of advertising. They range from classified advertisements in a local newspaper for a second hand washing machine to a multi-million pound press and TV advertising campaign to launch a new product.

In Britain we can trace national advertising back to the seventeenth century, in journals such as the *London Gazette* and the *Tatler*. With the expansion of markets which came with the Industrial Revolution, manufacturers realised that it was necessary to appeal directly to the general public. As living standards improved more luxury goods were produced. It was not necessary for consumers to buy these goods, they had a wide range of alternatives being offered to them and firms could no longer take their market for granted.

The desire of manufacturers to inform and influence the general public was helped by the growth of newspapers and magazines and later by the development of cinemas and public transport, all offering opportunities for firms to advertise their products. Further important developments have been the introduction of commercial television in 1955 and commercial radio in 1973.

There are many different groups who make use of advertising to reach a larger audience than would be possible by personal contact.

Small firms will spend little on advertising and are likely to concentrate on local media such as local newspapers, directories such as *Thomson Local Directory* and possibly local radio. At the other extreme there are major national and multinational companies who may spend many millions on advertising.

In 1983, for example, Proctor and Gamble spent nearly £46 m on advertising, mainly on TV for products such as Ariel, Bold, Bounce, and Head and Shoulders. Mars was the second

Advertising media.

1 List some of the reasons why each of the following might want to advertise.

Example: A private individual

Reasons for advertising:

- To sell second hand goods
- To find a job
- To announce an engagement
- To seek a flat mate

a The organisers of a sporting event.
b A charitable organisation.
c The government.
d A college of further education.
e A political party.
f A manufacturer.

2 Try to find examples of adverts produced by each of the above groups.

largest advertiser, spending over £27m on advertising Mars Bars, Bounty, and other confectionery products. In the public sector the Electricity Council spent over £19 m on advertising central heating, cookers, fridges etc. In retailing the Co-operative retail societies spent over £13 m promoting their services to the public.

Types of advertisement

Although there are no clear cut distinctions, it is possible to identify a number of different types of advertisement:

- **Informative advertisements** – These aim to make the public aware of a product's existence and purpose. They may provide technical information to help the consumer make a better choice.
- **Persuasive advertisements** – These seek to persuade the public to buy a product. They may, for example, present a glamorous image for the product in the hope that a consumer will identify with this image and buy the product. This is often known as the 'hard sell'.
- **Combative advertisements** – These attempt to expand one firm's share of the market at the expense of its rivals. This type of advertising has proved to be rather controversial in recent years with some firms making unreasonable claims about the benefits of their product over those of rival firms.
- **Generic advertising** – This is where a group of manufacturers get together to promote

a product type rather than an individual brand. This may be done through a trade association or marketing board such as the Milk Marketing Board.
- **Corporate advertising** – This is where a company promotes its own name rather than a specific product. This has the advantage that a whole range of products can be indirectly promoted through a single advertisement.

1 Collect examples of each of the types of advertisement listed above.
2 After studying the examples you have collected, write a short paragraph on the wording to be used in a newspaper advertisement for:

a an informative advertisement for a weedkiller
b a persuasive advertisement for after-shave
c a combative advertisement for a car
d a generic advertisement for coffee
e a corporate advertisement for ICI.

Advertising media

Advertising media means the method (or medium) used to communicate with the public. The best known media are the newspapers and television, but there are many others including commercial radio, direct mail, the cinema and

posters. The actual medium chosen will depend on a number of factors:

● The nature of the product – Most products are bought by a particular section of the population and the medium used should be the most effective for reaching this section. A crane-hire firm, for example, would advertise in the trade press of the building industry whereas a manufacturer of cosmetics may concentrate its advertising on women's magazines.

● Is the market national or local? – Local radio and local newspapers would be the best way of advertising a local car showroom, but national newspapers and magazines might be more cost effective in promoting breakfast cereals.

● Is the intention to reach a new market or to support an existing market? – Advertising financial services such as unit trusts may seem to be best achieved by using newspapers such as the *Financial Times*, but a new market could be tapped by advertising in the *News of the World*.

● Would a moving advertisement be an advantage? – Some products are made more attractive to the consumer if they can be seen in use. Toys, for example, benefit from being advertised on TV where a child can be shown playing with them. In the same way, colour advertisements are more suitable for some products such as food items. As a result newspaper colour supplements or magazines may be preferred to black and white newspaper advertisements.

● How effective has the medium been in the past? – Firms should attempt to measure the effectiveness of the medium they chose although this may prove difficult.

● How much does the firm want to pay? – It is necessary to make some estimate of the benefits expected from advertising and the cost.

A distinction is sometimes made between **above the line** advertising and **below the line** advertising. Above the line advertising is where the media pay a commission to an agency when an advertisement is placed with them. Examples include the press, TV and radio. With below the line advertising no commission is paid by the media and agencies make their money by charging the client a percentage on top of costs. Examples include direct mail, package design and exhibitions.

Figure 10: Advertising expenditure by media (1960)

	1960	
	£m	%
National newspapers	64	19.8
Regional newspapers	77	23.8
Magazines and periodicals	40	12.4
Trade & technical	31	9.6
Other	17	5.2
TOTAL PRESS	229	70.9
TV	72	22.3
Poster & transport	16	5.0
Cinema	5	1.5
Radio	1	0.3
TOTAL	323	100

Source: *Statistical Yearbook* Advertising Association

1 Using the figures for 1960, draw a pie chart to illustrate the breakdown of advertising expenditure between press,

Figure 11: Advertising expenditure by media (1985)

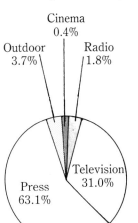

Source: Advertising Association

TV, outdoor (poster and transport), cinema and radio advertising.

2 Compare the figures for 1985 with those for 1960 and comment on the changes that have taken place.

Medium	Advantages	Disadvantages
National Newspaper	● National coverage. ● Reader can refer back. ● Relatively cheap.	● No movement or sound. ● Normally limited to black and white.
Regional Newspaper	● Good for regional campaigns and test marketing. ● Can be linked to local conditions.	● Cost per reader higher than national newspapers. ● Reproduction, layout etc. may be poor.
Magazines	● Colour advertisements possible. ● Targeting possible with specialist magazines. ● Advertising can be linked to features. ● Magazines may be referred to at a later date.	● A long time exists between advertisements being placed and magazine being printed. ● Competitive products are also being advertised. ● No movement or sound.
Television	● Colour can be used. ● Sound and movement possible. ● Can demonstrate the product in use. ● All groups of consumers can be reached.	● Relatively expensive. ● May cause irritation. ● Many consumers may not watch commercials.
Radio	● Enables use of sound. ● Most consumer groups covered.	● Not visual. ● No copy of material.
Cinema	● Colour, sound and movement can be used. ● Advertisements can be highly localised.	● Cinema audiences falling. ● Coverage restricted – audiences mainly young.
Posters	● National campaigns possible. ● Most groups covered. ● May encourage impulse buying through location close to shops	● Limited amount of information. ● Difficult to measure effectiveness.
Direct Mail	● Can be selective. ● Scope for originality. ● Effectiveness can be measured.	● Requires up to date mailing lists. ● Advertising mail may be thrown away unread.

An advertising agency

Advertising is a specialised undertaking and a great deal of money can be wasted if it is not carried out by experts. Even large firms with their own marketing departments may take the job of launching a new product to a specialist advertising agency.

Agencies were originally employed by the media, usually newspapers, to sell advertising space. To help sell space to manufacturers they offered advice on writing and designing advertisements. Later the idea of space broking developed whereby firms bought blocks of advertising space and resold this space in small units to advertisers. One of the earliest agencies of this type was Reynell and Son, dating back to 1812. Now there are over a thousand agencies offering a range of marketing services to customers, including market research, packaging design, public relations and advertising. The largest is Saatchi and Saatchi Garland Compton, employing over five hundred people and handling accounts worth £114,000,000.

Agencies have a number of advantages over a marketing department within a company. They will have expertise in producing TV and radio commercials which are highly specialised, they have access to the skilled personnel necessary to produce advertisements, including film directors, cameramen and technicians and because they are independent of the client, they are able to offer unbiased advice as to how a product should be promoted.

Within a large agency there will be a range of specialists. They may well be divided up into groups, each responsible for a number of clients, or in some cases one major client. Each client is known as an 'account' and a typical account group is illustrated in Figure 12.

Figure 12: A typical account group

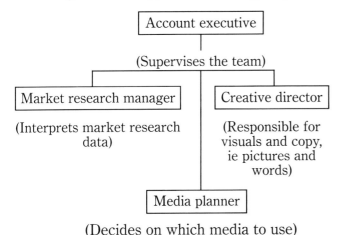

(Decides on which media to use)

The control of advertising

Given the power of advertising and the opportunities for abuse, it follows that the industry should be regulated in some way so as to protect the public. This regulation is a combination of legal controls and self regulation.

There are two important bodies involved in the control of the industry. These are the Code of Advertising Practice (CAP) Committee and the Advertising Standards Authority (ASA). The CAP Committee is made up of representatives of the trade associations involved in advertising. These include the Advertising Association and the Association of Mail Order Publishers. This body is responsible for preparing, amending and enforcing a code of practice for advertisers. This code of practice provides a set of rules for advertisers. The code of practice is supervised by the ASA. This is an independent body in that it does not consist of members of the industry. Their job is to protect the public interest and they deal with complaints from the public – as many as eight thousand a year. It is financed by a levy paid by the media on advertising expenditure.

The British Code of Advertising Practice, first published in 1961, spells out what makes a good advertisement:

● All advertisements should be legal, decent, honest and truthful.
● All advertisements should be prepared with a sense of responsibility both to the consumer and to society.
● All advertisements should conform to the principles of fair competition generally accepted in business.

The code also sets down rules relating to particular types of advertisement where the dangers of harmful advertising are seen to be greatest.

An extract from the code is given in Figure 14.

Figure 13: Advertising Standards Authority advertisements

Figure 14: Extract from British Code of Advertising Practice

Section C.X
Children

General

1.1   Direct appeals or exhortations to buy should not be made to children unless the product advertised is one likely to be of interest to them and one which they could reasonably be expected to afford for themselves.

1.2   Advertisements should not encourage children to make themselves a nuisance to their parents, or anyone else, with the aim of persuading them to buy an advertised product.

1.3   No advertisement should cause children to believe that they will be inferior to other children, or unpopular with them, if they do not buy a particular product, or have it bought for them.

1.4   No advertisement for a commercial product should suggest to children that, if they do not buy it and encourage others to do so, they will be failing in their duty or lacking in loyalty.

1.5   Advertisements addressed to children should make it easy for a child to judge the true size of a product (preferaby by showing it in relation to some common object) and should take care to avoid any confusion between the characteristics of real-life and toy copies of them.

1.6   Where the results obtainable by the use of a product are shown, these should not exaggerate what is attainable by an ordinary child.

1.7   Advertisements addressed to children should, wherever possible, give the price of the advertised product.

Source: Advertising Standards Authority

The ASA regularly runs advertising campaigns to inform the public of its existence and its purpose. The advertisements invite consumers to complain to the ASA about any advertising they feel to be wrong in some way. Complaints are investigated and regular case reports are published giving details of the result of the investigations. The ASA also make checks on a sample of other advertisements to make sure that they follow the guidelines.

It should be noted that the ASA is only responsible for press, poster and cinema advertising. Television and radio advertising is controlled by the Independent Broadcasting Authority (IBA). The 1981 Broadcasting Act placed legal controls on advertising on commercial television and independent radio. The IBA had to:

● exclude from broadcasting any advertisement which would be likely to mislead
● draw up and from time to time review the Code of Advertising Standards and Practice (in consultation with the Home Secretary)
● make sure advertisers comply with the code.

As with the ASA, the public can complain to the IBA if they are unhappy about an advertisement seen on TV or heard on radio.

In groups of four, take on the role of the ASA and decide whether you agree with each complaint. The complaints are real but not all were upheld.

You should be able to provide reasons for your decisions.

Basis of Complaint: A member of the public objected to a classified local press advertisement which stated 'A1 DISCOS, £25, also self hire discos'. On making enquiries, the complainant was informed that the cost of a disco was greater than £25. He also pointed out the advertiser's brochure did not feature a disco at this price.

Basis of Complaint: Two members of the public objected to a national press advertisement for the Alfa 33 headlined 'Life begins at 33', and which depicted a car not in contact with the road. The advertisement continued by stating 'A true five door sports saloon that can take you to 60 mph in 9.7 seconds and on to 116 mph with the precise handling, sure footed cornering and that driving sensation for which Alfa Romeo is renowned'. The complainants considered the advertisement likely to encourage illegal and dangerous driving practices.

Basis of Complaint: A member of the public objected to a leaflet, distributed in a local shopping area, inviting children to meet 'Una Stubbs, TV's Aunt Sally in Worzel Gummidge'. The leaflet also included details of other promotional items that would be available. The complainant pointed out that street canvassers approached accompanied children and informed them of the offer, which was subject to an account being opened in their name. The complainant questioned the suitability of such a direct approach to children.

Basis of Complaint: A member of the public objected to a local press advertisement for mirrored wardrobes headlined 'DOUBLE THE SIZE OF YOUR BEDROOM for £25'. The advertisement qualified the offer by stating that the fitments '...can be yours for only £30 deposit and 12 interest-free payments of £25 TOTAL PRICE £330'.

Source: Advertising Standards Authority

An example of the guidance notes provided for advertisers is given below. It relates to commercials for children's products.

'Children should normally be able to judge the size of toys by relation to some known object such as a child's hand.

Demonstrations of a toy in use should accurately represent what a normal child would experience using it. Similarly, shots of toys which are not self-propelled moving on their own account may be shown only if the film also demonstrates clearly how they are propelled in real play. Sound effects, say of the toy's real counterpart, should not be used in a way which would wrongly imply that the toy makes similar sounds.'

Figure 15: Carbolic Smoke Ball

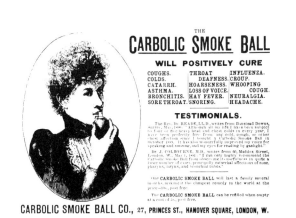

THE
CARBOLIC SMOKE BALL

WILL POSITIVELY CURE

COUGHS.	THROAT	INFLUENZA.
COLDS.	DEAFNESS.	CROUP.
CATARRH.	HOARSENESS.	WHOOPING
ASTHMA.	LOSS OF VOICE.	COUGH.
BRONCHITIS.	HAY FEVER.	NEURALGIA.
SORE THROAT.	SNORING.	HEADACHE.

TESTIMONIALS.

CARBOLIC SMOKE BALL CO., 27, PRINCES ST., HANOVER SQUARE, LONDON, W.

1 Imagine that this advertisement was to appear today in a national newspaper. Why would it no longer be acceptable?
2 Write a letter of complaint to the ASA about this advertisement.

Criticisms of advertising

Advertising must be judged on its effect on the public as a whole and not just on whether it helps a business to increase its profits. On this basis advertising is often criticised as being wasteful and unnecessary.

It is argued that good quality products will sell themselves and advertising is therefore an attempt to persuade consumers to buy poor quality goods. Supporters of advertising, however, would say that, however good a product is, the consumer still needs to be given information about the product and advertising is a way of providing this information. Although advertising can certainly help to persuade consumers to try a new product, many extensively advertised products have failed.

Given the high cost of a TV commercial, it would appear that some advertising costs must be passed on to the consumer in the form of higher prices. It has been argued that for every pound spent on washing powder, at least thirty pence goes to cover the cost of advertising. Those in the advertising industry would argue that advertising keeps costs down by expanding the market for a product, allowing firms to benefit from economies of scale.

Does advertising create a false need for a product? We may not need a car which is capable of travelling at 120 mph, for example, but advertising for a new car may promote this as a desirable feature. It could be argued, however, that this view underestimates the ability of the public to make up their own minds about the goods that they buy.

Large established firms are able to spend a great deal of money advertising their products. This makes it very difficult for new firms to enter the market and therefore reduces competition.

It is argued by many that advertisements provide inaccurate information to the public. They deal in opinion rather than fact and distort the truth. We have seen that, as a result of these criticisms, there are strict guidelines laid down on advertising practice.

THE MAKERS OF "WONDER WHITE" ARE PLEASED TO INFORM YOU THAT THE COST OF THIS ADVERTISEMENT IS HIDDEN IN THE PRICE OF EACH PACKET YOU BUY. THANK YOU AND GOOD NIGHT.

Benefits of advertising

A good advertising campaign will increase the firm's sales, which in turn may lead to increased employment and possibly lower prices through economies of scale. Advertising also provides essential revenue for the research and development of new products.

Advertising also provides the consumer with information about the products. Assuming this information is accurate, the risk of making a rash, ill-informed decision is reduced. Consumers can be informed if new products are in existence.

In the case of service industries, output cannot be stored and advertising is one way of regulating demand. British Telecom, for example, use advertising to promote off peak telephone calls as this helps to spread demand more evenly.

Advertising helps to pay for newspapers, commercial television and even supports sporting and cultural events.

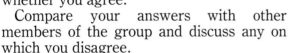

Read each one of the statements about advertising carefully and say whether you agree.

Compare your answers with other members of the group and discuss any on which you disagree.

a 'Advertising misleads the public.'
b 'Advertising is a valuable source of information about products.'
c 'Advertising makes products more expensive than they need to be.'
d 'Without advertising our choice of TV and radio programmes would be greatly reduced.'
e 'Advertising encourages competition between firms.'
f 'Advertising exploits the gullibility of the public.'
g 'Advertising helps to reduce unemployment.'
h 'Advertising encourages people to buy products they don't need.'
i 'Commercial breaks during TV programmes are annoying.'
j 'Advertising encourages people to go into debt.'

Sales promotion

Sales promotions are defined by the CAP committee as:

'...those marketing techniques which are used, usually on a temporary basis, to make goods and services more attractive to the consumer by providing some additional benefit whether in cash or in kind'.

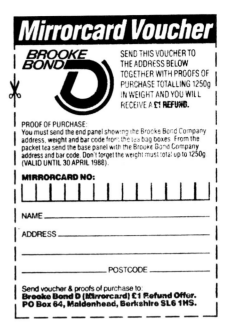

Vouchers are one example of sales promotion.

These promotions include:

● **Premium offers**, eg gifts in exchange for tokens and/or money, reduced prices, bonus packs or multi-pack offers such as 'buy two and get one free'.
● **Free offers or 'banded' offers**, eg a free wine glass with five gallons of petrol.
● **Distribution of vouchers, coupons or free samples.**
● **Personality promotions**, eg where a character is used to promote a product, such as the Dulux dog.
● **Charity linked promotions**, eg the consumer sends some proof of purchase to the company who make a charity donation in return.
● **Prize promotions**, eg newspaper prize bingo games.

As with advertising, there is a form of self regulation by means of the British Code of Sales Promotion Practice published by the CAP Committee. An extract from this code is reproduced in Figure 16.

Sales promotions are a short-term method of increasing sales. They provide the consumer with an incentive to buy now.

There are a number of reasons why a firm will choose to use sales promotion rather than using advertisements on TV or in the press. Promotions may be better at getting consumers to try new products, particularly if free samples are given. Some promotions are used to encourage repeat purchases of a product on the assumption that once a consumer has got into the habit of

Figure 16: British Code of Sales Promotion Practice

How the Code helps Promoters and Protects the Consumer

Let's look at some specific areas of concern.

First, *Protection of Privacy* Promoters should always respect consumer's right to reasonable privacy. It follows that promotions should not cause consumers trouble or annoyance. For example, mailing lists should be accurate and if a consumer asks for his or her name to be removed from such a list every effort should be made to ensure that this is done.

Clearly *Children and Young People* must be protected. The Code defines a child or young peson as one under 16 years of age. Promotions which are likely to attract them should not offer gifts or prizes which are unsuitable for people below 16.

It is also important of course, in promotions with more general appeal, to avoid offering gifts or prizes which might cause offence or be found undesirable. And, whether they are offered to children or adults, promotional products should always be safe.

The Code also has provisions on the way sales promotions are *Presented or Publicised*. Publicity should never be misleading. To ensure that it is not, all advertising material which supports the promotion should be checked both against the law and against the British Code of Advertising Practice.

Any consumer taking part in a promotion is interested in the *Quality* of what is on offer. The Code rules that all promotional products should reach satisfactory standards of safety, durability and performance in use and that any guarantee etc., should be clearly explained.

Promoters should avoid *Exaggeration*. Consumers – particularly when they have no opportunity to examine promotional products in advance – should not be led to over-estimate the quality or desirability of what is offered to them.

Source: Advertising Standards Authority

using a particular brand they will continue to do so. The offer of 'collectables' such as sets of wine glasses from petrol stations is one way of doing this.

Promotions may help to gain a firm extra display space in retail outlets, as the retailer also benefits from special offers being made by the manufacturer. Customers will feel that they are getting a better deal from the retailer and new customers may be attracted. Sometimes special offers are linked to individual retailers, notably large ones such as Boots and Asda.

Promotions may also be used to boost the sales of a product which is in decline. A well thought out promotional campaign can renew the interest of the salesforce, retailers and consumers. If a product is to be discontinued, promotions are also a good way of getting rid of stocks.

Study the list of promotions and answer the questions that follow.

1 State briefly what you think the main benefits would be of each of these promotions.
2 List as many examples as you can of each form of promotion.

   a A free bar of soap with each deodorant spray bought.
   b Large price reductions for a limited period.
   c Free samples delivered through the door.
   d Wildlife cards in packets of teabags.
   e A personal appearance by an author in a book shop.

Point of sale promotions

Because of the need to influence consumers when they are making up their minds about what to buy, many sales promotions operate at the point of sale itself. These point of sale promotions can take many forms. Display cards are often fixed on shelves or suspended from ceilings to direct the consumer's attention to the product. Window displays, display stands, window stickers and videos are amongst the many devices the promoters have available to them.

1 Outline briefly how you might promote the following:

   a A new LP in a record shop.
   b A new book by a best-selling author in a book shop.
   c A new wine in a super-market
   d A new type of screwdriver in a do-it-yourself shop.

2 The next time you visit a supermarket, make a list of the various ways in which firms attempt to attract the attention of the shopper and to promote their products.

One benefit of point of sale promotions to the retailer is that they bring customers into the shop. Some retailers use price promotions to attract customers by selling some items at cost price or even at a loss. These are known as **loss leaders** and the idea is that customers will be attracted by the low prices but will buy other goods once they are in the store.

Regular promotions also make shopping more interesting and increase customers' loyalty to the store. Some large supermarkets, for example, will run regular competitions for customers and offer free samples of items such as wine and cheese to shoppers.

Customers may also be encouraged to buy more than they intended when they first entered the store. One survey of housewives showed that they made 45% more purchases than they intended, the highest impulse purchases being cakes and biscuits. It concluded that shoppers make a list of basic essentials but rely on displays to remind them of other goods which they need.

The main benefits to the manufacturer are that they gain a good position on the supermarket shelves and a competitive advantage over their rivals. Within any shop there are some areas which are better for displaying a product than others. In supermarkets the prime selling spots are the ends of the aisles, the shelves at eye level and the checkouts. Special display stands and publicity material may help a firm to get its products into these good positions.

Research suggests that most customers have not made a firm decision as to which brand to buy when they enter the shop and so point of sale promotions can be an important influence. It is vital for a firm to know how its product is being sold. One firm significantly increased its sales once it realised that its packs were being stacked on the shelves with the ends facing outwards. The ends of the pack carried no information about the product, not even the company name. By placing a sticker on the end of the pack the customer's attention was attracted to the product and sales increased at the expense of the rival brands.

Public relations

As with sales promotions, public relations can put life back into fading products, aid the introduction of new products and provide publicity for a firm's product range.

Public relations (PR) involves providing the public with information about a firm and its activities and making sure the public knows about the company's strengths and achievements. It is important for a firm to build up a good reputation, but this takes a great deal of time. The use of newspapers and radio can speed up this process.

A major benefit of features in newspapers and on the radio is that they are more likely to be believed than advertisements, which are seen to be biased. Another advantage is that the firm is not limited to a small advertisement or a thirty second commercial to inform and educate the public. If they can have their product featured in a newspaper article or on a TV programme they can obtain much greater coverage.

An important part of PR is customer relations. It is essential to retain existing customers. Dissatisfied customers must be promptly dealt with to protect the company's reputation. Many large firms will have a customer relations department to deal with enquiries and complaints.

PR can also be used to influence 'pressure groups' such as shareholders and politicians who may put pressure on the company in some way. In attempting to influence these groups a firm is likely to be promoting its own image, (the 'corporate' image), rather than simply promoting individual products.

Promoting a corporate image

A corporate image is the view that people have of a company as a whole, rather than the individual products that it sells. Increasingly firms are recognising the advantages of actively promoting this image. A common form of corporate publicity is the use of company **logos** which might appear on promotional material, in advertising, on buildings, on packaging, on the side of vehicles or on staff uniforms. Another is the sponsorship of sport or cultural events.

A **corporate identity** may be created which can have a number of advantages for the firm. It may promote a feeling of belonging amongst employees, for example, and this is particularly important if the organisation is large.

New products introduced by the company may be linked to the company's particular strengths, and so the products will be more quickly accepted by the public. 'The 'sword' logo from Dettol, for example, has proved to be a major asset to the company in promoting new products. In addition, repetition is a very effective way of advertising and when the public continually see a company's name or logo they feel as if they know the company and can trust its products.

A company must always remember that times and attitudes change and therefore the company's image must change as well. A great deal

Figure 17: Company logos

1 With which companies do you associate each of the logos in Figure 17?
2 Where would you expect to see these logos displayed?

3 Design a logo for use by your school on note-paper, exercise books etc.

of money may need to be spent to change a company's image. A major bank, for example, may need to spend millions of pounds creating a new identity for itself as an 'Action Bank' or a 'Listening Bank'.

There are, of course, problems with a corporate identity. It may be that a company does not want to link together the products it sells. Cadbury, for example, were very unsure as to whether they should link the new milk substitute product 'Marvel' with the company name when they were advertising Diary Milk Chocolate as containing 'a pint and a half of full cream milk'. Similarly if a product is unsuccessful it may have a harmful effect on the company's other products.

Part 5   Distribution

Distribution is a significant element of a firm's costs as Figure 18 illustrates. It therefore requires careful control by management. This involves consideration of the stages through which the product passes before reaching the consumer (**the channel of distribution**) and the storage and delivery of the product itself (**the physical distribution**).

Figure 18: Distribution costs as a percentage of sales revenue

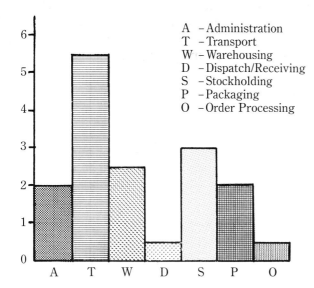

A – Administration
T – Transport
W – Warehousing
D – Dispatch/Receiving
S – Stockholding
P – Packaging
O – Order Processing

Source: The Henley Centre for Forecasting Ltd

Channels of distribution

Many small firms sell direct to the consumer on local markets. A market gardener, for example, may sell his produce on the local fruit and vegetable market. Most larger firms, however, have a national market or even an international market with customers scattered over a wide area. It is necessary, therefore, to set up a 'channel of distribution' between producers and consumers. Four of the most common channels of distribution are shown in Figure 19.

Figure 19: Channels of distribution

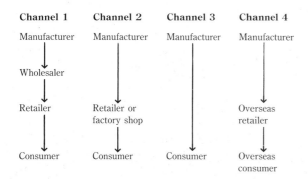

The first channel of distribution is the most common. In Britain, for example, about 40% of all foodstuffs are distributed by **wholesalers**. Wholesalers buy in bulk from manufacturers. They may specialise in a particular product group or they may carry a wide range of different goods. The wholesaler then transports the goods to the retailer who sells them to the consumer.

Wholesalers have a number of important functions:

● They break bulk – Wholesalers buy in large quantities from manufacturers and then sell to retailers in much smaller quantities. This benefits the manufacturer, who only has to make one large delivery to the wholesaler rather than many smaller and more expensive deliveries to shops.

Figure 20: Distribution without wholesaler

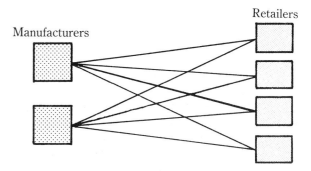

Figure 21: Distribution with wholesaler

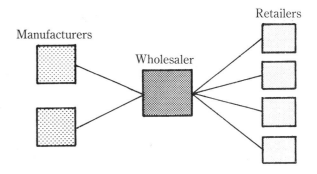

● They are able to give retailers advice on the state of the market. If they sell to a number of shops in the area, they are in a good position to comment on changing demand for particular products.
● They reduce the need for retailers to hold large stocks in their shops as the wholesaler can usually provide speedy delivery of most items.
● The wholesaler may provide credit to the retailer.

Because wholesalers do not actively sell their products, manufacturers often prefer to control their own selling by going directly to the retailer or the consumer. This has meant that the volume of trade handled by wholesalers has started to decline.

The second channel of distribution represents a more recent development. Here the finished good is despatched from the factory to either a factory shop or direct to an independent retail outlet, missing out the wholesaler completely. This gives the manufacturer greater control over the conditions under which its products are sold and the quality of service offered by the retailer.

The third channel is the simplest and represents **direct selling** by the manufacturer to the consumer. This is the oldest method of selling but has been increasing in popularity in recent years. One reason for its popularity is that it avoids the need for wholesalers and retailers who require profit margins and so raise the price of the product to the customer. A disadvantage is the cost to the manufacturer of holding stocks. This method of distribution is popular for high value capital goods, where there are few buyers and where products have to be demonstrated and after-sales service offered, eg electrical goods.

The fourth distribution channel tends to be associated with larger firms who sell a large proportion of their goods overseas. Export orders are easier to win if a firm appoints agents overseas who act as the firm's representatives. Foreign customers have a point of contact for both sales and service in their own country and the firm does not have to make expensive overseas sales visits or rely on visiting foreign buyers.

Choice of distribution channel

In choosing a channel of distribution a manufacturer will ask a number of important questions:

● Who are the customers? – They could be the general public, industry or institutions such as hospitals and schools.
● How wide is the market? – Mail order may be used when customers are scattered over a wide area.
● How often are purchases made? – Mail order and direct selling may also be used for goods which are not bought on a regular basis.
● What do consumers expect? – Avon sell cosmetics door to door and Tupperware sell household goods by party plan in response to consumer preference.
● What type of products are being sold? – New products may require a less 'traditional' channel of distribution because retailers may be unwilling to stock them.
● Do the products need demonstration? – Manufacturers may prefer to sell them themselves.
● Are the goods perishable? – In this case goods require a rapid channel of distribution.
● What is the image of the product? – The manufacturer may restrict the sale of goods to department stores if it wishes to project an exclusive image.

Types of retail outlet

There are many different types of retail outlet. The independent trader was the earliest form of retailer, selling a range of products within a relatively small area. Independent retailers have a number of advantages. They can offer a personal service to customers and are convenient because they serve the local area. They can also

Types of retail outlet.

offer a wide range of products to meet individual needs and often open long hours to suit the customer. They may even provide credit facilities and a delivery service.

This form of retailing is declining however, particularly with the increase in car ownership making the location of the retail outlet a less important factor. Being general stores they lack the expertise of the specialist retailer who is also able to obtain the benefits of bulk buying. As a result many small independent retailers have gone out of business in favour of larger retail outlets. This decline is illustrated in Figure 22 below.

Outlet	Description	Examples
Supermarkets	Self-service stores of more than 400 square metres with at least three checkouts. Sell goods with high, regular demand – mainly foodstuffs. Buy direct from manufacturers. Use low prices and special offers to increase turnover.	Tescos, Sainsburys
Hypermarkets	Usually out of town with extensive parking. Large supermarkets over 5,000 square metres with over 15 checkouts. Self-service, usually on one level, offering a range of goods from foodstuffs to consumer durables.	Asda
Co-operatives	Established in Rochdale 1844 based on the principle of customer ownership. Profits distributed to members according to value of purchases.	Local Co-ops
Department stores	Normally in town centres, carrying a wide variety of goods under one roof with specific departments dealing with particular groups of goods. May have services such as restaurants, delivery, credit etc.	Debenhams, Lewis's
Multiple stores	Groups of shops specialising in particular types of products. Normally buy direct, and pass on cost saving in the form of lower prices. May be owned by manufacturers themselves.	Burtons, Dolcis
Variety chains	Carry wide range of unrelated goods but normally specialise in 'convenience' or impulse items.	Woolworths, Boots
Discount stores	Usually sell consumer durables. Offer low prices but often with no delivery and no credit.	Comet, Argos
Voluntary wholesale chains	To counter the threat of large scale operations, independent retailers subscribe to a wholesale operation offering services such as advertising, bulk buying and own label products.	Spar, VG
Mail order	a Direct sales by manufacturer to consumer who responds to advertisements in the press or on TV.	K-Tel, Which?
	b Mail order houses – offering convenience, credit, privacy and the ability to return goods ordered from catalogues.	Kays, John Mills

Figure 22: Share of retail trade

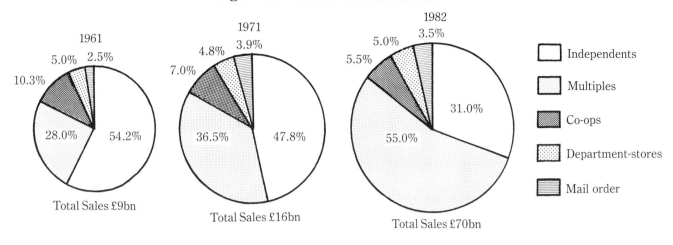

1961
5.0%   2.5%
10.3%
28.0%   54.2%

Total Sales £9bn

1971
4.8%   3.9%
7.0%
36.5%   47.8%

Total Sales £16bn

1982
5.0%   3.5%
5.5%
31.0%
55.0%

Total Sales £70bn

☐ Independents
☐ Multiples
▨ Co-ops
☷ Department-stores
☰ Mail order

Source: *Business Monitor SDO25 Retailing* Business
Statistics Office

1 How many different types of retail outlet can you spot in the photographs?

2 Draw a plan of your local high street or shopping precinct indicating the different types of retail outlet.

Other forms of selling include:
● Mobile outlets – Traditionally milk, coal and ice cream but also soft drinks, fast food etc.
● Vending machines – Not only sweets but also books and pre-packed meals.
● Door-to-door – Normally associated with brushes and encyclopaedias but now including insurance and double glazing.
● Party plans – Parties given for friends and neighbours to demonstrate and sell products such as Tupperware, jewellery and children's clothes.

Developments in retailing

Because of various changes in social behaviour and the costs of distributing products, there have been a number of developments in retailing during recent years. Important changes include the way in which customers pay for goods and the changes in retailing techniques which have resulted from greater automation.

Another marked trend has been the extension of **self-service** which is no longer confined to food but also can be found in garages and many other outlets. A further growth area has been in agencies who do not buy goods themselves but act on behalf of another firm or group of firms and charge commission. The most common examples are travel and insurance agents.

Money shops have also spread rapidly. Unlike the more formal commercial banks, they offer loans and other financial services in outlets

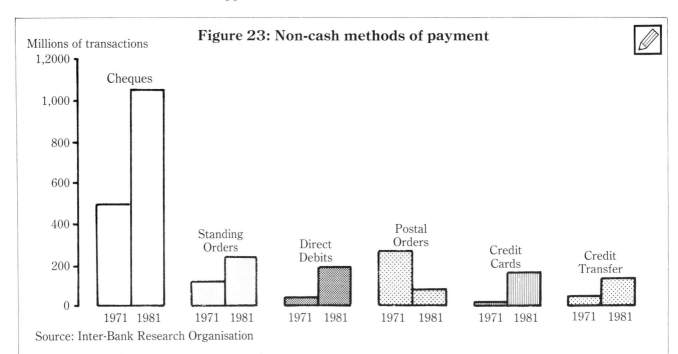

Figure 23: Non-cash methods of payment

Millions of transactions

Source: Inter-Bank Research Organisation

Retailing techniques are becoming more sophisticated with the greater use of electronic point of sales (EPOS) systems and scanning equipment. One method of electronic scanning involves passing a customer's purchases over a laser beam which reads the price symbol known as a bar code. The advantage to the consumer lies in greater accuracy, a faster service and a detailed receipt at the checkout. The equipment is basically designed, however, to help retailers monitor stocks and sales more effectively. In the future, the idea will probably be extended to electronic funds transfer at the point of sale or 'cashless' shopping. Rather than paying by cash, cheque or credit card, a customer will insert a plastic card into a terminal at the checkout and tap out a personal identification number allowing the sum to be instantly debited from the customer's account and credited to the retailer's account.

Source: Adapted from *Barclays Review* November 1985.

1   What is meant by cashless shopping?
2   What will be the effect of modern retailing techniques on:

   a the retailer?
   b the customer?

3   Describe the changes that took place in non-cash methods of payment over the period 1971 to 1981. How can these changes be explained?

very much like shops. The intention is to encourage people (who might be put off by the formality of traditional financial institutions) to make use of their services. This is an image which the commercial banks are trying hard to overcome. A similar development is likely to be the sale of shares and other forms of investment through retailers to meet the growing demand brought about by privatisation. Marks and Spencer is an example of a retailer experimenting in this area.

Another development has been the growth of **own label** products. These are goods sold under the brand name of the retailer although not normally produced by them. The best known example is the St Michael brand of Marks and Spencer, but supermarkets such as Tesco and Sainsbury also sell own brand products. The advantages are that loyalty to the outlet can be increased, the power of the major manufacturers is reduced and the store can be improved through co-ordinated packaging.

Diversification of outlets has also increased with shops moving into non-traditional products such as Tesco Home and Wear and also the development of the 'shop within a shop'. This is where shops may lease space to other retailers or to manufacturers. Fashion clothing, for example, is often sold in this way and specialist outlets such as camera shops may operate within department stores.

A final development has been the growth of **franchising**. This is where a company (the franchiser) provides the name, the product and

**Figure 24:
A franchise advertisement**

Join the world's most successful business-micro retail operation by becoming a ComputerLand franchisee.

If your ambition in life is to have your own company, this could be just the opportunity you've been looking for.

As a ComputerLand franchisee, you would not only be the owner of an independent business. You would also have the resources and buying power of a major chain.

<u>Why ComputerLand?</u>

The value of business computers sold in Western Europe soared from $2bn in 1983 to nearly $3.3bn by the next year, and is expected to reach $13bn by 1988. And of all the outlets for this prodigious growth, ComputerLand is the most successful.

Just 147 centres around the world in 1980. Over 800 today!

It is as part of this continuing expansion programme that we are now looking for enterprising and ambitious business people to set up their own retail outlets under the name of ComputerLand.

<u>Alright – how much?</u>

The total investment you'll need will obviously depend on the location of your premises, but it is unlikely to be less than £200,000, of which

fifty percent must be liquid assets.

You will, in addition, need to have management and selling experience, and an understanding of company finance.

<u>In return...</u>

It will be <u>your</u> business. But you will be able to count on a huge amount of backing from ComputerLand.

We'll help you with locating and fitting out your premises, provide training for you and your staff, give you advice on setting up accounting and stock-control systems, and back you with national advertising and marketing campaigns.

<u>Write now.</u>

If the idea of owning a share in the world's fastest-growing business appeals to you, write to: Brian Reade, Franchise Development Manager, ComputerLand UK Regional Office, 518 Elder House, Elder Gate, Central Milton Keynes, BUCKS MK9 1LR or telephone: 0908 664244.

**The most helpful people
in business micros.**

Source: Computerland Europe SA

1 Explain what is meant by franchising.
2 What are the advantages of owning a franchise such as the one advertised?

the know how to another company (the franchisee) who actually sells the product. The franchisee retains a degree of independence whilst at the same time benefiting from some economies of scale such as national advertising and bulk buying. Wimpey Bars operate in this way as do Kentucky Fried Chicken outlets. In fact many household names are franchise operations.

Physical distribution

Physical distribution involves the transporting, storage, and handling of goods and is an impor-

tant part of the marketing mix. It is a significant element of cost and hence the price of the product and decisions on such factors as pack size, warehouse location and method of transportation are all vital in giving a firm a competitive edge over its rivals.

Distribution can be used as part of the firms promotion. Fast, efficient and inexpensive delivery can be made part of the promotional package with facilities such as telephone ordering and same day delivery being offered to customers.

Distribution by road and rail.

Transport, in all its various forms, is a major aid to industry. It helps workers to travel to their place of work, it allows raw materials to be delivered to manufacturers and it enables finished products to be distributed to consumers both in this country and overseas.

The means of transport chosen by a particular firm will depend on a number of factors including the type of good to be transported, the need for speed in delivery and the distance over which goods are to be moved.

Road transport

98% of consumer goods and 80% of other materials are carried by road. Road transport also accounts for over 90% of passenger traffic. This form of transport has continued to grow steadily.

A marked development in road transport has been the increased use of third party express carriers rather than a firm having to use its own vehicles. These carriers, such as BRS, provide a quick, efficient and often cheaper service.

6% of goods vehicles carry 60% of the freight which is carried by road. This means that most freight is carried by heavy lorries with the resulting problems of congestion, pollution and damage to buildings.

---

1 List the actions that have been taken in your area to reduce the problems of heavy lorries.
2 Write a letter to a local newspaper about:

   a the damage being done to old buildings in your village by heavy lorries
   b a local shopkeeper's reaction to a proposed by-pass which will reduce traffic in the town centre but will also reduce passing trade.

Advantages of road transport

● Deliveries can be made 'door to door'.
● Delivery over short distances is rapid.
● The road network covers the whole country.

Disadvantages of road transport

● Causes congestion in towns and cities.
● Affected by weather conditions.
● Slower than rail over long distances.
● Only relatively small loads can be carried.

Rail transport

Rail transport handles around 10% of freight, most of which is bulky and involves products where rapid delivery is not essential. Rail transport is currently expanding with the use of 'containers' which can link road, rail and sea transport. These standard sized containers can be loaded at the factory and taken by road to a rail terminal where special equipment is available for transferring the containers onto rail wagons. They can then be transported rapidly, often over-night, to a rail terminal near to their destination or to docks in the case of goods being exported overseas.

Advantages of rail transport

● Faster than road over long distances.
● Fewer problems of pollution and congestion.
● Can transport large and heavy loads.

Disadvantages of rail transport

● Many parts of the country inaccessible by rail.
● More expensive over shorter distances.
● Cannot offer a door to door service.

Air transport

We tend to associate air transport with passengers rather than freight. Many large multinational companies have been attracted to locations close to international airports so that executives may commute easily between countries. Increasing use is also being made of this rapid form of transportation for carrying goods over long distances.

Advantages of air transport

● It is extremely rapid.
● It can be more cost effective over long distances.
● Greater security is provided for expensive items.

Disadvantages of air transport

● It is not appropriate for bulky goods.
● Delays may be caused by adverse weather conditions.
● Must be linked to other forms of transport to and from airports.

Sea transport

Apart from air transport, the main link with overseas markets is by sea. There are numerous forms of sea transport, some of which carry mainly passengers, eg ocean liners, some of which carry mainly freight, eg oil tankers and others which carry both, eg ferries.

Advantages of sea transport	Disadvantages of sea transport
● Containers can be handled easily and fully loaded lorries transported. ● Purpose-built ships such as oil tankers and bulk grain carriers can be used. ● It is generally cheaper than air transport.	● It is a slow form of transport. ● Loss or damage may be caused in loading and unloading. ● Other forms of transport must be used to take goods to and from docks.

Part 6   Market pricing

As we have seen, marketing is about satisfying customers' needs, and making a profit at the same time. Price is clearly an important factor in achieving this. Profit is revenue earned from selling goods minus the cost of producing them.

Revenue is dependent on the price of the goods and the quantity sold. Price is not the only influence on sales, however. We have already seen how advertising can influence a consumer's choice.

Consumer demand

The link between the price and the quantity sold can be shown by a demand curve. This shows, in the form of a diagram, how much of a good would be bought at each of a series of prices.

Demand can be defined as the amount of a good which consumers will buy at a given price over a period of time.

The demand curve normally slopes downwards. This shows that more goods are bought at lower prices. There are one or two exceptions to this rule. These include shares, goods with a snob value, and basic food items. People may buy smaller quantities of these goods as the price falls.

The following demand curve illustrates the demand for potatoes on a market stall. If a price of 100p were charged for each kilogram, only 200 kg would be sold. If the price were only 20p the demand would be 1,000 kg.

Supply

We have already seen how we can represent the amount that buyers will purchase of a product by a demand curve. In the same way, the willingness of sellers to sell a product can be illustrated by a supply curve. Supply is the amount of goods

Figure 25: A typical demand curve

Price per kg(p)	Demand(kgs)
100	200
80	400
60	600
40	800
20	1000

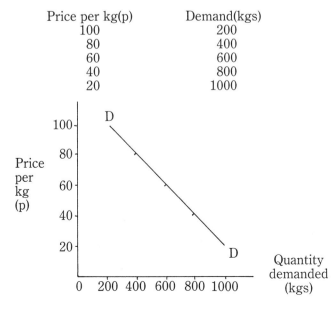

Figure 26: A typical supply curve

Price per kg(p)	Supply(kgs)
100	1000
80	800
60	600
40	400
20	200

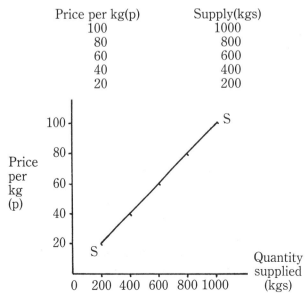

which will be offered for sale at a given price over a period of time. Generally speaking, supply will be higher at higher prices as it becomes more profitable for businesses to produce and sell products.

A typical supply curve is illustrated in Figure 26.

Factors influencing demand and supply

As we stated earlier, price is not the only factor which will influence the level of demand or supply. Those factors which cause more or less of a good to be demanded or supplied at a particular price are called the **conditions of demand or supply**. Changes in these conditions will cause more or less of a good to be demanded at the same price and result in a movement of the curve. For example, if people have higher incomes they may buy 800 kg of potatoes at a price of 60p rather than 600 kg.

The factors influencing demand and supply

Demand

- Population size and structure.
- Income levels.
- Advertising.
- Price of competitive goods.
- Price of complementary goods.

Supply

- Costs of production.
- Weather conditions.
- Strikes.
- Wars.
- New production techniques.

1   What effect would the following have on the demand for Ford Escort cars?

   a A change in tastes towards larger cars such as the Sierra.
   b A '*Which?*' report praising the reliability of Escorts.
   c An advertising campaign for the Austin Metro.
   d A fall in the price of petrol.
   e Improved public transport.

2   Use the following questionnaire to investigate the factors which influence the demand for cinema seats.

You may wish to add further factors to this list.

   a Choose a sample of students and ask them to tick the appropriate box for each factor.
   b Present your results in the form of a diagram or table.

Demand factors	Very important	Important	Not very important
The price of admission The popularity of the film The cost of home videos The quality of TV programmes The location of the cinema			

Market prices

A situation where an individual seller has no control over price is rare but examples do exist. An individual trader on the Stock Exchange, for example, is unlikely to be able to influence the price of a particular share. In this case price is set at a level at which buyers and sellers are prepared to deal.

Figure 27: Demand and supply of potatoes

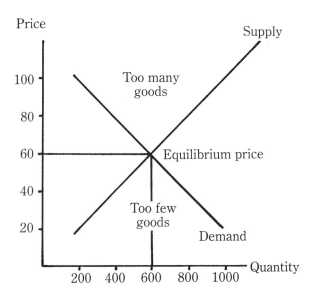

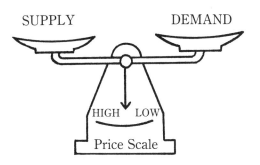

Supply and demand set price

more supply→low price←less demand
less supply→high price←more demand

This idea of prices being determined by demand and supply helps us to understand some of the factors which cause prices to change. In the example in Figure 27, at a price of 40p the demand for potatoes is for 800 kg but only 400 kg are supplied. Shortages will result and prices will rise. At a price of 80p there will be a demand for 400 kg, but 800 kg will be offered for sale. Stocks will build up and prices will have to be reduced to clear the stocks.

Only at a price of 60p will the amount supplied be equal to the amount demanded. This is the equilibrium or market price. Anything which changes consumers' willingness to buy or suppliers' willingness to sell will shift the curves and cause the market price to change.

1 A small village grocer sells butter for 65p for ½ lb. The nearest competition is in the local market town 10 miles away. In this town there are a number of grocers selling butter for 62p for ½ lb. A supermarket in a large town 5 miles away sells butter at 60p for ½ lb.

Explain why there are three different prices for butter.
2 Use supply and demand diagrams for potatoes to illustrate the following:
   a Bad weather resulting in a poor potato crop.
   b A change in tastes with increased consumption of pasta rather than potatoes.
   c An advertising campaign by the Potato Marketing Board.

Fixing a price

In most cases, firms have some influence on price. Generally speaking, firms will set a price which is high enough to cover their costs of production, but not so high as to result in too many customers being lost to competitors.

Firms normally use a method pricing known as **cost plus**. This involves calculating the cost of producing a good and then adding on a reasonable profit margin.

The firm needs to decide how big a **mark-up** it is going to charge on top of its costs of production. There are a wide range of factors which will influence the mark-up that a firm chooses. Some possible pricing policies are listed below:

● Penetration pricing – A low price to gain a large share of the market or to gain acceptance for a new product.
● Skimming – A high price aimed at a quick recovery of costs.

● Differential pricing – Charging different prices to different customers based on order size or type of customer.

● Promotional pricing – Temporary cuts in price to increase sales.

● Competitive pricing – A price in line with that being charged by competitors.

● Psychological pricing – The use of prices such as £3.99 rather than £4.00.

QUICK QUIZ

1. Give a brief definition of 'marketing'.
2. What are the five stages of market research?
3. List three ways in which a market can be split up, (segmented).
4. What is meant by a random sample?
5. What is the difference between 'primary' and 'secondary' data?
6. List three methods of field research.
7. Name the four elements of the marketing mix.
8. What are the five stages of the product life cycle?
9. Briefly describe three 'extension strategies' open to a firm.
10. What is meant by each of the following terms:
    a Informative advertising?
    b Persuasive advertising?
    c Corporate advertising?
11. Give two advantages and two disadvantages of advertising using:
    a national newapapers
    b radio
    c television.
12. List three functions of an advertising agency.
13. What do the following initials stand for? ASA CAP IBA
14. Give examples of four kinds of sales promotion.
15. Give a brief definition of 'public relations'.
16. What is meant by each of the following terms:
    a Channel of distribution?
    b Physical distribution?
17. Identify three factors which would influence the choice of channel of distribution for a product.
18. Name four functions of a wholesaler.
19. Give four factors which would increase the demand for a product.
20. Give examples of five possible pricing policies a firm could use.

Case Study: The Ford Motor Company

Britain's first Fords were shipped from New York in 1903. Eight years later, the Ford Motor Company (England) Limited was established as a first step towards building the phenomenally successful Model T in a former tram factory at Trafford Park, Manchester.

Right from the start, Trafford Park adopted the revolutionary mass-production methods pioneered by Henry Ford. Britain's first moving production line enabled the factory in 1914 to assemble up to 21 chassis an hour. From 3000 vehicles in 1912 Trafford Park's output soared to 6000 in 1913, and made the Model T Britain's best-selling car with nearly 30% of the rapidly-growing market.

Trafford Park was extended as demand soared after the First World War. But it was already clear that Ford needed a modern factory designed for operations on a vast scale. The hunt ended in 1924, when £150,000 was paid for a 500-acre site on the River Thames, near the Essex village of Dagenham. Many experts were convinced that the land was unsuitable, but Ford invested £5m – a vast amount of money at that time – to create what was then Britain's and Europe's biggest car factory.

It had been chosen because Henry Ford appreciated the value of building factories with deep-water berthing facilities. A private wharf suitable for ships handling up to 10,500 tons of cargo gave Dagenham direct access to the world's seaways. Meanwhile, the London County Council was making the Essex village into a town by building 25,000 homes on Britain's biggest housing estate.

Dagenham produced its first Ford on October 1, 1931, when the nation's economy was in the grip of a terrible depression. The press hailed the factory as 'a magnificent gesture of faith in Britain's commercial future'.

In 1985, Ford of Britain plants produced 317,689 cars, 101,407 commercial vehicles, 36,051 tractors and 22,445 component packs.

Source: *Yesterday, Today, Tomorrow* Ford Motor Company Ltd

This case study shows that Ford had to make three major decisions:

- **The method of production** – Should cars be produced by hand or by mass production?
- **The scale of production** – Should they produce a small number of cars or aim for a mass market?
- **The location of production** – Where should they build their factory?

1 From the case study, list any of the factors which could have influenced the Ford Motor Company's decision on the method, scale and location of production.

Part 1   The method of production

In any firm there is a need to organise work to ensure that it is carried out profitably and efficiently. The people responsible for carrying this out are known as the **production personnel**.

Production involves using raw materials to produce finished products which are sold to the customer. Most firms, however, are just one link in the chain which joins raw materials to consumers. Their production process starts with materials that have already been produced by another firm. The first task of the production department will therefore be to decide what the firm will produce itself, and what it will buy from other suppliers.

Figure 1: The production process

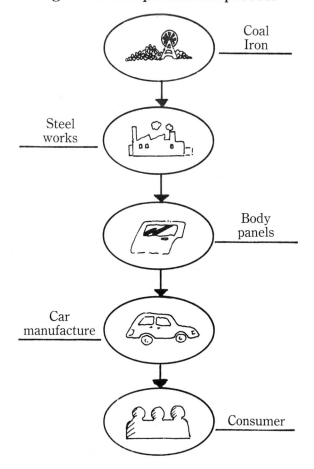

Types of production

The way in which a company will be organised will depend on the method of production that is used. There are basically three methods of production used by firms in manufacturing industry.

Job production

This refers to goods that are manufactured in single units and to the customer's own specification. An example would be bespoke tailoring, where two suits are never identical – each being individually tailored to the customer's shape and taste.

Batch production

This is where groups of similar items are produced at the same time. A good example of this kind of production would be a small bakery, where a range of breads and cakes are produced in batches.

Flow production

This is where one product, or a small range of products, pass through a number of operations continuously and in very large numbers. Good examples of these mass-produced products include motor cars and television sets.

Flow production

Organisation of resources

The resources used by a company include the following:

● Land.
● Buildings.
● Raw materials and components.
● Machinery.
● Labour.

These resources must be organised in the most efficient way possible to ensure that profits are earned.

Land

All firms need land in order to produce. Firms need to be located somewhere, whether it is an office in the centre of town, a factory building on the outskirts or a garden shed at the proprietor's home. As with all the firm's resources, land has a cost. This cost includes the purchase price or the price of a lease on the land and also the rates paid to the local authority each year.

A lease is an agreement which gives someone the use of land for a fixed period after which it returns to the original owner. A great deal of commercial property is leased rather than being bought outright.

Buildings

Decisions have to be made on the size and type of buildings which will be needed. The scale or size of the firm and the type of production will obviously be important influences on these decisions. Factory buildings will need to be large enough not only to cope with present output, but also to allow scope for expansion. If the accommodation is too big, however, then this will be costly in terms of rent and rates.

Other factors which need to be considered include the cost of heating and lighting the premises, the availability of suitable storage space, the ease with which goods can be moved around the building, access for deliveries and parking for employees.

Raw materials and components

A firm will need to make sure that it has enough raw materials and components to meet the planned level of production. This will involve holding stocks, but this is expensive. A balance must be found between the costs and the benefits of stock holding.

There are a number of benefits of keeping a stock of raw materials and components:

● The company can buy in bulk and this will often result in lower prices.
● The company will have reserves to allow production to continue, even if delivery from suppliers is delayed.
● The pattern of demand may be unpredictable and the company may wish to increase production at short notice.
● Holding stocks is a safeguard against price increases.

Holding stocks involves a number of costs to the company:

● The cost of rent and rates of warehouse facilities.
● The wages of warehouse staff.
● The possibility that stocks may become out of date and therefore difficult to sell.
● Insurance and security costs which may be high if the stocks being held are valuable.
● The risk of pilfering. Most thefts from retailers, for example, are by staff rather than customers.
● Money is tied up in stock which could have been earning income for the firm.
● Perishable goods will deteriorate if held for too long.

Stock control

As a result of these costs, stock control is an important job for the production department. Their main responsibility is to ensure that the organisation's stocks are kept at the right level so as to avoid both understocking and overstocking.

It will be the job of the stock control section to decide on what raw materials and components need to be kept in stock, the quantities of each item which is to be held in stock, how much to order and when an order should be placed:

● **The maximum stock level** – This is the agreed maximum. It is set in order to prevent overstocking and should take account of the storage space available, the cost of stock and the rate at which it is used.
● **The minimum stock level** – An agreed lower limit below which stock should not fall. Its purpose is to cushion the effect of delays and disruptions in supply.
● **The re-order level** – The level at which stock should be re-ordered. It must take into account the delivery time from suppliers.
● **The order quantity** – This is the quantity required to return stocks to their maximum level.

Stock control graphs

It is useful to be able to represent the changes in stock levels on a graph. The stock control graph for alternators is shown in Figure 2.

Point A indicates that at the beginning of the month there are 52 alternators in stock. The line then traces the change in stock over a period of 80 days. As we move along this line we can see how the stock of alternators falls by two each day. After 20 days the stock will have fallen to 12. This is as low as the firm wants its stock to fall.

If it takes ten days for its suppliers to deliver alternators, an order would have to be placed ten days before stocks reached this minimum level, ie after 10 days.

Figure 2: Stock control graph

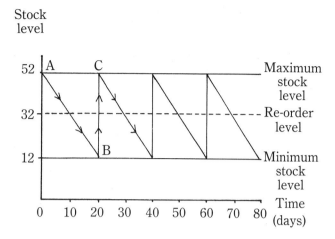

When the new stock of alternators arrives, stocks are returned to the maximum level again.

Machinery

Much of the machinery used by a firm may be highly specialised and expensive. In order to make the best use of it, it may be necessary to have a **shift work** system. This is where one group of workers will work for a set number of hours and then they will be replaced by a second group who work the next shift.

Glass and steel manufacturing require twenty-four hour working. A three shift system is used, with one group of workers working from say 6.00 to 14.00, a second group from 14.00 to 22.00 and a third group from 22.00 to 6.00 the next day.

As well as ensuring that the most efficient use is made of machinery, a decision has to be made as to how much machinery to employ. There are many ways of combining resources in order to produce a particular good. The firm may decide on a **labour intensive** method of production, where a great deal of labour is used compared with the amount of machinery. At the other extreme would be an automated production line

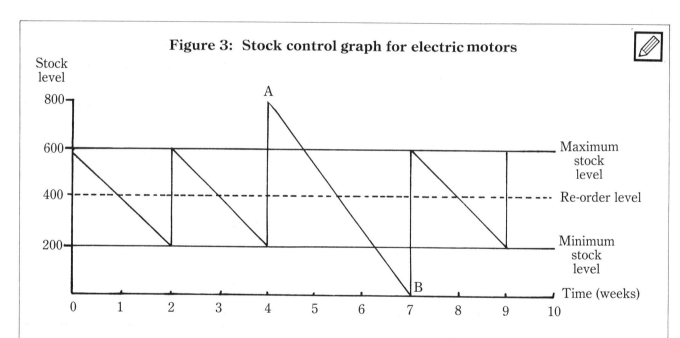

Study the stock control graph for electric motors which are used in the production of a refrigerator and then answer the questions that follow.

1 What is the weekly usage of motors?
2 What is the normal delivery time from the suppliers?
3 What is:

    a the maximum stock level?
    b the minimum stock level?
    c the re-order level?

4 Give two possible reasons to explain the stock level at point A.
5 Give reasons for the changes in the stock level between points A and B.
6 Compile the list of factors that might influence the level at which the maximum, minimum and re-order stock levels are set.
7 What advantages are there to the firm in adopting a good system of stock control?

where very few workers are required. This is known as **capital intensive** production.

Labour

Even with capital intensive production, some labour will be required to operate and maintain machines and to offer support services.

We can make a distinction between **direct** labour, which is employed on the shop floor and **indirect** labour, which offers back-up services. This indirect labour includes clerks, secretaries, supervisors and drivers.

The **quantity** of labour is not the only thing the business needs to consider. There should also be an attempt to ensure that the **quality** of labour is improved through careful recruitment and training. The objective of the business must be to ensure that productivity, that is output per worker, is maximised.

Production, sales and capacity

We have so far concentrated on how the company will try to organise its resources so as to produce as efficiently as possible. This implies that there is sufficient demand for the firm's output to enable it to work at full capacity.

Full capacity output is that level of production achieved when all the resources of the firm are being fully utilised, ie plant and machinery are being used to the limit and workers are fully employed.

It is rare, however, for firms to be working at full capacity. This will be particularly true when the economy is in a recession, with high levels of unemployment and low levels of demand for goods and services.

This means that resources will be lying idle and the company will still have to meet costs such as depreciation on unused machinery and rent on unused buildings.

A particular problem is when sales are not spread evenly throughout the year but are concentrated in a particular month or season, as for example, in the motor industry.

Production services

In addition to those personnel directly involved in organising production, there will be other staff offering support services.

Design

Product design is important as both an aid to increasing sales and to increasing profitability.

'Two hundred Austin Rover workers are to be made redundant as a result of the group's decision, announced yesterday, to reduce production of all models by 10%.'

News of the redundancies comes only nine months after Austin Rover took on 600 extra workers at Longbridge and its other car plant at Cowley, Oxford, to increase production.

The 10% reduction follows the highest output at Cowley and Longbridge for several years, in anticipation of the peak sales month of August, when some 20% of Britain's yearly car sales are made.

To build up stocks for August, Austin Rover raised its output in the first six months of this year to 257,000 vehicles, 35% more than in the first half of 1984.

But production cuts may not bring stocks back to normal levels. The company's other contingency plans are believed to include closing its factories for a week at the end of September and introducing further incentives for its dealers in the autumn.

Source: Adapted from *The Guardian* August 20 1985

Read the above extract carefully and answer the questions which follow.

1 a Why does the industry experience peak sales in August?
   b At what other times of year would you expect sales to be high?

2 Draw graphs to illustrate the likely pattern of production and stock levels over a 12 month period. (Use the same axes for both graphs.)

3 a What methods are open to Austin Rover to help bring stock levels back to normal?
   b Note down the advantages and disadvantages of each method.

Designers will be concerned with a number of factors:

- How the product looks.
- How efficiently it works.
- How economical it is to produce.
- How easily it can be repaired and serviced.
- How safe it is.

Work study

Once production is underway, it is still possible to find ways of making the process more efficient.

Work study is the technique of measuring performance, usually by timing individual activities. These measurements can be used to provide the basis for bonus schemes. They also help in finding ways of improving production in order to make it more efficient.

Quality control

There are two main aspects of quality control. The first is to ensure that the company's products meet the specifications that the company has set. Secondly, it is often necessary to ensure that products meet official standards. The British Standards Institute, for example, provides standards for a wide range of products. Goods meeting these standards carry the BSI 'Kite Mark'.

BSI Kitemark

1 Find as many examples as you can of products which carry the BSI 'Kite mark'.
2 Design a publicity leaflet to promote the work of the British Standards Institute to the general public.

Inspection can be carried out by the workers themselves as part of the production routine. A firm may also have special **quality inspectors** whose sole responsibility is to check on the quality of the products being produced.

Inspection can take three forms. The firm may inspect the raw materials and components that it buys in from other firms, the work in progress at various stages as it passes through the factory and also the final product to ensure that it meets the necessary standards.

Sometimes it is possible to test all of the firm's output but, in the case of mass production, it may only be possible to test a sample. This sample may be tested 'to destruction' to make sure that standards of safety and durability are met.

Maintenance

It is important for the efficient running of the organisation that machines are kept in good working order and production lines are kept running. This, together with the repair of buildings, will be the responsibility of the maintenance staff.

In smaller firms and when specialist skills are required, outside contractors may be brought in to do repair work. Larger firms will normally have their own maintenance staff to carry out routine work. Much of the work of the maintenance staff will be preventative. That is to say, replacing parts before they wear out and interrupt production. A firm may find it cheaper, for example, to change all its light bulbs at once rather than replacing each one as it fails. With certain processes it may be necessary to close down the whole plant in order to carry out maintenance work and this is usually organised to coincide with weekends or annual holidays.

Research and development

Research and the development of new products are essential for any successful business. A company cannot rely on existing products always being in demand. It must continually seek to improve its products and add new products to its range.

This is particularly true of firms in the high-tech sector where change is very rapid, as this quote from the managing director of Hewlett-Packard Ltd illustrates:

'Hewlett-Packard invests about ten per cent of revenue in research and development. Currently this amounts to about £100 m each year and results in a new product being introduced almost every working day.'

Products must be designed to meet the wishes of the consumer.

New product development relies a great deal on team work. Both the marketing and the production departments will be involved. The marketing department will be concerned with research into what customers want and what they are prepared to pay. The production department will be concerned with how products can be designed to meet the wishes of the consumer.

There are a number of stages involved in the development of a new product.

Market research

The first step is to find out what the market will be for a new product. Who are the likely customers? What are their needs? What are they prepared to pay? What competition is there in the market?

Preparing the product brief

The company's product development team will need to be given details of what the product should be able to do and what it should cost to produce. This 'brief' will be based on the findings of the market research.

Development of the product

This will involve producing detailed drawings from which prototypes can be made. A prototype is a model of the product which can be used for testing.

Tests will be carried out and modifications made until the product meets the standards that have been set. As a result of this testing, many new products are abandoned as they are either too expensive or technically too difficult to make. In the case of some products such as drugs, the testing can last for many years. Even then, some unsafe drugs may still find their way onto the market.

The length of time taken to develop a product will vary. A balance must be found between getting the product onto the market quickly to beat competitors and making sure the product is safe and efficient.

Consumer trails

Once the product has been successfully developed, the marketing department will normally want to try the product out on a sample of consumers before the company goes into mass production.

Patenting

If the new product is in some way different from other products on the market, the company may want to protect their idea by applying for a patent.

A patent is granted by the Government Patent Office. It prevents other companies from using an invention for up to 20 years without the permission of the owner of the patent. A document is issued which describes the invention and defines the protection that will be provided by the patent.

An invention which can be patented, is anything which is new and not obvious. This may be a new machine, a new product or new production process.

Applying for a patent is a long, and often costly operation. Many smaller firms therefore, decide against applying for a patent and rely on selling as many products as possible at a premium price before competitors can copy their ideas.

The product launch

The final stage is to launch the product onto the market. There is still an element of risk at this stage, however much research has gone into ensuring that the product meets the needs of the consumer.

Figure 4: The fate of new product ideas

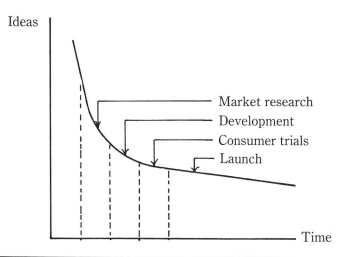

Part 2   The scale of production

Our first problem in looking at the scale of the firm is to decide on how we measure scale or size. There are a number of alternative ways to measure the size of a firm:

● The number of people employed. This could be misleading, however, as a firm may have few workers but a great deal of capital equipment, eg an automated car plant.
● The value of the firm's output. The problem here is that a small firm may produce goods of very high value, eg a diamond mine.
● The capital employed. Even this could give a misleading picture if land or labour were more important factors of production than capital, eg agriculture.

The 1981 Companies Act used all three of these measures of size. It concluded that a firm could be considered to be large (or small) if at least two of these measures agreed. A firm with a high value of output and a great deal of capital, for example, would be considered to be large even if there were few employees.

Industrial concentration

Industrial concentration refers to the number of firms in a particular industry. Many industries are dominated by a relatively small number of large firms.

In 1909, the country's largest 100 companies produced just 16% of manufacturing output. By the 1970s, this figure had risen to 40% and by the 1980s to 50%.

Figure 5: Industrial concentration

Share of UK production by the top five companies in selected

industries (1980)	%
Tobacco	100
Artificial fibres	94
Motor vehicles	91
Asbestos goods	89
Cement, lime and plaster	86
Electric cables	80
Office machinery	70
Bread and biscuits	65
Glass	63
Brewing	60

Source: Census of Production

Figure 5 shows the degree of industrial concentration in a number of key industries. Suggest some reasons why these industries are dominated by a small number of large firms.

There are a number of reasons why this trend towards larger firms is likely to continue.

Economies of scale

There are a number of advantages available to a large firm which result from its size. These advantages produce cash savings which make large firms more competitive and able to expand their market share at the expense of smaller scale producers.

Risk bearing economies

Large firms can operate in a number of different markets and can produce a range of different products. They can therefore spread their risks and withstand a fall in sales in any one market or for any one product.

They can also survive problems that cannot be insured against such as strikes or machinery breakdowns.

Financial economies

There are more sources of finance available to large firms and financial institutions will offer favourable terms as the risk of lending to a large organisation is less. They tend to be more 'credit worthy' as they have greater security to offer.

Marketing economies

These can further be broken down into buying economies and selling economies.

Large firms are able to buy in bulk and this is usually cheaper. In addition, they can employ specialist buyers who 'shop around' to get the best price for raw materials and components.

Selling economies result from a large firm's ability to sell in a national rather than a local market. The cost of using national newspapers or television for advertising is less than using local newspapers in proportion to the number of potential customers who will see the advertisement. A large firm is also able to employ specialist salesmen to ensure that its products have maximum distribution.

Technical economies

These result from a large firm's ability to use mass production techniques. Increased specialisation is possible, with significant cost savings resulting. More sophisticated capital equipment can also be used.

Managerial and administrative economies

Overheads, eg managerial and administrative costs, can be spread over a greater output as a firm expands.

It is also possible to employ specialist mana-gers to look after areas such as finance, personnel and legal matters.

There are, of course, disadvantages of large-scale enterprises. They tend to be rather bureaucratic and slow to respond to change in the market. Communications between individuals and groups within the organisation can often be poor and a large organisation is more difficult to control. Worker morale is often low because individual workers find it difficult to identify with the organisation. The result is poor industrial relations.

Mergers

A merger is the joining together of two or more firms to form a single organisation. It represents a more rapid method of growth than the natural expansion of a firm through investment. Growth in the number of mergers has been a major factor in concentrating industrial activity in the hands of a relatively small number of firms.

A distinction is sometimes made between a 'merger' and a 'takeover'. A merger is the voluntary joining together of two or more firms, whereas a takeover is where an outsider takes control of a firm through the purchase of its shares, often without the agreement of the directors of the firm being taken over. This is known as a 'hostile' takeover.

Figure 6: The merger process

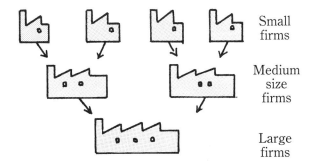

We can distinguish between three main types of merger. The first is a **vertical merger**. This is where two companies at different stages in the production process join together. It can involve a firm joining together with either a supplier or with a customer. A brewery, for example, will usually control a number of public houses where its products are sold.

A second type of merger is a **horizontal merger**. This is where two companies at the same stage of production join together. They may be competitors, such as when one shoe retailer joins with another, or they may produce complementary goods, as when a car manufacturer merges with a truck manufacturer. This is sometimes known as a **lateral** merger.

The final type of merger is the **conglomerate merger**. This occurs when two or more firms in different industries join together. The main motive for this type of merger is to spread the risks through diversification. Diversification means producing a range of different products and/or selling in a number of different markets.

Whereas in the nineteenth century 90% of mergers were horizontal and around 10% were vertical, most of the major mergers of the past decade have been conglomerate mergers.

Figure 7: Types of merger

Type		Nature	Motives
Vertical	**Forward**	A firm merges with another at a later stage of production	Control of retail outlets. Firm brought closer to the consumer.
	Backward	A firm merges with another at an earlier stage of production.	Control of supplies – supplies guaranteed. Better control over price.
Horizontal		A merger between firms at the same stage of production – producing competitive goods.	Increased market share. Economies of scale. Reduced competition. Excess capacity in the industry can be reduced.
Lateral		As above, but where firms produce allied goods.	Increased range of goods. Some economies of scale.
Conglomerate		Where firms producing non-competing and non-complementary goods join together.	Risks spread. Some economies of scale.

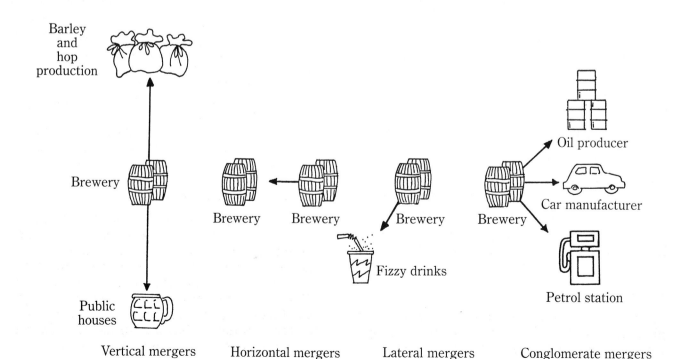

Vertical mergers   Horizontal mergers   Lateral mergers   Conglomerate mergers

BRITISH HOME STORES AND HABITAT AGREE ON £1.52BN MERGER

Habitat/Mothercare, the home furnishings and clothing group created by Sir Terence Conran, and British Home Stores, the food to lighting chain, yesterday agreed to a £1.52bn merger.

The merger – the latest in a series of deals to sweep the high street – will create a retailing group with a combined turnover of £1bn, nearly 800 stores and more than 30,000 employees.

The new company will embrace Habitat, Heals and Conrans in the home furnishing field, Mothercare, Now and Richards in the clothing and mother and baby area and the BHS chain of variety stores.

Mr Denis Cassidy, the managing director of BHS said, 'Over the past two years we have been looking at the future of retailing and looked at acquisitions and mergers alongside organic growth'.

The two companies will create a new holding company which will acquire their shares.

The combined group will have increased buying power with its suppliers. Habitat may expand further overseas while BHS could develop its financial services and home shopping.

The two companies will share their experience of electronic retailing and cost savings will be possible in the distribution network.

Source: Adapted from The *Financial Times* November 26 1985

Read the newspaper article and answer the questions which follow:

1 Explain the following terms used in the text:

   a Organic growth.
   b Holding company.

2 Discuss the benefits of the merger:

   a to customers
   b to employees
   c to the management of the two firms.

your eggs in one basket and to rely too heavily on one product or on one market. By operating on a large scale with many different products and markets, a firm is able to spread its risks. If one particular industry goes into decline or if there is a recession in one economy then the company can switch its resources to other products or other markets.

To overcome the problems of running a large organisation, there is usually some form of decentralisation of management. Each firm within the company may operate independently in terms of day to day decision making. Long-term planning, however, will be in the hands of a holding company.

Because firms will often continue to trade under their own names after a merger has taken place, the extent of industrial concentration is not always obvious. Did you know, for example, that Settlers, Phensic, Vosene, Silvikrin, Lucozade and Quosh are just some of the brand names used by the Beecham company?

Make a list of all the different brands of washing powder found on supermarket shelves. Examine the packets to find out how many different manufacturers there are.

New high-technology industries

The newer science-based industries are often very capital intensive. This means that the cost of setting up in business will be very high. Small firms would find it difficult to raise the finance to purchase the equipment needed and to carry out the research and development necessary to compete in a rapidly changing market.

As a result, many of the high-technology industries are dominated by a few very large manufacturers. Recent experience in the home computer market has illustrated the difficulty that smaller firms have in staying in the market in the face of competition from the major manufacturers.

The growth of markets

Over the years, there has been a growth in both home and overseas markets. The most significant factor has been the expansion of overseas trade with increases in world population, better means of transport and narrowing cultural differences between countries. This has meant that standardised products can be sold in many different markets allowing firms to gain the maximum benefits from mass production.

Diversification

As we have seen, one form of merger is a conglomerate merger. This is a means whereby a firm can spread its risks. It is not wise to have all

The need to compete in international markets has meant that firms have had to grow in order to survive. Small firms would find it very difficult to enter international markets for goods such as motor cars and computers, which are dominated by large multinational corporations.

The small firm

There are a number of limitations on the extent to which firms can grow in size, either naturally or through mergers. The first restriction is the size of the market. Certain markets are very specialised or are limited geographically. In these markets, large-scale production would not be possible and small firms tend to dominate.

What size must a firm be to be classed as small? This is not an easy question to answer since, as we have seen, the size of a firm can be measured in many different ways. For example, it might be argued that a firm which employs less than 100 people or sells goods valued at less than £50,000 in any one year should be classed as 'small'. Clearly, there is no one answer to the question.

In 1971, the Bolton Committee of Inquiry on Small Firms reported that it preferred a statistical definition which varied from industry to industry. In manufacturing, Bolton defined a small firm as one which employed 200 people or less and in retailing it was one with a total sales revenue for the year of £50,000 or less. A firm in the road transport industry was said to be small if it had five or less vehicles.

Given that so many problems exist, it may seem surprising that small businesses still survive. Not only do they survive, however, but in some industries they dominate. In manufacturing industry alone, around 95% of firms employ less than 200 people. It should be noted, however, that these firms account for less than 20% of employment and output.

Small firms survive for several reasons. Firstly the demand for many items is quite small and production of these goods or services is therefore best undertaken on a small-scale. Even when demand is large, there may be some industries where there are no real benefits from large-scale production. In these industries small firms can compete on an equal basis.

Large firms tend to make standardised products rather than catering to the customer's individual tastes. This is not the case with small firms who can normally offer customers non-standard products. A good example of this is to be found in the motor car industry, where large firms such as British Leyland only offer highly

Advantages of small firms

- Good employee relationships result in better communications and fewer strikes.
- Decision-making is quicker and easier since access to senior management is better.
- They tend to be both more innovative and adaptable and are more willing to change to exploit new markets.
- They are often best placed to serve local markets.

Disadvantages of small firms

- Lack of capital for expansion.
- Market research and product development are often impossible owing to lack of finance.
- They cannot afford to employ specialists such as accountants and people with legal training, the owner being a 'jack of all trades'.
- They do not enjoy the economies of scale available to large firms.

standardised cars. In contrast, small motor car manufacturers can tailor a car to a customer's own requirements.

Small firms tend to offer the personal service that most people prefer. This can be clearly seen in retailing, where small corner shops are able to offer a friendly service to customers and may even offer credit facilities.

Small firms have also been helped a great deal by government policy. In recent years, governments have placed great stress on the importance of small firms to the economy. They see the small firm sector as providing an outlet for individual creativity and feel that they can make a significant contribution to reducing unemployment. Since 1979 the Department of Trade and Industry has been involved in a whole range of measures aimed at helping the small businessman.

The Enterprise Allowance scheme is the best example of how committed the government is to small businesses. The scheme, which was launched in April 1983, encourages jobless people to start their own businesses. Participants in the scheme receive £40 per week. This provides them with an income whilst their business is starting up and before it begins to show a profit.

Applicants must have been unemployed for the last thirteen weeks, be currently in receipt of either unemployment or supplementary benefit, be over the age of eighteen and have at least £1,000 to contribute to the business. The allowance is given for only one year. The scheme is run by the Manpower Services Commission. In addition to the Enterprise Allowance scheme, the government offers a range of tax and other benefits to small businesses.

Part 3   Location of production

One of the most important decisions that will need to be made by a firm is where to locate production.

Factors influencing location

Historically, industries were located in particular areas because of the availability of raw materials. Extractive industries such as mining and quarry-ing can only be located where deposits are found. Other industries using large quantities of raw materials save on transport costs by producing near to suppliers. Hence iron and steel based industries such as engineering and shipbuilding were located close to iron and steel production. Industries relying on imported raw materials located near to ports, eg sugar refineries in Liverpool.

Transport costs can also be saved by locating

Figure 8: Factors influencing location

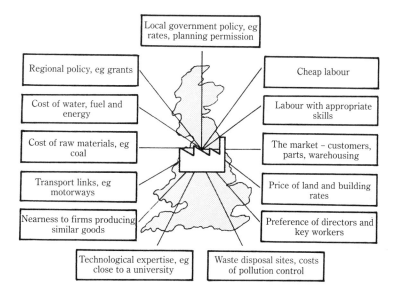

Local government policy, eg rates, planning permission

Regional policy, eg grants

Cost of water, fuel and energy

Cost of raw materials, eg coal

Transport links, eg motorways

Nearness to firms producing similar goods

Cheap labour

Labour with appropriate skills

The market – customers, parts, warehousing

Price of land and building rates

Preference of directors and key workers

Technological expertise, eg close to a university

Waste disposal sites, costs of pollution control

near to markets. In the case of a national market, savings can be made by locating near large centres of population, eg consumer goods industries are attracted to the area around London.

The nature of the product will help determine location. Bulky raw materials will lead firms to locate near to raw material supplies, whereas where the final product is bulky or fragile the firm will tend to locate near to the market.

---

1   Which of the following industries would you expect to locate near to their market and which near to raw materials?

   a Market gardening.
   b Sugar refining.
   c Consumer durables.
   d Biscuits.
   e Metal boxes.
   f Heavy engineering.

2   Which industries are the major employers in your area? Try to find out why individual firms originally decided to locate in your area. (You may want to produce a questionnaire, setting out a number of possible reasons, to be sent to local firms.)

Another important factor in determining location used to be the availability of power. A good example of the location of industry near to power supplies is provided by the cotton and woollen industries. When water mills provided the power, the industry was located in the Pennine Valleys of Lancashire and Yorkshire. Later, the invention of steam engines led to the industry moving to areas where coal was plentiful. Power sources are no longer a significant factor because of the general availability of gas and electricity.

Transport was also an important historical factor in determining the location of industry. At first, the canals led to industrial growth along their banks during the Industrial Revolution – a notable example being the growth of the Potteries around Stoke. Later, the railways opened up new areas. The present motorway system has led to the development of new industrial areas and new towns. The use of bulk carriers has also led to the increased importance of areas around ports. Rotterdam in Holland is a classic example.

The concentration of industry in particular areas tends to create its own advantages.

One advantage is the availability of skilled labour. If labour is skilled, it reduces the need for in-plant training. Labour is not the most mobile factor and many people remain within a few miles of their place of birth. The result is a ready supply of labour with experience in local industries. Further education colleges base courses on the requirements of the area they serve, providing new generations of skilled workers.

Another advantage is the development of subsidiary industries. Firms will grow up to serve the major industry in that area. Transport and marketing firms, for example, will grow up geared to the needs of the major industry. Banks will understand the problems faced by industry in an area. Specialist markets may also grow up to serve particular industries.

These advantages may lead to industries remaining in a particular area long after the original advantages, such as the availability of raw materials, have ceased to apply, eg High Wycombe was a major centre for the furniture industry because of the availability of beech wood from the Chilterns. Local wood is no longer important, but the availability of skilled labour still attracts firms to the area.

Industrial inertia is the term used to describe the tendency for firms to locate in a particular area long after the original advantages have disappeared. This tendency, however, can cause problems. The decline of an industry, due say to technological developments, leads to severe unemployment in the area where the industry was located. Often this unemployed labour force has specific skills not suitable for other industries and expensive retraining has to be carried out. This has led to a great increase in government intervention in the location of industry in recent years.

Regional policy

The industries which formed the basis of the Industrial Revolution in Britain, such as textiles, iron and steel, coal and shipbuilding, located near to raw materials and early economic development was based in the North.

Over the years, and most notably since the 1930s, these industries have declined. Newer industries have grown up to take their place, but these industries have been attracted to the South to be close to the major centres of population and European markets.

This has meant that, although unemployment is a problem for the whole country, the level of unemployment is much higher in some regions than in others. As a result, successive British governments since 1945 have given financial incentives to firms setting up in the depressed regions.

Government policies currently consist of the payment of regional development grants and the operation of enterprise zones.

Regional development grants

These grants are available to firms who set up or expand capacity in **development areas**. These areas are illustrated in Figure 9. The level of grant is currently set at 15% of the firm's capital expenditure, or in the region of £3000 for each new job created (whichever the higher sum). Most of these grants are for manufacturing industry although some service activities, mainly business services, also qualify.

Grants are also available on a selective basis for projects in all the **assisted areas** which create or safeguard employment. Service industries may qualify for selective assistance as well as manufacturing industry. These assisted areas are also shown in Figure 9. The level of these grants will vary and will depend on the nature of the project. Support is available towards capital costs and for training.

Enterprise zones

These are small geographical areas where firms are encouraged to expand. They were first introduced in 1981 and were based on areas of physical and economic decay.

These areas offer rate free accommodation for up to ten years and there is reduced interference from outside authorities in matters such as planning regulations. Government requests for statistical information are reduced. There are also additional tax advantages for firms locating in enterprise zones.

A criticism of this scheme is that service and distribution rather than manufacturing firms have tended to be attracted to these areas because of exemption from rates. It has also been argued that some firms have simply moved into the enterprise zones from areas outside with no overall increase in jobs.

At this stage it is dificult to say just how effective this scheme has been in creating new jobs and aiding the development of the assisted areas in general.

Figure 9: Regional assistance

Figure 10: The first eleven enterprise zones

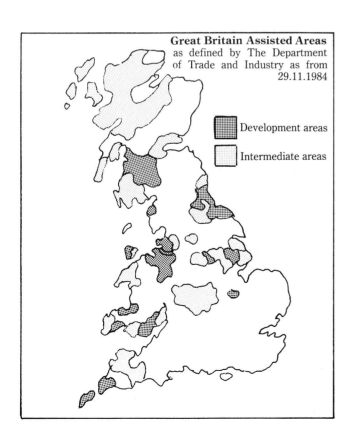

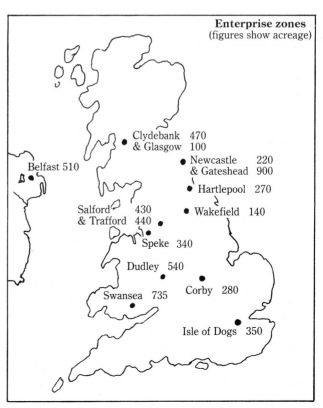

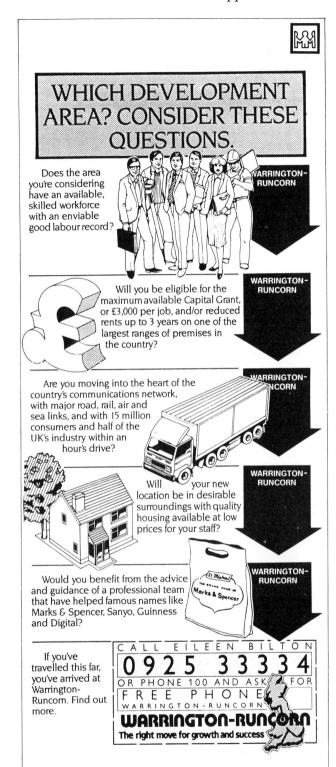

1 Read the advertisement and describe, in your own words, the benefits being offered by Warrington-Runcorn.
2 In groups, produce an advertisement for your own area. Outline the attractions available to new businesses locating in the area and decide on the incentives you could offer to help attract them.

Criticisms of regional policy

There are a number of criticisms of government regional policy. Some people argue that firms should locate where it is economic.

Grants are intended to move firms away from the best locations and they therefore encourage an inefficient use of resources.

Even if it is agreed that the unemployment problems of some parts of the country need special attention, it is not necessarily true to say that the present system is the best way of dealing with the problem.

A great deal of aid goes towards the cost of capital which will encourage capital intensive firms rather than those that employ a lot of labour. The present legislation, however, limits capital grants to £10,000 for each new job created which goes some way towards overcoming this problem.

Two conflicting criticisms of the present system are that not enough is spent on regional assistance and that the cost of creating new jobs has been too high (£40,000 per job has been quoted).

Supporters of government policy argue that the regional imbalance would have been much worse without state help. The critics argue that some regions still have far higher unemployment than others and so the policy has clearly not worked.

Arrange a class debate with speakers for and against the motion:

'Firms should be left to make their own decisions on location without interference from the government.'

QUICK QUIZ

1. Distinguish between job production, batch production and flow production.
2. What factors need to be taken into account in designing a factory building?
3. List three reasons why a firm may want to hold stocks of raw materials and components.
4. What are the main costs associated with holding stocks?
5. Briefly describe the work of the following production support staff:

   a Designers.
   b Work study engineers.
   c Quality controllers.
   d Maintenance workers.
   e Product researchers.

6. What are the benefits of taking out a patent on a new product?
7. Name three ways in which the size of a firm can be measured.

8. Explain briefly the following 'economies of scale':

   a Risk bearing economies.
   b Financial economies.
   c Marketing economies.
   d Technical economies.
   e Managerial economies.

9. What are the disadvantages of large-scale enterprise?
10. Briefly explain and give an example of each of the following:

    a A vertical merger.
    b A horizontal merger.
    c A conglomerate merger.

11. Give three advantages and three disadvantages of a small firm.
12. List six factors which will influence a firm's decision as to where to locate a factory.
13. What are the benefits of locating within an enterprise zone?

Case Study: Happiness is a new laundry

After three generations the Clegg family decided it was time to move its laundry to new premises. The old plant had every available space crammed to the limit, there was no room to grow and the building was in such a bad state that women sometimes had to iron sheets while sheltering under umbrellas stuck on poles.

And so, four years ago Cleggs moved to a brand new custom-built laundry in Rainhill, near Liverpool. Not only was it custom-built to the management's specifications but also to the workers'. It was the factory staff who chose the carpet in the canteen, the showers in the washrooms and even the colour of the walls. They also helped to decide where different facilities would be sited and contributed to the design of their own workspaces.

The takeover a couple of years ago by the Charles Baynes group has not changed that at all. Employee involvement is still a very important part of the way Cleggs operates, with everyone on first-name terms.

Since the move, staff numbers have doubled, so that now there are around 100 production staff (about 40 of whom work on a part-time or casual basis) and nearly 30 office staff.

All the employees in the laundry are classified as general workers; that is, they may be employed on any of the processes in the plant. This helps to give their work more variety and keep them interested in what they are doing.

Of the present staff, 24 joined as Youth Opportunities Programme trainees but the majority either applied direct to the company or were recruited from the local job centre.

As to the future, expansion remains very much part of Cleggs' plans.

Source: *Employment News*

Cleggs' laundry illustrates how the success of a business depends on the people who work in it and we can see how this has influenced the way in which the laundry has been managed. Management involves getting things done through people.

1 What would you pick out from the case study as examples of good management?
2 If you were asked to design your own workplace, what factors would you take into consideration?

Part 1   Labour needs

Employees are likely to be a major cost for any organisation and these costs must be controlled in the same way as raw materials or overhead costs. Changing technology also means that the company's needs will change, both in terms of the number of employees required and the skills they must possess. This will affect the way in which the firm recruits new workers and the way in which it trains its existing workforce.

A firm must first decide on the number of workers it needs. If a firm has too many workers, it could reduce staff by **natural wastage**. This involves not replacing workers who leave the company and usually has union support as it does not make workers redundant. However, the workers who leave may be in shortage areas, and this can cause problems, especially if other workers cannot be retrained to fill the gaps left. Companies may try to speed up natural wastage by encouraging early retirement.

The alternative to natural wastage is compulsory redundancy. Certain legal conditions must be met where redundancies are announced, and employees who have been with the company a long time may receive substantial redundancy payments.

To reduce the cost and to obtain union support, the principle of 'last in, first out' tends to be applied. This means that it is the newest recruits who are first to be made redundant. If these are mainly younger workers then it may be easier for them to find other jobs, but from the point of view of the company, it does not guarantee that they keep the most efficient employees.

Labour turnover

Labour turnover is the movement of employees into and out of the firm. A high level of labour turnover is usually seen as a serious problem.

Causes of labour turnover

All firms will experience some turnover of labour and this can have benefits. Movement of staff brings new blood into the organisation and improves the chances of promotion for employees. Unavoidable causes of labour turnover include resignation due to ill health, pregnancy and domestic circumstances. There will also be those employees who reach the age of retirement, those who are dismissed for misconduct and those made redundant due to a fall in the firm's labour requirements.

It is the avoidable causes of labour turnover which are the main concern of management. If a company is to make any progress in reducing labour turnover, it must attempt to discover which groups of workers are more likely to leave and take the necessary action. Voluntary resignation tends to be more common in large organisations than in smaller ones and in urban areas rather than rural areas. Younger employees are also more likely to resign than older ones.

There are a number of common characteristics found in groups of workers with a high labour turnover:

- Low pay compared with similar jobs elsewhere in the same area.
- Fluctuating pay due to the uncertainty of overtime, bonuses etc.
- Irregular work creating stress on some occasions and boredom on others.
- Lack of achievement and poor prospects of promotion.
- Lack of familiarity with the workplace or the demands of full-time employment.

The cost of labour turnover

There are a number of costs which the firm will have to bear as a result of high levels of labour turnover. The most obvious costs are those associated with recruitment. These costs will include advertising, interviewing and training. There will be other costs, however, which may be even greater.

A high level of labour turnover results in lost production. It is rare for a vacancy to be filled immediately when people leave. The result may be that machines stand idle and production is lost. In addition, a new recruit will take time to reach the level of skill of the worker who is leaving and this results in an overall reduction in productivity.

Morale amongst the workforce is low when staff keep coming and going and there is no time for a team spirit to develop. Supervisors in particular become frustrated with the need to be continually training new staff.

A great deal of management time will be wasted reorganising production to cope with fluctuating staffing levels and planning output becomes very difficult. As a result, there is a need to find solutions to the problems of high labour turnover.

Reducing labour turnover

Evidence suggests that for most companies the greatest labour turnover is found amongst new recruits. The aim should be to ensure that new recruits are going to fit in and to ease the process of adjustment.

The second most vulnerable group are those who are in the early stages of their careers and are seeking promotion. A certain amount of movement within this group is probably desirable, but a firm must make sure that it adopts a system of staff development which avoids too much movement. This could include training, internal promotion and appraisal which will identify the needs of individual employees.

In addition, employers should try to maintain good communications with the shop floor to avoid management becoming too remote from the workforce. Management and supervisory training is also important to teach the skills of man management and grievance and disciplinary procedures should be designed so that employees know where they stand.

The managing director of a medium sized engineering firm is concerned at the high level of labour turnover. He has asked you, as personnel manager, to prepare a report setting out:

a the possible causes of the high level of labour turnover
b the costs to the firm
c recommendations for dealing with the problem.

Part 2 Recruitment

It is important for any business to recruit the right people. If the right people are recruited then they are likely to stay with the firm. If the wrong people are recruited then they will either leave and force the firm to go through the expensive recruitment procedure again, or even worse, they will stay but do their job badly.

Any system of recruitment used by a firm should have three features:

● Effective in choosing the right candidate.
● Cheap to operate.
● Fair to all candidates.

Job descriptions

The first stage of recruitment is to decide on the job that needs to be done and then to decide the type of person you are looking for to do it.

The first task is therefore to produce a **job**
description which, as the name suggests, gives an outline of what is involved in a particular job. It will include an outline of the tasks which are to be carried out and the responsibilities of the person doing the job.

Job specification

Once a description of the job has been produced, it should then be possible to describe the kind of person you would want to fill that job. This involves drawing up a **job or personnel specification**.

This will obviously help in making a selection from the applications received for a job.

One system which is often used in drawing up a specification is the **seven-point-plan**. This involves setting out the details of an ideal candidate under seven main headings as illustrated in Figure 2.

Produce a brief job description for a teacher setting out:

a the main purpose of the job
b the tasks which need to be carried out
c the position of the post holder within the organisation.

Figure 1 provides an example to help you.

Figure 1: A job description

Job title: Office Services Supervisor

Department: Administration

Main purpose of job: To ensure the provision of efficient typing, reprographic and switchboard services to company personnel.

Scope of job: Responsible to: administration manager.
Responsible for: five staff equipment to value of £30,000.

Main duties:

1 To allocate suitable personnel to switchboard, telex, offset printer and photocopiers, as required.
2 To ensure the provision and maintenance of an accurate and efficient typing and reprographic service by:

   a receiving and recording work for typing and reproduction
   b deciding priority of work
   c allocating work
   d deciding most appropriate and efficient method of reproducing documents
   e checking a sample of work for accuracy and presentation
   f typing and operating machines as necessary to cover for absent staff.

3 To ensure the maintenance and upkeep of equipment.
4 To collate control information on departmental costs, etc.
5 To order stationery, reprographic chemicals and other materials, recording use and maintaining suitable stock levels.
6 To train and assist in selection of new staff.

Source: *ACAS Advisory Booklet No.6*

Figure 2: A personnel specification

Essential	Desirable
1 Physical make-up Good health record. Acceptable bearing and speech. No serious uncorrected impairment of sight.	Pleasant appearance, bearing and speech.
2 Attainments GCSE level English language (grade A–C) or equivalent. Ability to type, and to operate office machines. Experience of general office work.	GCSE level maths (grade A–C) or equivalent. RSA II typing. Experience of using simple statistical information. Experience of staff supervision.
3 General intelligence Above average.	
4 Special aptitudes Reasonable manual dexterity. Facility with figures.	
5 Interests	Social activities.
6 Disposition Persuasive and influential. Self-reliant.	Good degree of acceptability, dependability and self-reliance. Steady under pressure.
7 Circumstances No special circumstances.	

Source: *ACAS Advisory Booklet Number 6*

Methods of recruitment

Having decided on the kind of person required for a particular job, the firm must decide how it is going to recruit.

Internal candidates

The firm needs to decide if the job will be filled from inside the organisation or from outside.

Recruiting from within the organisation has a number of advantages. By offering promotion to employees, it encourages them to stay with the firm and to undertake training to help them progress up the promotional ladder. The person recruited to the job will already be familiar with the company, its products and the people who work there. They should therefore be able to settle in more quickly to the new job.

Just as an internal candidate will know more about the company, those responsible for recruitment will know far more about the strengths and weaknesses of an internal candidate than they will about somebody from outside the firm. This will help them to ensure that the person appointed to a particular job will be able to do the tasks required and will reduce the risk of recruiting the wrong person.

However, those candidates not appointed from within a firm may feel resentful and there may be accusations of favouritism. A newly promoted employee may find it difficult to work with colleagues who previously worked alongside him or her, but who are now subordinates.

It may also be desirable to bring in 'new blood'. An outsider brought into an organisation can take an unbiased approach to their job and can often bring new ideas into the company. It has been suggested that a 15% to 20% turnover of staff in any company is desirable.

Give three examples of jobs that might be advertised:

a internally
b locally
c nationally
d internationally.

Figure 3: Job advertisements

External advertising

Having decided on how widely to advertise, the company must decide on the method it will use. In making this decision, the firm will have to balance the cost of advertising against the need to attract a high quality of applicant. The ease

---

Collect copies of a local newspaper for a period of four weeks. This could be less if there is a local evening paper.

1 What types of job are advertised most often?
(Divide jobs into groups such as clerical, factory work, catering jobs etc.)

2 Is there any connection between the size of the advertisement and the salary being offered? Adverts do not always say what salary is on offer so you will need to limit your sample to those that do.

3 One problem you may have come up against in the previous question is the offering of various 'perks' such as company cars and pension schemes.

List the various 'perks' being offered together with the types of job offering these incentives.

Why do you think that companies offer these incentives rather than just paying a higher salary?

4 Design an advertisement for a job as a nurse. You will need to decide on such things as the size of the advertisement, the salary being offered, the type of person required and what form the application should take.

NB Beware of discrimination.

---

with which the right type of person can be attracted clearly depends very much on the nature of the job on offer. Whilst it will be easy to recruit unskilled workers locally, there may be shortages of some skills in the area, requiring much more extensive advertising.

By far the cheapest way of advertising a post is by **word of mouth**. Existing employees may inform friends and relatives of job vacancies and encourage them to apply. As well as being cheap, this creates a good community feeling amongst employees, many of whom will know each other socially.

It does, however, limit applications to local people and the employer may be accused of unlawful discrimination (in terms of sex or race) and favouritism.

Many employers advertise vacancies in **local schools and colleges**. They may ask careers teachers to recommend students who would be suitable for a particular job. Many schools now produce profiles of school leavers, setting out their strengths and weaknesses. Employers have encouraged this as it helps them to match candidates for a job with the personnel specifications that have been drawn up for that job.

YTS has given employers the opportunity to get to know more about a school leaver before offering permanent employment. Many employers do not recruit directly from school at sixteen, but may take on a number of YTS trainees with a view to retaining those who have impressed them over the two years of the scheme.

Local newspapers are another common method of recruiting people who live in a particular area. The cost of advertising is quite modest, but the local paper is read by most people who are looking for jobs locally. The size of the advertisement will often reflect the importance of the job being offered.

As well as advertising in local publications, an employer may consider advertising a post in **national newspapers** or in **specialist magazines**. These advertisements will be more costly but will reach more people and will attract more applicants. Teaching posts, for example, could be advertised within the school, possibly in local newspapers, and in many cases in *The Guardian* or *The Times Educational Supplement* which have national circulations.

A quick way of filling vacancies is to make use of the local **job centre**. A job centre is staffed by specialists who offer a range of services to people seeking employment and to employers. They handle both temporary and permanent jobs and display details of job vacancies in their offices. Anyone expressing an interest in an advertised job can be referred to the employer for interview. If an employer has a vacancy which needs to be filled quickly, the job centre can draw up a list of suitable candidates from its files from which the employer can then choose.

In addition to job centres there are also **commercial employment agencies** in many towns. These agencies tend to specialise in a particular type of job such as secretarial or computing jobs. Many of them deal with temporary rather than full-time jobs. They keep a list of suitable staff who are referred to employers. The employer pays a fee to the agency but saves the cost of advertising and selecting staff for itself. A number of these agencies specialise in professional appointments, eg accountants.

In the same way, one branch of the Government Employment Service also deals with professionally qualified people. This is the **Professional and Executive Recruitment** branch which specialises in managerial and professional posts.

An extension of the recruitment consultancy services which is available to companies is an **executive search organisation**. An organisation of this type may approach people already in jobs who they feel would be suitable for a vacancy which has been referred to them by a client. This is often known as 'head hunting' and is usually restricted to senior managerial posts.

Put yourself in the position of an unemployed secretary. You have good typing and shorthand speeds and five years experience in a typing pool. You have not worked for a number of years whilst bringing up a family but now you want to return to work.

1 List the possible sources of information about local jobs.
2 Using as many of these sources of information as possible, produce a list of all the suitable jobs currently on offer. You may wish to visit the local job centre and to make use of the local newspapers.
3 Compare your lists with those produced by other members of the class to see if you have missed any jobs.
4 Choose one of these jobs and write (or type) a letter of application stating why you think you should be considered for the post.

Selection

Having advertised and received applications for a post, the next stage is to make a selection. Some employers will ask candidates to contact them by telephone and others will ask for a letter of application. This may help selection if an ability to speak clearly on the telephone or to write letters is an important part of the job. In most cases, however, employers use standard application forms as the first stage of selection. This gives the advantage that the employer can compare the qualifications and achievements of applicants, as well as their ability to write neatly and accurately. Employers will sift through the applications and then make a 'short list'.

The next step will be to take up references. Candidates will normally be asked to provide the names of people who can say something about their ability to do a job. These people may be teachers, doctors or previous employers.

Once references are received, assuming they are favourable, candidates are called for an interview or a test. A formal test has the advantage of being objective. It does not rely on the opinion of the employer. However, there is a limit to the amount of information that can be gained and employers may wish to meet candidates. In this case, an interview will be used in order to assess a candidate's personality and find out more information about them.

Interviews are not always reliable, particularly if they are short and the person being interviewed is nervous. A skilled interviewer can soon put a candidate at ease, however, and a great deal of information can be obtained. An interviewer will often take this opportunity to obtain more details about points mentioned in the application form. There will usually also be an opportunity for the candidate to ask questions about the job and about the company.

For unskilled jobs the **personnel department** may carry out the interviews, but with more senior posts the managers or supervisors will be involved. This has the advantage that managers and supervisors will share in the decision as to who should work under them. A disadvantage is that they are not likely to be skilled interviewers and may even be rather nervous themselves.

---

1 Design an application form suitable for one of the secretarial job advertisements used for the last activity.
2 Each member of the group should fill in a copy of the form. You will have to make up suitable experience and qualifications but try to make the other information as factual as possible.
3 Choose one member of the class to act as an interviewer and another to be the applicant. Act out an interview based on the applicant's completed form.
4 Discuss what you have learned about job applications and interviews.

Appointment

Having selected the best candidate, an appointment can be made. When an employee joins a company he or she must be offered, within thirteen weeks, a **contract of employment**. This contract sets out the conditions under which a person is employed and will contain details of the following:

- The name of the employer and employee.
- The title of the job that the employee is to do.
- The date when employment began.
- How the rate of pay is to be calculated.

- When payment will be made, eg weekly or monthly.
- Hours of work and overtime arrangements.
- Holiday entitlement and holiday pay.
- Sick pay.
- Pension rights.
- Disciplinary rules.
- Grievance procedures.

The contract protects the interests of the worker. If an employer wants to end this contract he must give prior warning. This is known as the period of **notice** and the length of this period is determined by the length of time the employee has been with the company.

A contract of employment places a responsibility on both the employer and employee. The employer has duties in areas such as health, safety, training and supervision. An employee has a duty to co-operate with his employer in meeting these obligations and a duty to do his job in a way that does not endanger other workers.

Induction

After they have been appointed, new employees need to be inducted into the company. Induction is helping employees to settle in to their new jobs and their new place of work. They will need to adjust to new people, new surroundings and a new company as well as getting to know a new job. This will happen in time without help, but a formal induction programme can speed this up.

As a team of tutors with responsibility for first year students, you have been asked to devise a one week induction programme for new entrants into the school.

The programme should help them to:

a get to know each other and the staff who will teach them
b get to know the school
c find out about the school rules.

Your programme should include activities and should not be simply a series of lectures.

Helping an employee to settle in quickly is in the interests of the company. The new employee will be more productive once he or she has settled down and it is obviously important that safety rules are learned as soon as possible. Employees who have not been helped to adjust to their new surroundings may feel unhappy and may even leave the company within a few weeks of starting. The costly process of recruiting will then have to start all over again.

A good induction programme will help new entrants to develop a loyalty to the company, which will not only encourage them to stay but will also increase their efficiency as they have a better understanding of the company's aims. At the other extreme, an unhappy employee can create an unsettled atmosphere which will have an undesirable effect on fellow workers. To achieve this sense of loyalty, recruits should be told about the work of the company and how their job contributes to its success.

Induction will vary considerably between firms. Candidates will be provided with some information about a job before they are interviewed and further information may be provided at the interview itself. The first day at work is also important and it is at this stage that the new recruit is often introduced to his or her workmates. In many companies, this first introduction is the only induction that the new recruit will get, whilst in others there will be a more formal programme lasting a few days or even weeks.

Induction training may include some or all of the following:

● Talks given by managers or supervisors on aspects such as company regulations.
● Written information covering things such as fire and safety regulations.
● Films or slides may be used to help describe the company and its products.
● Visits may be organised to other factories or branches of the company or to the head office.
● Tours may be arranged within the plant to visit different departments and to meet key personnel.
● Group discussions may be held where a number of new recruits can share their problems.

Part 3 Training

It has often been stated in recent years that Britain has the worst trained workforce in Western Europe, yet training is vital to the success of industry.

Benefits of training

A well-trained workforce will have a number of major benefits for a firm. The most obvious one is that training helps to increase productivity. If workers receive formal training in their job then the quantity and quality of work they produce will increase.

Training will also create a more flexible workforce, able to do more jobs and able to respond to changes in the nature of jobs within the firm. Gone are the days when apprentices learned a skill and worked as craftsmen within one industry, or even one firm, for the whole of their working lives. Jobs change as modern technology is introduced and workers need to be retrained to learn the new skills which are needed. This does not only apply to manufacturing industry but also to the service sector. The use of word processors, for example, has changed the nature of secretarial work a great deal in recent years.

Training within a firm can also improve job satisfaction and morale. Most employees like to feel that they are making progress within the organisation and training provides an opportunity for individuals to improve themselves and learn new skills. They have more opportunity to gain promotion and a chance to earn higher wages.

Finally, training in such topics as health and safety is vital for all employees. Many firms offer first aid courses and safety training to workers and some even offer a range of welfare courses such as lectures for employees preparing for retirement.

Forms of training

Training can take many forms. It isn't limited to shop floor workers learning craft skills. The type of training varies depending on the company's policy and the skills to be learned. The simplest method is 'sitting next to Nellie' where a new employee is shown what to do by an experienced worker.

Obtain a copy of the prospectus from the local college of further education and study the courses on offer.

1 List the skills for which training is offered.
2 For each course briefly describe the following:

    a The type of trainees most likely to attend the course. (Note in particular the difference between trainees on part-time courses and those on full-time courses.)

    b The qualifications which can be obtained at the end of the course.

    c The types of job available locally in which trainees could be employed on completing the course.

Training which is carried out in the workplace is known as **on-the-job** training. It has the advantage that the training offered is linked to the firm's needs, but has the disadvantage that 'Nellie's' productivity is reduced whilst the new employee is being trained and, unless the firm has a training department, the training is likely to be given by someone who is not an experienced instructor.

The introduction of new technology has resulted in a decline in traditional crafts and in the apprentice training associated with these crafts. Craft training does, however, still take place in trades such as plumbing, electrical work and engineering. This training may be offered in skill centres run by the Manpower Services Commission or in further education colleges. Many of these courses lead to formal qualifications such as City and Guilds Certificates.

Off-the-job training of this type may be appropriate when the work is of a semi-skilled nature. These jobs have no formal apprenticeship scheme, but a general education alone is not sufficient. An example would be a shorthand typist, who would need training in shorthand, keyboarding and office practice. Some training would be provided at the place of work, but this is likely to be limited to practice on the equipment used in the office and instruction in the way that a particular office is organised. More formal training will be provided by a technical college or a private secretarial school. This training may take place before the employee goes into a new job, or the employer may encourage new employees to attend evening classes or may give them time off work to attend on a day release basis.

For many industries, the main type of training for employment is through the Youth Training

---

YTS a go-go!

SUE SMITH and Sarah Pickard have gone Gah-ga over YTS. Gah-ga is the name of the band they have just joined as backing vocalists.

They are employed under YTS by the two founder members of the band, Owen Downey and Keith Bell of Chesterfield in Derbyshire, who set up their promotions company, Itz Fixx with help from the Enterprise Allowance Scheme, in November last year.

In order to qualify, the two young entrepreneurs had to convince the Manpower Services Commission that the girls would get proper training. This is being provided by Response, a local independent training body who have been decreed an Approved Training Organisation by the MSC.

The girls receive training in all aspects of performing – guitar and keyboard lessons, choreography, and advice on the business side. 'We believe it's the first of its kind,' says Owen.

Sarah has always had musical ambitions, but until the YTS offer, had had no success. Just before the band's first gig in Barnstaple, she admitted, 'I'm really nervous,' but it won't dampen her ambition. 'We're after a recording contract next. We want to make it to the top.' They're ready to go-go!

Source: Employment News March 1987

1 Collect literature on the YTS schemes in your area for your file. The careers service should be able to help you.
2 Study the article and answer the following questions:

    a Why do you think Owen and Keith employed the two girls on YTS rather than offering them full-time jobs?

    b Why does the training include business advice?

    c How does the Enterprise Allowance Scheme operate? (You should be able to find out from a job centre or a library).

Scheme. The two year YTS scheme started in 1986 and is financed by the government's Manpower Services Commission (MSC). It provides a combination of on-the-job and off-the-job training for sixteen and seventeen year old school leavers.

The scheme is run by managing agents who find work placements for trainees and pay them an allowance whilst they are training. Off-the-job training is provided by colleges or other training bodies and should lead to the award of a nationally recognised qualification.

The growth of the tertiary or service sector of industry has resulted in the need for training in **social skills**. Training is needed for those entering the caring services, such as nursing and social work, but also for those who deal with the public as part of their job. British Rail, for example, recently put all their employees through a courtesy course to improve their image with the public. Again this type of training will be a mixture of 'in house' training offered by the employer and training in colleges.

Another group of workers who require training in dealing with people are supervisors and managers, who have to deal with other employees as part of their work. Supervisory and management training has expanded rapidly in recent years with increased awareness that skills such as leadership, decision making and organisation can be taught and are not simply natural abilities.

Management training is often carried out within the firm or by specialist organisations offering a short course for managers. Larger organisations may have their own staff college where training is carried out. These colleges usually offer residential courses and have the advantage that managers and supervisors can get away from the day-to-day demands of their work and concentrate on improving their managerial skills.

Staff appraisal

In many large firms, staff appraisal is part of staff development. It usually takes the form of a regular meeting between an employee and a line manager where the employee's progress is discussed.

There are a number of reasons for carrying out an appraisal of this type. The first is to see how well an employee is doing and to discuss the ways in which work can be improved. The discussion will also provide information on the training needs of the employee and it will provide the manager with information about the employee's strengths and weaknesses which may be of help when considering promotion. In some firms salary increases are dependent on the outcome of a review of the employee's work over the year.

There are also a number of problems with staff appraisal. Some employees will not like being criticised even if the intention is to help them to get on. Some managers may be reluctant to criticise employees and staff appraisal becomes little more than an annual ten minute chat with the boss.

Despite these and other problems, some form of staff appraisal is a useful part of a programme of staff development and is being introduced into more and more firms.

As the training officer for a large building society you receive the following memo from the managing director.

From: Managing director
To: Training officer

Staff development for trainee managers

As you will be aware, a group of ten school leavers will join the society at the end of June on completing their 'A' levels. I would like you to produce a report giving me details of your proposed staff development programme for these new recruits. In particular I would like details of:

a any induction programme that is planned
b training offered within the branches
c any proposals to use the society's staff college in Oxford
d the assistance that will be offered to help the trainee managers to obtain the Building Society Association examinations.

Write the report outlined in the letter from the managing director.

It may be of some help to study the extract from the training programme for Metal Box finance trainees in Figure 4.

Your careers teacher or local building society manager may also be able to help with details of the training needs of building society employees.

Figure 4: Metal Box plc: Extract from graduate training programme

Induction course

Our two months induction course aims to help you find out all about us and our operations. Most graduates joining the company take part in this course; for certain specialists, a shorter period may be sufficient, and in some cases elements of the course are more appropriately taken in later training.

The course begins in head office with a week's introduction to the company. This is followed by a week improving your basic communication skills before going on to a series of factory-based group projects. Typical projects introduce you to the problems of personnel, production and commercial management.

Later, you will spend one week on an outdoor Endeavour Training Course, before returning to head office for final sessions on resources, finance, personnel, marketing, raw materials and research and development.

Finance traineeships

Finance trainees follow the general two month induction course. They then move on for their professional training, normally at a factory under the supervision of the factory accountant. Practical exposure to all accounting operations is augmented by private study pursued by a correspondence course or day release at a local college.

The training programme lasts two years and covers the accountancy aspects as laid down by the professional bodies, eg ICMA:

The training period will also provide a detailed knowledge of the factory operation by attachments to production and service departments.

The period following the two year training programme will depend to a certain extent on the individual and the factory situation. A third year is often required before a professional accountancy qualification can be gained.

Source: Metal Box plc *Graduate Prospect 1987*

Part 4 Salaries and motivation

It would be impossible to study the place of people in business without considering wages and salaries. Although the difference between wages and salaries is not as clear cut as it used to be, we usually consider wages to be weekly payments to manual workers and salaries to be monthly payments to clerical and managerial staff.

Payment systems

The simplest payment system is the one based on the number of hours worked, ie **time rates**. This system is simple and cheap to administer and employees are certain how much they will receive each month. The system, however, may not provide an incentive to work harder, as workers get the same rate per hour no matter how hard they work. Supervision is required to make sure workers are not doing as little as possible.

There are some situations where time rates may be used. It is not always possible to measure the output or performance of individual workers, such as nurses or teachers. In other jobs, quality rather quantity is more desirable and so time rates would prevent the need to hurry the job.

Payment by results (PBR) is the system most commonly used as an alternative to time rates where an employer wants to encourage greater productivity. This method is usually used for production workers whose output is easily measured. However, other workers, such as salesmen, may also be paid according to their performance.

Where payment is a fixed amount for each unit of output this is known as **piece work**. The employee can work at his own pace and extra effort will result in extra financial reward under this system. Output can further be increased if employees can find quicker ways of organising and carrying out a task. Because employers know how much they are paying out in labour

costs for each unit produced, piece work also makes cost calculations simpler.

There are problems with this system, however. An individual worker's wages may be affected by factors outside his or her control. A strike elsewhere in the plant or a delay in receiving supplies of raw materials will prevent an employee earning as much as he or she would otherwise have done. There may also be resentment amongst workers, particularly between those on time rates and those on piece rates, as earnings may differ significantly.

Although less supervision is required to ensure that workers are working hard enough, there may be a need for supervision so that quality is maintained and that safety standards do not suffer as employees seek to produce as many units as possible.

A further problem arises in trying to get agreement on the rate per unit which is to be paid and there are often bitter disagreements between management and unions as to what is the right rate for the job. The issue is further complicated when new technology is introduced, which increases output with no extra effort on the part of the employees. Management would normally try to reduce the piece rate but unions would

Payment systems – piece rates and time rates.

demand some compensation for their members because the nature of their jobs had changed.

Where it is impossible to measure the output of an individual employee, a system of **group PBR** may be used. Here the output of the group is measured and the bonus pay is divided amongst the group. This has the added advantage of encouraging employees to work together but there will often be accusations that one or two members of the group are not pulling their weight.

A group PBR scheme could pay bonuses based on total output or the value of sales. This system encourages workers to see themselves as part of the organisation as a whole and they benefit directly from any changes in work practices which make the organisation more efficient. Individual workers may not work as hard, however, and the system can be rather complex and difficult to understand.

A further extension of this principle is **profit sharing**, when employees receive a bonus based on the profits of the company. As with the previously described scheme, the individual worker has an interest in ensuring the overall efficiency and profitability of the organisation. There is the added advantage that if the scheme is linked to the issue of shares to employees they may have the added incentive of being part owners of the business in which they work.

Take-home pay

The payment systems we have described already allow total or **gross pay** to be calculated. This is not how much the worker will take home each week or month, however. Various deductions are made from gross pay to arrive at the **net pay**. In most cases these deductions are made by the employer before the employee receives payment. This is known as the **pay as you earn** (PAYE) system.

The first deduction is income tax. All employees are allowed to earn a certain amount 'tax free.' This is known as a personal allowance and extra allowances are available if you have a dependant, for example, a relative. In addition there are other allowances which might be available for such things as the cost of buying special clothing for work.

When all allowances are taken into account an individual will be given a tax code by the Inland Revenue. This code is made up from the total allowances figure. The last number is removed from the total and replaced by a letter indicating an employees circumstances, eg

H for a married man's allowance
L for a single person's allowance

Each individual who receives an income fills in an annual tax return, giving details of personal circumstances relevant to the calculation of the tax code. The code for that year is then notified to the individual and to his or her employer. This code, when used together with a tax guide provided to employers, allows them to calculate the deductions to be made for taxes out of the employee's wage.

Tax is paid at the basic rate on taxable income up to a certain level and at a higher rate on income above this level. At the time of writing tax rates and allowances were as follows:

Figure 5: Tax allowances

Tax thresholds (Allowances)	1988/89
Single person's allowance	£2,605
Wife's earned income allowance	£2,605
Married allowance	£4,095

Simplified tax calculation

A married man receives an annual income of £20,000 pa. He has to purchase tools for his trade valued at £55 but has no other allowable expenses.

		£
Tax code:	Personal allowance (married man)	4,095
	Add expenses	+ 55
	Total allowances	= 4,150
	Tax code	415H
Taxable income:	Gross income	20,000
	Less tax free income	− 4,150
	Taxable income	= 15,850
Tax payable:	25% of £15,850	= 3,962·50

Income tax is not the only deduction from total income. The next biggest deduction is normally National Insurance. This is a contribution towards the cost of benefits such as unemployment benefit, sickness benefit, family allowance and flat rate pensions. Both employers and employees make a contribution to this scheme and the size of this contribution is linked to the level of earnings.

As well as contibuting to the flat rate old age pension, employers normally contribute to an occupational pension scheme which provides an

Figure 6: Take-home pay

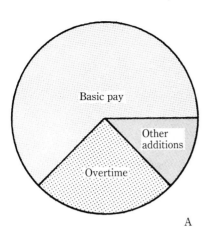

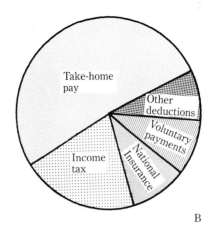

A

B

Figure 7: A pay slip

NAME			W/E			
WORKS/DEPT. No			Code No.			
			Tax Week No.			

GROSS WAGES TO DATE		TAX DEDUCTED TO DATE		WAGES DUE FOR WEEK	£	p.
£	p.	£	p.	BASIC		
				HRS. O/T @		
				HRS. O/T @		

DEDUCTIONS | | £ | p.
Superannuation.............................
National Insurance.........................
Standard rate at...........................%
Reduced rate at............................%

INCOME TAX....................................
OTHER DEDUCTIONS............................

HRS. O/T @
BONUS, HOLIDAY, XMAS
SICK PAY
OTHER PAYMENT

GROSS

DEDUCTIONS

INCOME TAX REFUND

NET £

extra payment above the minimum. Employees usually make a payment towards these schemes as well and this is a further deduction from income.

In Figure 6, the first diagram shows how gross pay is made up and the second diagram shows deductions from gross pay. It can be seen that take-home pay for most people is little more than half of their gross pay.

Figure 7 illustrates a typical pay slip which records gross pay, deductions and take home pay. Employers use tax tables to calculate how much to deduct from wages.

Wage determination

Why do some people earn more than others? There are many factors which will influence the level of earnings of individuals. These include the value to society of the goods they produce or the service they provide, their training and qualifications, their working conditions and the power of the trade unions which bargain for wages on their behalf.

List the main factors which you think are likely to influence the earnings of workers in a particular occupation.

Choose up to five occupations with which you are familiar and give a score out of ten for each of the factors you have listed.

Add up the total scores for each job and compare this with the actual earnings of workers. You will be able to find these figures in *Employment Gazette*. Do your findings suggest that some factors are more important than others in determining income?

Figure 8: Factors influencing earnings

Job factor (Max score 10)	Occupation	
	Nurse	Building labourer
Value of product/service	8	4
Qualifications	3	1
Physical effort	5	9
Total score		
Earnings		

Job evaluation

The technique of breaking down a job into the tasks involved, and the skills and experience required, is known as **job evaluation**. We have already seen how this allows us to draw up a job description and a job specification. We can also use it as a means of determining wages.

It will be clear from the previous activity, that decisions have to be made as to the importance of the various factors you have picked out as being relevant, and it is quite likely that you have disagreed with the scoring in Figure 8. Another problem is that it is the job which is evaluated and not the person doing it. In many cases, however, the nature of a job will vary a great deal according to who is actually doing it.

Job evaluation helps to reduce discrimination on the basis of sex and race, because anyone in a particular job will earn the wage which has been agreed for that job. The system should also reduce disagreements on wage differences between groups of workers. This will be the case particularly where the workers or their representatives have been directly involved.

Job evaluation also provides valuable information to help the firm with selection, training and promotion of employees and it also helps to highlight situations where workers are placed in jobs which are not in line with their abilities.

Common methods of job evaluation include:

- **Job ranking** – This involves looking at a job as a whole and then comparing it with other jobs. A list of jobs in order of difficulty and responsibility is produced and jobs are then grouped into grades which form the basis of pay scales.
- **Job grading** – This works the opposite way around with grades being determined first. Descriptions of each grade are produced and selected jobs chosen as being typical of each grade. By comparing other jobs with these so called benchmark jobs, they can be placed in the appropriate grade.
- **Points rating** – This is the most sophisticated method which involves breaking down each job into 'factors' such as responsibility and training. Points are then awarded for each factor in a similar way to the exercise completed earlier.

Factors are weighted according to the importance attached to them and a job can then be ranked on the basis of its points score.

Other factors determining wages

We have see that wages may be influenced by a range of job factors, but the actual wages earned by a particular employee will be affected by many other things not related to the nature of the particular job being carried out. Briefly these include the following:

- The power of trade unions in the industry as a whole.
- The profitability of the company.
- The payment system in operation, eg piece work, bonuses.
- The demand and supply of workers with a particular skill in the labour market.
- Government policy on incomes, particularly where the government is the employer.
- The experience of the individual worker.
- Promotion prospects, ie where prospects are good, initial pay may be low.

Non-financial rewards

A glance through any page of job advertisements, particularly for higher paid jobs, will show that there are other rewards offered by employers in addition to the basic salary. These additional rewards are often referred to as 'perks' and they have become so widespread that they are now taxed in the same way as if extra income had been paid.

Study the list of executive perks and answer the questions which follow.

Figure 9: Executive perks

Benefit	Percentage of executives
Life assurance	92
Full use of car	80
Medical insurance	74
Subsidised lunches	56
Bonus scheme	44
Share option scheme	36
Subsidised phone	35

1 Why are 'perks' most commonly found in higher paid jobs?
2 Carry out your own survey of advertisements appearing in the national press. List the benefits being offered and record the number of times each one is found.
    Present this information in the form of a diagram or table.

The production line

The expansion of mass production has done little to create the sort of working conditions necessary to motivate the workforce. The process of division of labour described earlier has led to many jobs becoming boring and repetitive with little job satisfaction.

This lack of involvement of employees in their work leads to problems such as absenteeism, high labour turnover, low productivity, poor quality work and industrial unrest.

One solution adopted by a small number of firms has been to reorganise production and to move away from the assembly line.

A well-publicised example of this was the Volvo plant at Kalmar in Sweden, opened in 1974. This plant replaced the production line with teams of workers, each responsible for a complete section of a car. One team, for example, would assemble the whole steering system and another the electrical system.

The team decided between themselves on how the work was to be distributed and they had some control over the pace of their work and the timing of breaks. By this means the monotony of the traditional production line was done away with.

The management's hope was that the new teamwork approach would improve efficiency and the quality of work by putting greater responsibility on the workers themselves. At the same time it was hoped to reduce labour turnover and absenteeism. The stress of the production line would be reduced and employees would be able to identify with the company and its product.

The experiment was an expensive one, involving a much higher initial investment than would have been required for a traditional car plant. In addition, productivity was generally lower and the experiment was not, therefore, altogether successful. It did, however, lead to further experiments in work organisation including the use of job rotation, job enrichment and job enlargement.

Job rotation

This involves changing jobs at regular intervals. This could mean moving onto a different part of the production line or to a new department. By this means boredom is reduced unless rotation is from one tedious job to another. It also helps provide a more flexible workforce with experience of more than one operation. Production is lost, however, as workers have to adjust to new skills and unions have not always been supportive of schemes of this type.

Job enrichment

It has been argued that work should be organised in such a way as to give the employee greater responsibility, to provide the employee with a sense of achievement, to give some form of recognition for work done as well as offering better prospects of promotion.

Read the following article and answer the questions which follow:

Girls, wives, factory lives

Churchmans was a declining part of Imperial Tobacco, producing pipe and loose tobaccos. It was a small factory. Most of the 140 women worked in the weighing and packing departments, the labour-intensive areas. The largest of these, the machine weighing room, was filled with long weighing machines.

Each machine contained six scales, each with a little light which went on to register the correct weight of tobacco. Each weigher picks up tiny lumps of tobacco which she drops into a hole – sometimes taking back a few shreds – until the exact weight is reached. A counter records her performance. The machines clatter all day from 7.30am to 4.30pm except for a 15 minute breakfast break and an hour for lunch, recording all the time. Failure in performance standard or speed leads to a warning, and downgrading to a lower 'proficiency pay rate'. Keeping up with the machines or the performance rates and coping with monotony – that was what factory work was about.

PAT: We get good wages, I think I'm lucky to be working here. We ought to be grateful for having jobs.

But the money didn't mean that they were not bored.

PATTI: I'd like to see them here, I'd like to see the manager on a weighing machine for a week.

MARY: Not a week! An hour would be enough!

As the women talked to me, it became clear that a 'good' factory was one where you found mates. The work could never be 'good'. Older women find the younger generation 'more defiant' than they used to be. There are quick witted insults, jibes, competition. The supervisors' job is to contain these outbursts, to maintain work discipline. They find it hard to handle.

STEVEN: (chargehand, machine weighing room): I say, if they want to act like children, I shall have to treat them like children.

Being treated like children is part of factory life, part of relations with men – including union men.

1   What does this article tell you about:
   a The problems of the production line?
   b The particular problems faced by women?

2   How was work organised in the factory to obtain maximum output from the workforce?

3   What could the company have done to improve working conditions for its employees?

Source: Adapted from *New Society* 22 October 1981

Job enrichment is designed to achieve these aims by giving the employee some responsibility for work planning and reducing supervision. The employee is required to carry out more varied tasks and, where possible, an employee is responsible for a complete unit of work.

This could involve giving an employee responsibility for quality control or for the ordering of materials, or giving a machine operator responsibility for routine maintenance. In this way a new dimension is added to the work.

There are clearly some jobs where it would be impossible to apply these principles. There may also be union objections to workers doing more than one job. Evidence suggests that job enrichment is most appropriate in administrative, clerical, supervisory and technical positions.

Job enlargement

Possibly the least satisfactory means of re-organising work. It involves giving the employee more work to do which is of a similar nature. Instead of operators performing a single task they may complete several tasks. This increases the variety of the job being undertaken and it may help to overcome boredom. Unless it is coupled with increased financial rewards, however, it is unlikely to be welcomed. It is also technically, less efficient and therefore not favoured by management.

The theory of motivation

It will be clear from our consideration of the production line that the main problem in motivating the workforce is that the needs of the individual are not necessarily the needs of the organisation. Business has therefore drawn on the research of scientists to look at the factors most likely to overcome this possible conflict.

Douglas McGregor

The emphasis on financial reward together with strict supervision as the best way of ensuring maximum productivity, is based on certain assumptions about the nature of employees.

McGregor called these traditional assumptions Theory X. According to this theory most people do not like work, are reluctant to take on responsibility, and want decisions to be made for them.

McGregor himself favoured Theory Y which assumed that most people find work natural, enjoy taking on responsibility and want to play some part in decision making.

If this theory is correct, then less supervision is required as workers are capable of motivating themselves if the right working conditions exist.

A. H. Maslow

Maslow stated that man has a 'hierarchy' of needs. That is, there are many needs on different levels.

At the base of this hierarchy are the needs for food and shelter. At the next level come the so-called safety needs including physical and economic security. These needs dominated during the nineteenth century when survival and security against unemployment were the main concern of the workforce.

With increased living standards and the rise of the welfare state in the twentieth century, the higher needs have become increasingly important in motivating the workforce.

The first of these are the social needs, such as the desire for social and welfare activities in the workplace and for a sense of belonging. The next level involves the so called esteem needs including self respect, personal achievement, and status. The final level is referred to as 'self actualisation' and includes the desire for power. As each level of need is satisfied then the next level becomes more important in motivating the individual. If you are well-fed, for example, you would be prepared to give up a meal every now and again in favour of satisfying other needs.

Figure 10: The hierarchy of needs

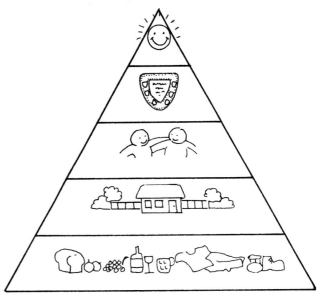

Self actualisation	–	Desire for self-fulfilment, creativity, power.
Esteem needs	–	Success, self-respect, personal achievement, status.
Social needs	–	Identification, social and welfare activities in the workplace.
Safety needs	–	Physical and economic security.
Physiological needs	–	Hunger, thirst, sex, rest.

F. Herzberg

Herzberg arrived at much the same conclusions as Maslow in his book, *The Motivation to Work*. He asked workers what it was about their work that gave them the greatest satisfaction.

The answers Herzberg received were of five main types:

● When a task had been successfully completed.
● When achievement had been praised or rewarded.
● Where responsibility or trust had been given.
● Where they had been promoted.
● Where the tasks to be undertaken were interesting.

Herzberg also identified a number of factors which were most likely to cause discontent. These are referred to as **hygiene factors**, as dealing with them prevents unwanted outcomes in much the same way as personal hygiene prevents unpleasant results.

Whilst those factors which motivate the workforce relate to the work itself, the hygiene factors relate to the conditions within which work takes place. These factors include pay, working conditions and levels of supervision. All of these factors are taken for granted until something goes wrong, in which case it can result in industrial unrest.

I was the Chairman of the Board until I found out about the rates for overtime.

Source: *Punch 1946*

Money as a motivator

Employees are paid money in exchange for the work that they do in helping the firm to produce goods or provide services. There are other rewards for working including job satisfaction, but for most people the major reward is financial.

Money is therefore the main incentive to work, but does it guarantee that employees work as efficiently as possible?

Wage systems such as payment by results encourage workers to put in more effort, but the incentive only lasts as long as the money is there. It doesn't change an employees attitude towards work. As a result many firms have looked for other ways of encouraging workers to work harder.

Variations on the payment by results theme have often been used, including bonus schemes and profit sharing schemes all designed to encourage increased productivity. Encouraging employees to become shareholders has been another method of giving workers a greater feeling of commitment to the firm.

It has been argued, however, that the needs of employees are not simply for financial reward. An employer must look at other ways in which employees can be motivated.

Part 5 Workplace communication

Communication between people is obviously a vital activity within an organisation and good communication not only aids motivation but also improves overall efficiency. The main emphasis of this section will be on communication between managers and employees.

Larger companies, with over 250 employees, are required by the 1982 Employment Act to describe, in their **directors report**, the action that they have taken over the year to increase employee involvement in the company. This would include information provided to employees on matters which are of importance to them and possibly the degree of involvement of employees in decision making.

An example from the Annual Report of Proctor and Gamble is given in Figure 11. You should be able to find other examples for yourselves.

Figure 11: Extract from Proctor & Gamble Annual Report

Employee involvement

Face-to-face, two-way communication between employees and their management continues to be at the heart of employee involvement in Proctor & Gamble Limited. It is facilitated by a management structure in which there are usually no more than ten or so employees to one manager; contact is close and real.

This open, two-way communication is critical in involving employees as appropriate in decision-making processes and, in turn, achieving greater commitment to results. It also increases the company's ability to manage change.

Works Councils, made up of management and elected non-management representatives, provide an additional involvement forum at our Trafford Park and West Thurrock plants.

We have continued with regular internal publications to all employees. These include a factual business review, a house magazine, and explanatory booklets on the company's employee plans, policies and benefits.

The purpose of communication

Workplace communication is the passing of information and instructions which help the organisation to operate efficiently. From the point of view of the management, it increases efficiency by ensuring that more informed decisions are taken. There is also more likelihood of these decisions being accepted by the employees if they have been involved in some way.

Employees are likely to be better motivated and more committed to their work if the system of communication is efficient and job satisfaction will be increased. Industrial relations should also improve with greater mutual trust and understanding if information flows freely within the organisation.

The attitude of employees towards their work has changed over the years as has the nature of the work that they undertake. As organisations have become larger and more complex and as employees have begun to demand more from their work than simply a weekly pay packet, the need for co-operation between management and employees has grown. The relationship is no longer simply one of managers passing down instructions to subordinates.

The purpose of communication is therefore far wider than simply instructing the workforce. Information must flow from management to employees and, just as importantly, it must flow from the employees to managers if decision making is to be more effective.

Communication also includes **negotiation** and this could involve individual employees negotiating personal objectives for the coming year, departments negotiating with each other for resources or management negotiating with trade unions over pay and conditions. In each case, an efficient communication system will help to reduce conflict.

In some firms communication between management and employees may involve **consultation** where employees or their representatives are directly involved in the decision making process.

In dealing with this changing process of communication, we will need to consider the nature of the **message** which is passed, the **medium** or 'method' that is being used to pass on the message and the **channel** along which the message passes.

The message

The message is the content of the communication between managers and employees and can take two main forms, information and instructions. Instructions flow downwards from managers or supervisors to subordinates. The way in which this form of communication is handled is obviously very important. If instructions are not communicated properly then at best they 'will be ignored, and at worst there will be serious industrial relations problems.

Information should also flow from management to the workforce. Some information is required by law. This includes information about employees' conditions of employment set out in documents such as the **Contract of Employment, Health and Safety regulations** and **statements on disciplinary procedures**. Further information will be provided on the nature of an employee's job, including technical information about the work and the equipment to be used and general information on the organisation of the department. In addition, information may be provided on the organisation as a whole including the company's products and achievements. This information is often communicated during an induction course.

It is important to note that the flow of information should not be one way. Employees should have the opportunity to react to the information they have been given and they may themselves have valuable information to pass on.

This 'feedback' helps to ensure that the message has been understood. Noting the reactions of employees is also a good way of anticipating problems that may arise in the future. The reaction of a shop floor worker to the proposed introduction of a new machine may warn management of possible union opposition or practical problems which may arise such as the problem of noise.

Because employees are more closely involved with production and in many cases are in close contact with the consumer, they can often make a valuable contribution to the organisation of work and to policy decisions. Firms have recognised this in a number of ways, from the use of suggestion boxes with rewards for good ideas, to more formal systems for involving workers in decision making, possibly through worker representatives on boards of directors.

The medium

There are a number of ways in which a message can be passed from one person to another. Some of these are oral methods and some are written. The best method will depend on the nature of the message.

Oral methods

Oral methods have the advantage of being quick and allowing immediate response. Misunderstanding can be reduced as instructions and information can be questioned. In addition, reactions can be noted.

Problems may arise, however, because there is no written record of the message which can be referred to later. Also, when the message has to pass down a long chain, there is the possibility of distortion.

Oral methods of communication include **meetings** such as departmental meetings, mass meetings of the workforce, inter-departmental and board meetings.

Other forms of oral communication include **face-to-face** communication, where a supervisor or manager passes on instructions to an employee, and casual conversations during which information is passed from one person to another. Interviews are also included, whether they are for a job or annual assessment interviews.

Telephone conversations are a very common form of oral communication. This method has the disadvantage that, unlike face-to-face communication it is more difficult to judge the reaction of the recipient of the message or the attitude of the person passing the message on. A person's facial expression can help a great deal in interpreting a message and telephone conversations are therefore more likely to be misinterpreted because of the absence of these clues.

Written methods

Written methods have the advantage that the message is permanent and can be referred to at any time. Greater detail can be provided than would be possible using oral methods as detail which is not written down will quickly be forgotten. Information is also likely to be more accurate as greater care will be taken in presenting the information. Written methods are also more appropriate where there is a wide audience for a particular message. If you wanted to contact the whole workforce, for example, it would not be advisable to rely on word of mouth.

Figure 12: Non-verbal communication

Written methods of communication include **handbooks** and **manuals** produced for reference purposes and dealing with personnel matters or technical details. A company may also produce regular **employee newsletters** to keep workers informed about company activities. **Circulars** can be used to inform workers of special events or to provide important information. Where it is essential that an employee is given a particular piece of information, a personal letter may be sent.

Much internal written communication takes place by means of **memoranda**. A 'memo' as it is usually called, is a form of letter but is not usually private. Copies may be sent to a number of people to keep them informed. This is the most common form of written communication between managers in an organisation.

Another common method of keeping management informed is by means of **reports**. These may be technical or financial reports and they normally deal with specific problems, outlining the various options available and making recommendations. These reports are often discussed at management or director's meetings.

The **annual report and accounts** of a company is a financial report which is made available to shareholders as well as managers and in many cases the report, or a specially produced summary, is made available to employees to keep them informed as to the company's financial position.

We saw earlier that a disadvantage of oral communication is that there is no permanent record of information, instructions or decisions. In the case of meetings this is often overcome by the keeping of **minutes**.

The minutes of a meeting are a record of the main items discussed and any conclusions or decisions reached. Where there is a regular series of meetings, one of the first items on the agenda is usually the approval of the minutes of the last meeting and any other matters arising from these minutes. The minutes provide a permanent record of what went on at the meeting and can be filed for future reference.

Draw up a chart which summarises the different methods of communication and the advantages and disadvantages of each.

Choice of medium/method

A number of factors will determine the best choice of medium for any particular message. A number of questions need to be asked:

- Is the message confidential?
- Is speed important?
- Who is to receive the message?
- Is a permanent record required?
- Is the message complicated or lengthy?
- How much will it cost to send the message?

Use these questions to decide on the best medium for the following messages:

a An official warning to an employee for continual lateness.
b A reminder to the personnel department to arrange an interview.
c Detailed specifications of a new product.
d Arrangements for an urgent meeting.

The channel

Messages can travel along different routes within the organisation. Some follow the formal organisational structure between one level in the hierarchy and another (known as vertical communication) or between one department and another (known as horizontal communication). Messages may also follow the less formal route which we often refer to as the 'grapevine'.

Vertical communication

The traditional form of vertical communication is the passing of instructions from superiors to subordinates. As we have seen, however, there is a growing recognition of the importance of an upward flow of information and comments.

Vertical communication tends to place a great burden on supervisors and middle management

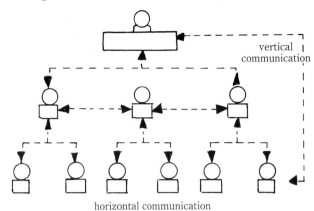

Figure 13: Formal communications

through whom the messages are normally passed. They must receive information, interpret it, decide which messages are to be passed on and pass them on in a form which is understandable to the recipient. They should also take note of reactions to the information and instructions that they are being given.

Passing on information may well have a low priority with managers and supervisors who have more immediate problems to deal with. The result is that this may cause delay and even prevent information flowing through the system.

In parallel with the official lines of communication from management to employees, there is likely to be a direct link between trade unions or employers associations and top management, cutting out middle management. This strengthens the vertical flow of information. The main form of communication through this channel will be negotiations over pay and conditions.

Trade unions are themselves also responsible for establishing a two-way communication between the management and their membership. The views of the members should be accurately conveyed to management and information made available by the management as part of the bargaining process should be accurately reported to the membership. Unions have certain legal rights to information from the management but there is often a problem of confidentality. Some information would be of great value to competitors if it were freely available.

Horizontal communication

This is the type of communication which takes place between people at the same level within the organisation. Employees who work in the same department will obviously need to communicate with one another either face-to-face or using the telephone or memoranda. Communication also takes place between departments and it is here that most problems arise.

For communications to be effective, a great deal of co-operation is required, but in many firms departments are competitive rather than co-operative. The finance department, for example, may not tell the sales department that a particular customer is not paying its bills and the sales force may, as a result, be continuing to take orders for goods which may never be paid for.

A further problem of communication between departments is the use of technical language. Nobody wants their work to look easy and so experts tend to use technical language deliberately to baffle other people. This isn't limited to the production department as accountants and computer experts also have a language of their own.

Informal communication

Think up some interesting piece of information which is unlikely to do anyone any harm. Let three of your class mates pass on this information to friends outside the class – in confidence of course!

Check after a few days how many of the class have been let in on the 'secret'. Depending on the nature of the information you may find that it has been passed from class to class, between year groups and even to teachers and parents – so be careful what rumour you spread!

Information does not always flow along the formal vertical or horizontal channels but may link people with no obvious relationship within the organisation. The so called 'grapevine' can be seen in operation in the staff canteen and at social gatherings. Sales representatives are important agents in the grapevine as they tend to wander between departments picking up and passing on information. Secretaries are also likely to meet and chat with colleagues in other departments and pass on interesting pieces of information.

The type of information most likely to be passed on in this way is rumour and gossip. This will often be deliberately distorted to make a better story and it allows those who are unhappy in their work to get their own back on those they dislike.

Most gossip does little real harm to the organisation as a whole but rumours of plant closures, redundancies or new working practices can often lead to unrest and even strike action. To avoid this a firm needs the trust of its workforce, which is only achieved by making information freely available wherever this is practical.

The grapevine can even be used in a constructive way. By feeding information into the grapevine it is possible to test staff reactions without having to make a formal statement. Informal channels can also be used to get around bottlenecks in the system which are preventing information passing along the official channels.

Rumour can also be a forewarning of future problems. A salesman may have the feeling that a customer is not doing too well, for example. He may not be willing to pass this information on formally, but hints dropped in the right ears will warn the company to keep an eye on that particular customer and to take quick action if bills are not paid.

External communication

As well as communicating with other members of the organisation, it is necessary to communicate with outsiders such as customers, suppliers and the government. Letters and telephone calls are the most common forms of external communication and we have already considered the advantages and disadvantages of each. More modern techniques, such as telex, attempt to combine the speed of the telephone message with the permanent record provided by a letter.

Other common forms of external communication include reports such as the annual report and accounts, which have wide circulation, advertisements aimed mainly at customers and press releases which are aimed at the general public and form part of a company's public relations.

Communication technology

Around 50% of Britain's workers are employed in offices. It has been calculated that if all the pieces of paper handled in the world's offices were laid end to end, they would stretch from here to the sun. These two statistics highlight the scope for new technology in the office.

Technology in the office

One of the most significant applications of new technology to offices has been the introduction of the word processor. This can do the work of many typists, allowing standard letters to be produced at the touch of a button and enabling corrections and alterations to be made to letters and reports with minimum effort.

Management can also be made more effective by the use of new technology. All Debenham's 69 stores, for example, are linked by a viewdata system. This can be used for sending messages from one manager to another and also allows executives at the London head office to analyse trading figures which are collected and updated every week from all 69 stores. It is hoped to improve the system still further to make infor-

---

Read the following article and answer the questions which follow:

The office of the future has already arrived for Ivor Cohen, managing director of Mullard. He sits at his desk surrounded by a battery of screens, keyboards and phones which give him immediate access to and control over his business empire.

If Cohen wants to find out sales or order figures he simply turns in his chair, asks the questions via the keyboard, and within seconds has the answer on his screen.

Another screen gives him up-to-the-minute information on such vital subjects as exchange rates, through the Prestel data base. It can also act as a personal diary and be used to send or receive messages to or from his staff.

Cohen thoroughly approves of the electronic revolution. 'This vastly improved access to information gives me and my managers the time to take real decisions, instead of having to fumble with a phone or bits of paper,' he says.

1 With the help of the article above, describe the benefits that a manager can obtain from the use of new technology.
2 Find out what you can about Prestel and the range of services on offer to businesses.

Source: Adapted from *The Sunday Times* January 23 1983

---

mation available on a daily basis. Directors also have access to information in their homes through their own terminals.

Telecommunications

Telecommunications equipment, such as Fax machines and modems, allowing computers to be linked via the telephone, has greatly speeded up communication between businesses. As the cost of such equipment has fallen, so its use has become more widespread.

Speed of communication has become increasingly important in modern business. Firms dealing in financial markets need minute by minute information on changes in share prices and currency rates. Contracts, orders and other documents need to be transmitted around the world in seconds. To enable this rapid communication to take place, the telecommunications industry has made maximum use of new technology.

Many specialist services are now available to business to aid communication:

- **Radiophones** – These allow contact with vehicles and are used widely by companies such as British Gas to contact service vans.
- **Radiopaging** – This is a system where a 'bleeper' is used to let someone know that there is a message for them.
- **Answering machines** – These allow messages to be recorded even when there is no one in to answer the telephone. They may be linked to a paging system.
- **Freefone** – Freefone numbers allow customers to contact a firm free of charge. It is often used by firms selling directly to the public and taking orders over the telephone.
- **Trade directories** – Directories such as *Yellow Pages* can be used for advertising as well as simply listing telephone numbers.
- **Teleconferencing** – This service allows more than two people to be linked by telephone. It helps overcome the delays and expense involved in having to get a group of people together in one place for a meeting.
- **Confravision** – This is a more sophisticated form of teleconferencing and allows sound and vision communications between studios located throughout the UK.
- **Facsimilie transmission (Fax)** – This system allows documents, letters, photographs, diagrams etc to be sent via the telephone system using special machines rather like photocopiers. Large firms may have their own Fax machines, but there are also agencies in larger towns which offer the use of Fax machines for a fee.

The new NEFAX-18

Fax machines greatly speed up communications between offices.

• **Telex** – This system offers the speed of the telephone and the permanent record available with a letter. Messages are typed into a teleprinter and transmitted using the telephone system to another machine where they are printed out.

• **Databases** – The telephone system can also be used to link together computers. Links to a national computer allow access to up-to-date news and information and the Prestel service allows two way communication with users being able to book plane tickets or to call up particular information.

What telecommunications equipment can help to deal with the following situations?

a A firm wants to confirm an order with a French customer within an hour.

b An architect urgently needs to send copies of a plan to a customer.

c A firm wishes to contact a service engineer who is in his van.

d A stockbroker wants information on current share prices.

e A direct sales firm wants to encourage customers to place orders over the telephone.

f A self-employed plumber wants to be able to receive telephone messages even though he is rarely at home.

Part 6   Worker participation and trade unions

One form of communication within an organisation may be the participation of workers in decision making. This participation can take a number of forms. At one extreme is the appointment of workers to the company's board of directors and at the other is some system of joint consultation, where representatives of management and workers form committees to discuss issues such as safety, welfare, and training. Another form of participation is co-ownership, where the workers hold shares in the company and are therefore part owners as well as employees.

Worker participation

Worker directors are not a new idea and as long ago as 1897 the South Metropolitan Gas Company had employees on the board of directors. Participation through worker directors has been suggested by many people and West Germany has had a system of two-tier boards for many years.

This system is favoured by the European Community. It involves a top level board similar to the traditional board of directors with a second level board on which workers are represented. Overall policy is retained by the top level board with responsibility for day-to-day management being delegated to the second tier board. This board is responsible for putting policies into action. It takes decisions on things such as investment and personnel matters.

The three main political parties in this country are broadly in favour of more worker involvement in decision making and the unions also support greater participation.

Organise and hold a debate dealing with the issue of worker directors. Choose a title such as:
'Workers should not be involved in management.'
The case for and against this motion should be presented by two teams, each consisting of one employer representative and one trade union representative.
The following quotations give some idea of the conflicting arguments.
'I will not sign any recommendation that deprives the shareholder of his ultimate voting power in the affairs of the company, although I accept that this power may almost never be used.'
Sir Jack Callard, Ex–ICI.
'If there is any hope of convincing the workers of the virtues of private enterprise the way to do it is to include them in decision making at the top.'
Jack Jones, Ex–TGWU

The amount of formal consultation with workers varies a great deal from company to company. Generally speaking, the UK tends to lag behind most of Western Europe. There are some companies, however, with a well developed system of consultation. Regular meetings between management and representatives of the workforce may be held to discuss matters of mutual

Figure 14: Worker's real and desired influence

	real influence			desired influence		
	quite a lot	some	little or none	quite a lot	some	little or none
	%	%	%	%	%	%
a General facilities (canteens, social club, toilets)	31	29	40	71	27	2
b Disciplinary matters	16	25	59	46	44	9
c Who gets laid off if redundancies are necessary	17	23	61	64	27	9
d Organisation of your own work	14	32	54	73	25	2
e Fixing of work standards	10	25	66	70	27	2
f Methods of payment	12	21	68	76	23	1
g Rate of pay	11	23	67	81	17	1
h Purchase of new machinery or equipment	3	14	83	41	42	17
i Allocation of overtime	11	16	73	56	36	7
j Safety matters	24	36	39	81	18	1

Source: *New Society*

concern, such as welfare and personnel policies. Studying the directors reports of a number of large companies will illustrate the range of consultative systems in use.

These reports will also show examples of the third type of participation, co-ownership or profit sharing. The offering of shares to the workforce either on favourable terms or as bonuses has been encouraged by the government in recent years. Again this is not a new idea with examples going back many years. The John Lewis Partnership, for example, introduced a profit sharing scheme in 1929. The logic of these schemes is clear, as it is argued that an employee will be more committed to a company in which he or she has a financial stake. Even if the shares issued to employees carry voting rights, however, the employees will have little influence over company policy and it has been argued that schemes of this type do not represent real participation.

Figure 14 illustrates the areas in which workers feel that they do have an influence over company policy and areas over which they would like to have an influence. The table is based on research from Strathclyde University.

You will see from Figure 14 that real influence is limited to areas such as general facilities **a** and safety matters **j** with no real influence over the organisation of work **d** or rate of pay **g**.

This illustrates the point that participation tends to be restricted to areas of common concern, rather than areas of conflict such as wages and job control. Where conflict exists the normal link between employers and employees is through trade unions and collective bargaining. This involves negotiation rather than consultation.

Trade unions and collective bargaining

Collective bargaining involves negotiation between representatives of the workforce, ie trade unions, and the representatives of the employers. The main issues which are negotiated are wages, conditions of work and security of employment. These negotiations often take place at national level but trade unions also have an important role to play at the place of work.

Unions are groups of workers who have banded together to protect their interests and to improve the position of their members as employees. Trade unions exist in almost all industries and occupations and in some industries almost all employees will be members of a union.

Trade unions represent around 12 m employees and there are over 400 different unions. Many have a large membership and their names are well known.

How many of the following unions do you recognise? Give their full name and the groups of workers that they represent:	
a NUM	**d** AUEW
b NUT	**e** NALGO
c TGWU	**f** GMWU

The origin of Trade Unions

Trade unions originated during the Industrial Revolution of the late eighteenth and early nineteenth century. They were originally illegal organisations, but over the years they gradually gained legal recognition as their numbers grew. A number of factors contributed to this growth of the union movement. For the first time large numbers of people worked together in mills, factories and mines. They were able to communicate with one another and they all shared common grievances. These grievances were basically low pay and poor working conditions.

The following extract from evidence given before the Royal Commission on Trade Unions in 1868 illustrates the conditions which existed for miners.

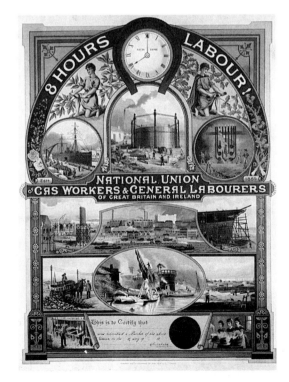

An example of a 'new union' poster from the 1880s.

Women and children pulling coal in a mine.

'The condition of the miner's boy then was to be raised about one o'clock or two o'clock in the morning if the distance was very far to travel, ... We remained then in the mine until five and six at night. It was an ironstone mine, very low, working about 18 inches and in some instances not quite so high...

We had to keep drawing the coal with these ropes over our shoulders and sometimes round the middle with a chain between our legs. Then there was always another behind pushing with his head. That work was done by boys such as I was from ten to eleven down to eight and I have known them as low as seven years old. A very great deal of our drawing, as we call it, was performed in the dark in consequence of the want of ventilation in the mines.'

Given these conditions, it is hardly surprising that workers, recognising that there was strength in numbers, banded together to fight for better standards.

Types of union

A **general union** represents workers in a wide range of industries and from a range of occupations. These unions usually represent unskilled and semi-skilled workers.

Skilled workers are more likely to join a **craft union**. Many of the oldest unions are of this type and they represent workers in a number of industries who share a common skill such as electricians.

Where workers in a specific industry are represented by a union whatever their particular skill then this is known as an **industrial union**. There are relatively few industrial unions in this country and in many industries employers have to negotiate with a number of different general and craft unions.

Where a union represents non-manual workers such as bank employees or civil servants, it is known as a **white collar union**. It is this type of union which has grown most rapidly in recent years with the growth in the tertiary sector of the economy.

Find an example of each of the four types of trade union.

The origin of trade unions

We tend to hear a great deal about the bad side of trade union activities such as the effect that strikes have on the general public. Wage bargaining is usually the only part of trade union affairs that receives publicity, but union membership offers a wide range of benefits to employees.

As we have seen, trade unions grew up out of a desire to improve the conditions of the employed workforce. Modern trade unions achieve this in three main ways.

They provide a range of personal services to members. These could include accident and sickness benefits, additional pensions, legal advice, training courses and protection against unfair dismissal.

They negotiate with employers on matters such as wages, working conditions and security of employment. This is known as collective bargaining and normally takes place at national level, with full-time union officials negotiating with representatives of the employers. Issues which are discussed could include national wage levels, apprenticeship and entry qualifications, the length of the working week and holiday entitlement. Bargaining can also take place at local level, with shop stewards negotiating with local management on issues such as health and safety and individual disciplinary matters.

At national level, unions can influence government policy by acting as a pressure group to 'lobby' MPs. This term is derived from the lobby in the House of Parliament where constituents or representatives of pressure groups can talk to their Member of Parliament. The unions also have political power, through their votes at the Labour Party Conference where the party's policies are debated.

Unions will attempt to influence government policy in areas of interest to their members. These areas include employment policy, health and safety legislation, equal opportunities and other industrial relations legislation. Much of this political lobbying is done through the TUC.

Design and draw a poster to be displayed in a factory encouraging workers to join a trade union. Your poster should set out some of the benefits of union membership.It should also be designed to be eye catching if it is to stand out from the other posters on display.

Trade unions can achieve their objectives in a number of ways. The most common techniques at their disposal include:

● **Working to rule**– This involves doing everything according to the rule book, which usually means that production is slowed down. This may also be supported by an overtime ban.

● **A token stoppage**–This could involve a one day strike or a union meeting called during working hours. Some unions have achieved success in recent years by calling a small number of key members out on strike, eg computer operators.

● **Restricting the supply of labour**–This is achieved by laying down entry requirements and rules on apprenticeship. In this way the union will be in a stronger bargaining position because their members cannot easily be replaced.

● **An official strike**–Where the withdrawal of labour has full union backing this is known as an official strike. In the past, many strikes have been unofficial. These are usually for short periods and are called by **shop stewards** as a result of some local grievance.

Drawbacks of trade union membership

Despite their many advantages, there has been a gradual fall in union membership in recent years. This is partly due to rising unemployment and

---

Follow a recent union dispute in a local or national newspaper and make brief notes under the following headings:

a The issues involved.
b The methods used by both sides to achieve their objectives.
c The final outcome.

---

the change in the pattern of employment towards part-time jobs and jobs traditionally held by women. There are other problems, however, which have led to adverse publicity for the union movement as a whole.

One problem relates to the lack of individual freedom of members. Each individual has to abide by the decisions of the majority. Therefore, if a strike is called, a member who does not agree may have to abide by the majority decision and withdraw his or her labour.

An added problem is that the union leadership may not be representative of the membership as a whole. It is often argued that union leaders are voted into office by a hard core of activists who lead the membership into industrial action against the wishes of the majority. To help to overcome this criticism, unions now have to elect their leaders by secret ballot.

An obvious answer would seem to be for a member who did not agree with union policy to leave the union. This is not always possible, however, as in some industries there is a **closed shop**. This is where there is an agreement between the employer and one or more trade unions that only union members will be employed. Failure to join an approved union will place the employee in breach of contract and he will lose his job. This does, however, give the advantage to the employer that they bargain with fewer unions and also reduces the chance of unofficial strike action.

Government legislation, such as the 1980 Employment Act, attempts to provide safeguards for employees where a closed shop is introduced.

A further argument levelled against trade unions is that they are too powerful, particularly when they represent workers in vital industries such as power and transport. It has been argued that workers in some industries should not be allowed to join unions at all because of the effect that this could have on public safety or national security.

Although major strikes in recent years have not supported the view that unions in vital industries can always achieve their aims through strike action, there has still been a trend towards

Figure 15: The role of the shop steward

Many people, even trade unionists, talk of the 'union' as some distant
body, too remote to be interested in the problems of individual workers.
It isn't. The union is your union. Your Union Steward is one of your
workmates and your Branch Secretary could be as well. They are there
to speak for their members on every issue which affects them on the
job with the exception of your basic pay, which is negotiated at national
level. So if you have a problem, or doubts about some aspect of your
job, go to your Union Steward for advice.

the use of legislation in the area of industrial relations designed to reduce the power of trade unions.

Union organisation

The running of a trade union is usually split between national officials and local members.

The local branch

Most unions have local branches to which members belong. The members will vote for local branch leaders and can attend meetings to discuss matters of interest to them. The main contact for most people with their union is the **shop steward**.

Shop stewards are elected by their workmates. They are not paid for their union work but are normally allowed time off to conduct union business. The shop steward is on hand to deal with problems as they arise at the place of work and can negotiate directly with local management.

Where there is more than one steward within a factory, then one will usually be chosen as the senior shop steward or **convener**. The convener will arrange (or convene) meetings of the shop stewards to discuss common problems.

The main activities of the shop stewards are to collect union subscriptions, to recruit members, to provide information to members and to provide a link between shop floor members and the national union. They will also deal with local disputes and may even call for industrial action with or without the support of the full-time union leaders.

The national union

Trade unions will also have a national organisation with full-time staff and a **national executive committee** elected by the membership. They manage the union's affairs and put its policies into practice. Each year the union will hold a conference to decide on policies for the coming year. Local branches will send representation (known as delegates) to these conferences. The branches will put forward matters for discussion and delegates will speak in support of these motions and will vote at the conference in accordance with the wishes of their members.

The Trade Union Congress (TUC)

The TUC is a body which represents the union movement as a whole. Over 100 unions are affiliated to the TUC including most of the largest unions. The best know activity of the TUC is that once a year it brings together representatives of the trade union movement to discuss issues which affect union members. This is the TUC conference which usually receives a great deal of publicity and extensive TV coverage. At this conference, the TUC General Council is appointed to manage TUC affairs. The TUC is the main policy-making body of the union movement and attempts to influence the government on trade union issues. It has little power over its individual members, however, and does not interfere in their day-to-day activities.

Employers' associations

Just as workers band together to form unions, so employers often group together to form employers' associations. Many are small local groups and the Department of Employment estimates that there are around 1,350 such groupings.

Employers' associations provide help to members on a wide range of industrial relations and trade matters. Amongst the services they provide are help with technical problems, public relations for the industry, research facilities, acting as a pressure group in promoting the industry at national or local level and bargaining with trade unions on national wage deals.

The Confederation of British Industry (CBI)

This is the employers' equivalent of the TUC and was established in 1965. The CBI acts as a national pressure group for employers, often commenting on government policy at its annual conference. It voices the opinion of employers on issues such as industrial relations, training and government economic policy.

The role of the government

In Britain, collective bargaining is essentially voluntary but, over the years, the government has become increasingly involved in the bargaining process and with industrial relations as a whole.

In 1974, for example, the government set up a collective bargaining machinery designed to help unions and employers when negotiations break down. This was the Advisory, Conciliation and Arbitration Service (ACAS).

Figure 16: ACAS publicity

WHAT is ACAS?

ACAS – the Advisory, Conciliation and Arbitration Service – is an independent body charged with the duty of promoting the improvement of industrial relations. It seeks to discharge this responsibility through the voluntary co-operation of employers, employees and their representatives and it has no powers of compulsion.

WHAT does ACAS do?

ACAS provides advisory and information services

Advice and practical assistance is available to everyone concerned with employment – employers, workers and their representatives – in organisations of all sizes in every sector of commerce and industry on matters such as:

- personnel policies and organisation
- labour turnover, absenteeism and manpower planning
- payment systems including productivity schemes and job evaluation
- industrial relations and employment legislation
- procedures for settling disputes and grievances
- recruitment, selection and induction
- equal pay and anti-discrimination legislation
- hours of work and other conditions of employment
- training in industrial relations.

ACAS provides conciliation in trade disputes

Conciliation is voluntary. The eventual level of settlement will be the joint decision of both parties. The conciliator cannot decide or even recommend what that settlement should be.

ACAS provides arbitration services if requested

Arbitration is also voluntary. An arbitrator or board of arbitration examines the case for each side and makes an award. Arbitration awards are not legally binding but since arbitration is chosen by both parties as a means of settlement such awards are morally binding. Before seeking arbitration efforts should be made to settle a dispute by conciliation.

ACAS provides mediation

Sometimes the parties to a dispute may ask for the help of an independent third party to mediate and make recommendations for a settlement or to suggest a basis for further discussion. If so ACAS may appoint a mediator.

1 List six issues on which ACAS is able to offer advice to employers.
2 Define the terms:

   a conciliation
   b arbitration
   c mediation.

3 Why is it thought necessary for the government to be involved in industrial relations?

Source: ACAS

Industrial tribunals

These are courts of law with a legally qualified chairman and representatives of employers and employees. They make legally binding rulings on issues such as discrimination, equal pay, and unfair dismissal where it has not been possible to reach agreement through arbitration.

QUICK QUIZ

1. What is meant by 'last in, first out'?
2. List three costs to a firm of a high level of labour turnover.
3. Distinguish between a 'job description' and a 'job specification'.
4. Give four reasons why an organisation might appoint from the existing workforce rather than from outside.
5. List four ways in which a job vacancy could be advertised.
6. What is the purpose of an induction programme for new employees?
7. What is meant by off-the-job training?
8. Give three advantages of piece rates as a method of wage payment.
9. List three deductions which are made from gross pay in order to arrive at net pay.
10. What is meant by job evaluation?
11. Give three examples of executive perks.
12. Briefly describe:

    a job rotation
    b job enrichment
    c job enlargement

13. List three possible barriers to effective internal communication.
14. List three ways in which modern technology has helped business communication.
15. What is a craft union? Give two examples.
16. List four techniques which can be used by trade unions to help them achieve their objectives.
17. What is meant by the term 'closed shop' in industrial relations?
18. Give three possible functions of an employers' association.

Case Study: Chess Mate

John Knight worked for a small engineering firm in Northampton, which he joined at the age of sixteen as an apprentice. He had always had a flair for art and enjoyed drawing and painting in his spare time. One day, in a local hobby shop, he bought a book on woodcarving and soon became engrossed in this hobby. One of his most successful projects was to carve and paint a complete chess set by hand.

His friends were so impressed that some of them asked him if they could buy sets from him to give as presents. John agreed and charged £10 for each set, which more than covered the cost of the wood he used. By the end of a year, John had produced 20 sets earning £200 and, as the cost of his materials was only around £40, he had made a profit of £160.

Then disaster struck. The company that employed John went into liquidation and he lost his job. John decided to set himself up in business and so 'Chess Mate' was formed. Using his redundancy pay he bought a second-hand lathe and, working from his garage, started to produce chess sets which he sold on a stall in the local market.

Business was brisk. In the period leading up to Christmas he sold up to twenty sets a week. Assuming that this level of sales would continue, John decided that he wanted to expand by taking on an assistant and buying a second lathe. To raise the extra money he needed, John visited his bank manager to try to arrange a loan. Although John had a good record with the bank, rarely having gone into the red, the bank manager insisted on seeing John's accounts.

Based on the figures that John provided, the bank manager advised him that he would have to sell 50 sets per week just to break even and pointed out that, because the demand for chess sets was likely to be seasonal he would need to hold quite large stocks.

John began to realise that business was not simply a matter of making products and selling them, you also had to get the finance right.

The story has a happy ending. John returned to producing highly individual chess sets which were sold through a number of specialist retailers. Some sets sold for over £200 and his business, whilst remaining small was very profitable.

1 John calculated that he had made £160 profit in his first year. Was this really all profit?
2 What financial records should John have kept?
3 Why was the bank manager reluctant to lend money to John for the expansion of his business?

Part 1 Sources of finance

Money is an important resource to the firm. Without it, the firm will be unable to pay its workers, buy raw materials or purchase machinery. Money flows through the organisation as it is received from customers and is passed on to workers or suppliers. A successful business will need to control both the inflow and the outflow of money. In larger firms this will be done by a **finance department** headed by a qualified accountant.

The job of the finance department is to keep records of payments and receipts and to make information available to help in decision making. We will consider record keeping and management information later, but first we will look in more detail at the flow of money within an organisation. A simplified diagram of this flow of money is shown in Figure 1.

Somebody must provide the money to start up the business in the first place. Extra finance may have to be introduced into the business if it is to develop and expand. The owners of the business can provide funds themselves from their own savings or funds can be provided from profits which are not taken out of the firm, but instead used to buy more resources. There are also a

number of possible sources of finance available to a firm from people outside the organisation.

Because firms will often have to pay for labour and raw materials before they sell their goods or services, there is always a risk that the money coming into the firm will be less than the money that has been paid out. Those people providing finance will therefore want a reward for taking the risk of not being repaid. This reward will take the form of **profit** if finance is provided by the owners of the business, or **interest** if it is provided by outsiders.

Figure 1: The money-go-round

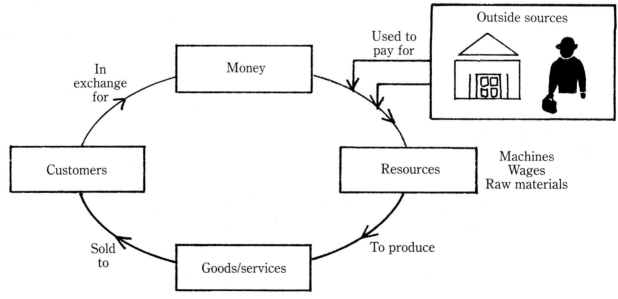

The issue of shares

As with John Knight's venture, a business usually begins by the owners putting in some of their own money. Once a firm has set up, growth can be achieved by 'ploughing back' some or all of the profits into the business.

Where the business takes the form of a **joint-stock company**, the owners are known as shareholders and the number of shares that each shareholder has indicates the proportion of the business that he or she owns.

When we look at a firm's balance sheet we will see an item called **issued share capital**, which shows the value of the shares that have been issued by a company. If a company wants to raise more finance it can ask its existing shareholders to provide more money by buying a new issue of shares or it can try to attract new shareholders. The **authorised share capital**, also indicated on the balance sheet, shows the maximum amount that can be raised in this way, although existing shareholders can vote in favour of an increase in this maximum figure.

Shareholders are not paid interest on their investment but instead they receive a share of the profit. This is known as the **dividend**. They cannot ask for their money back although in a public joint stock company they are free to sell their shares. The price of shares is not fixed, however, but depends on what buyers are prepared to pay. If a company stops trading and its assets are sold off, there is no guarantee that shareholders will get their money back. All the other people that the company owes money to must be repaid first.

Types of share

There are two main types of share, the most common being **ordinary shares** or **equities**. The holders of ordinary shares take a risk that the firm will not be profitable but when profits are high, so are the returns. Shareholders gain from increases in the market price of shares as well as from dividends. Ordinary shareholders also have some power in the running of the company through their votes at the annual general meeting.

The second type of share is known as a **preference share**. Holders of these shares have priority over ordinary shareholders in the payment of a dividend. Preference shares usually carry a fixed rate of return. This is paid out before ordinary shareholders receive anything. In some cases, preference shareholders may also receive any arrears of dividend owing from previous years (**cumulative preference shares**) or bonuses on top of the fixed rate of return when profits are high (**participating preference shares**). Preference shareholders also have priority for repayment if the company goes into liquidation.

Although the risks involved with holding preference shares may be much less than with ordinary shares, they rarely carry voting rights and ordinary shareholders will receive a much better return if profits are good.

Dividends

Dividends are a shareholder's 'share' of the company's profits. Not all profits are distributed to shareholders. Some are retained for taxation, the replacement of capital, for expansion or simply held as reserves for the future.

Dividends are calculated on the face value of shares and the declared dividend is not necessarily the rate of return an individual will

---

A company has a share capital of £500,000
This consists of:
   600,000 ordinary shares @ 50p
   200,000 5% cumulative preference shares @ £1

Assuming that all profits are paid out to shareholders as dividends, complete the following table:

Year	Profit to shareholders	Preference shareholders	Ordinary shareholders
1	16,000	£10,000 (5%)	£6,000 (2%)
2	8,000		
3	25,000		
4	50,000		

receive on his or her investment. This is because shares may change hands at a higher or lower price than the original face value. The actual rate of return based on the present market price is known as the **yield** on a share.

For example:

A share has a face value of £1.

A company declares a dividend of 10% (10p per share).

If the market price of the share is £2, what is the yield?

If you were to buy this share at £2 you would receive a 10p return on a 200p outlay. This represents a 5% return.

$$\frac{10p}{200p} \times 100\% = 5\%$$

Public joint-stock companies keep an up-to-date register of shareholders and are informed of any changes in the ownership of shares. Dividends are paid to registered shareholders after being approved at the annual general meeting of the company.

The Stock Exchange

The Stock Exchange is the market place where buyers and sellers of shares are brought together. It was on the floor of the Stock Exchange that shares were traditionally traded.

The origins of the Stock Exchange go back to the sixteenth century, when merchants would take a share in a trading expedition. They would provide funds for the voyage and share in the profits that were made. The risks were great but so were the possible profits. The shares that merchants had in these early companies, with names such as 'The Mysterie and Company of the Merchant Adventurers for the Discoverie of Regions, Dominions, Islands and Places Unknown', could be sold to someone else. This trade in shares grew up in the coffee houses around London's Royal Exchange.

In 1773, the most famous of the coffee houses, New Jonathans, became the Stock Exchange. Today, the market is very sophisticated and highly automated but its basic function remains the same. It provides investors with the opportunity to buy and sell shares by setting a price at which buyers and sellers are prepared to trade.

Because investors can sell their shares at any time, (although they will not always make a profit if share prices are falling), the existence of the Stock Exchange encourages people to invest in industry and therefore makes it easier for firms to raise money by issuing shares.

In addition, the Stock Exchange provides protection to the shareholder against fraud by setting out Codes of Practice which quoted companies must conform to. It also provides a way in which the performance of individual

Computerised share dealing.

Understanding the city page
SHARE PRICES

Highest price of share this year, ie £3.98

Lowest price of share this year, ie £1.85

Current share price (halfway between buy and sell price), ie £3.32

Change in share price since previous day, ie +1p

Price earnings ratio compares market price of share with earnings, ie price is 13.67 times the earnings per share

Yield. Each £100 invested in the company at the current market price will give a £3.30 return.

Ex-dividend shares sold without the right to receive the next dividend payment

1986 High	Low	Stock	Price		Change	Yld	P/E Ratio
204	165	Greenall Whitley	189			4.2	9.45
280	183	Greene King	259		-2	3.2	14.80
355	275	Guinness	298		+2	3.9	11.30
91	66	Highland Dist	68	xd	-1	4.6	13.15
469	384	Mansfield Brew	431		-3	2.7	17.53
114	77	Marston Thompson	111½		+0½	2.9	15.93
427	311	Merrydown Wine	405	xd		1.9	24.64
234	163	Scot & New Brew	199		-1	5.0	12.06
288	131	Sth African Bre	239	xd	+3	-	-
540	353	Vaux	473		-2	3.8	16.24
316	223	Whitbread A	256	xd		4.5	11.81
561	410	Wolv & Dudley	558			2.5	15.72
257	165	Young Brew N/V	248		-2	4.6	17.08

ELECTRICALS

1986 High	Low	Stock	Price		Change	Yld	P/E Ratio
396	185	AB Electronic	332		+1	4.3	17.31
93	43	AMS	55		+2	3.9	8.73
106	34	Acorn Computer	39		-1	0.0	2.74
240	133	Alphameric	214			1.3	21.73
30	17½	Amer Elec Comp	26½		-0½	4.8	16.36
150	36½	Amstrad	111		-1	0.5	11.64
368	210	Apd Holographics	359		+1	-	-
100	43	Apricot Comp	50		-3	0.0	8.46
300	226	Atlantic Comp	294		-1	1.4	9.40
79	50	Audio Fidelity	72		+1	0.0	23.00
22½	6½	Audiotronic	18¼			0.0	-
220	168	Auto Security	206	xd		1.1	14.04
370	235	BICC	254	xd	-2	6.2	14.34
138	65	BSR	80			3.1	5.34
595	375	Bowthorpe	553	xd	+1	1.9	19.08
195	70	Brikat	91	xd		6.6	7.40
112	89	Brown Boveri	95	xd	-1	5.3	9.02
104	62	CASE	89		-3	0.0	7.45
180	130	CML Micro	160			1.6	16.43
42	25	CPU Computers	32			0.0	19.16
313	193	Cambridge Elec	207	xd	-1	5.1	12.45
243	1	Cap Gp	196			1.1	24.84
57½	43	Chloride	54½		-0½	0.0	12.79
21¼	8½	Cifer	16			0.0	2.39
14½	8	Comb Tech	10½		-0½	2.9	-
353	203	Comcap	353		+5	0.7	17.58
53	30	Compsoft	40			0.0	6.70
162	84	Consultants	158		-2	1.1	30.74
172½	105	Conti Microwave	163		-2	2.0	19.13

1986 High	Low	Stock	Price		Change	Yld	P/E Ratio
385	308	Booker	339	xd	-2	5.3	14.67
75	36	Borthwick Thomas	72½		-1½	1.5	-
196	158	Cadbury-Sch			-1	4.7	21.47
245	141	Cliffords A	218			5.0	12.51
163	128	Dalepack	152			-	21.56
305	208	Dalgety	265	xd	-5	7.0	11.69
216	110¾	Fisher (Albert)	171	xd	+1	1.9	20.05
316	238	Fitch Lovell	262		+2	5.7	16.12
136	65	Freshbake	109½		+1½	2.6	18.28
263	188	Glass Glover	243			2.4	18.54
164	126	Hazlewood	153	xd	-1	1.8	21.95
242¼	135¾	Hillsdown	227	xd	+7	2.1	14.68
189	115	Hunter Saphir	182	xd	+1	2.2	22.43
300	122	Matthews (B)	279	xd	-1	1.6	25.09
300	243	Nthn Foods	247		+1	4.6	12.24
165	127	Park Foods	165			3.6	14.32
292	157	Ranks Hovis	283	xd	-4	3.3	13.67
800	605	Reckitt & Colman	833	xd	+4	2.9	17.98
532	365	Rowntree Mack	392	xd	+6	4.6	10.89
248	154	Somportex	218			0.0	-
658	502	Tate & Lyle	575		-3	5.7	11.69
70	40	Tavener Rutledge	46			0.0	6.57
325	216	Unigate	310	xd	-3	5.0	14.82
269	216	Utd Biscuits	233½	xd	+1½	6.8	12.64
159	134	Watson & Phillip	155		-1	6.3	19.40
90	34	Wold	35			2.5	31.25

INDUSTRIALS

1986 High	Low	Stock	Price		Change	Yld	P/E Ratio
260	179	AAH	238		+5	4.9	13.40
110	75½	Aaronson	93			6.5	10.30
28	19½	Anglo Nordic	23½			0.0	4.68
188	75	Appleyard	166		+1	5.2	-
258	225	Ass Paper	258			3.9	12.29
223	144	Attwoods	215		-2	3.3	16.46
393	263	Avon Rubber	371			2.5	9.31
465	375	B.E.T.	437		+1	5.6	15.86
289	117	BBA	127		-3	2.7	17.52
550	328	BPB	529	xd	-4	2.7	15.58
158	132	BTP	164		+1	4.6	18.58
330	241	BTR	269		-2	3.6	18.75
397	227	Barlow Rand	290	xd		-	-
241	170	Beatson Clarke	193		+5	5.5	13.24
120	58	Bedford (W)	111		+1	5.8	10.30
450	356	Beecham	424½	xd	+9½	4.0	17.64

Source: *The Independent*

1 Using a recent list of share prices, answer the following questions:

a Find a share which is at its lowest price this year.

b The Blue Circle share price was £6.50 on December 18 1986.
By how much has it changed since then?

c List three industrial shares which have a high yield. What would be the advantage of buying these shares?

d Some shares have a very low yield. What would be the benefit of buying these shares?

2 Class exercise

Split up into teams of three or four for this activity.
Each team has £1000 to invest in shares.
You can hold shares in up to five companies at any one time.
At the end of four weeks all shares will be sold.
The object is to make as much profit as possible from buying and selling shares.
You can ignore dividends and the cost of buying and selling.
You will need to keep a careful note of how the prices of your shares are changing and you will also have to design forms to keep a record of all your transactions.

companies, sectors of the economy or even the economy as a whole, can be measured.

This is done through the publication of share prices. If the price of shares in an individual company is falling, it may reflect poor profits or a lack of confidence in that company's future. Such things as rumours of a possible takeover will also affect a company's shares price. On a general level, a confident market with rising prices is known as **bull** market whereas a lack of

confidence leads to a **bear** market with falling prices.

A number of figures are published to provide information on the overall movement in share prices. The most recent index to be introduced is the Financial Times/Stock Exchange index which measures changes in the prices of the 100 largest companies' shares, and is updated minute by minute.

An hourly update is provided by the FT 30

index which measures changes in a representative sample of 30 shares. The value of this sample in 1935 was equal to 100. Although there have been some changes in the composition of the sample, the current value reflects the amount by which these share prices have increased since then. A value of 1000, for example, would mean that the 30 shares that make up the index are, on average, 10 times more expensive than in 1935. The Stock Exchange deals mainly in second-hand shares which have already been issued. There are four main ways in which shares in public joint-stock companies are issued:

● **An offer for sale** – Here shares are sold to an issuing house or stockbroker who then offers some or all of them to the public.

● **A prospectus issue** – This is where shares are offered directly to the public, following the publication of a prospectus which provides details of the company. Issuing houses will **underwrite** a share issue of this type for a fee. This means that they will buy up any of the shares not bought by the general public.

● **A placing** – Often when a company is issuing shares for the first time and demand from the public is likely to be limited, this method of issue is used. Issuing houses or stockbrokers contact selected clients such as pension funds and persuade them to buy the shares.

● **A rights issue** – This is where existing shareholders are offered the first chance to buy a new issue of shares. They are offered shares in proportion to their existing shareholding, eg one new share for every four already held. The shares are normally offered on favourable terms.

It will be clear from the description of the Stock Exchange that in the case of public joint-stock companies, the company does not sell shares directly to the public, but does so via a number of middle men and institutions.

Brokers

If a member of the public wants to buy or sell shares, the first step is to approach a broker. Most towns have firms of brokers offering their services to the public and the high street banks will also offer help and advice.

Until the reform of the Stock Exchange in 1986, the **Big Bang** as it was called, brokers had to deal with people known as **jobbers** who are rather like wholesalers of shares. They buy and sell shares on their own behalf, making a profit by selling shares at a higher price than they buy them for. They tend to specialise in particular types of share such as oil shares. Brokers make their living by charging a commission or fee when they buy and sell shares. It is their job to sell at the highest price possible and to buy at the lowest price they can find on the market.

The recent change in Stock Exchange rules allows brokers to cut out the middleman. If a broker has a client wanting to sell 100 ICI shares

---

These are the thirty companies which make up the current index. Those companies asterisked appeared in the original index of July 1935.

Allied Lyons
Associated Dairies
BTR
Beecham Group
Blue Circle Industries*
Boots
Bowater Corporation
British Insulated Callendar Cables
British Oxygen Group
British Petroleum
Cadbury Schweppes
Courtaulds*
Distillers*
General Electric*
Glaxo Group

Grand Metropolitan
Guest Keen and Nettlefolds*
Hawker Siddeley Group*
Imperial Chemical Industries*
Imperial Tobacco Group*
London Brick*
Lucas Industries
Marks and Spencer
P. and O. Steam Navigation
Plessey
Tate and Lyle
Thorn EMI
Trusthouse Forte
Tube Investments Group
Vickers*

1 How many of these names do you recognise?
2 With the help of the rest of the group, list as many as possible of the products and services provided by these companies.
3 Are there any important industries not represented in this list?

and another wanting to buy 100 ICI shares, it is no longer necessary for both transactions to be carried out via a jobber.

Issuing houses

The issuing houses are a group of merchant banks who arrange the details of a share issue. They have the expertise to advise on the issue price of shares and on the best way of ensuring that all shares are sold. They may also act as **underwriters** by guaranteeing to buy any shares not purchased by the general public or financial institutions. A large issue may be under-written by a group of issuing houses.

Institutional investors

The government estimates that, as a result of recent privatisation, there are approximately 8.5m small shareholders, around 20% of the adult population. Despite this, the continuing trend in share ownership is towards institutional investors. These are large organisations such as pension funds and insurance companies who hold shares in many different companies and in many different sectors of the economy. This is what is known as holding a **balanced portfolio**.

The majority of shares are now held by these institutions. They are mainly concerned with earning an income from their shares and do not normally exercise their rights of ownership such as attending and voting at annual general meetings. Figure 2 illustrates the importance of institutional shareholders to Unilever.

Figure 2: Proportion of ordinary share-holding in Unilever

Class of holder	Number of holdings	Amount of holdings £	%
Banks and discount companies	5,058	556,900	1
Financial trusts	55	65,767	—
Insurance companies	844	8,336,261	21
Investment trusts	139	320,717	1
Pension funds	163	2,510,022	6
Nominee companies	4,580	15,310,855	39
Other companies	1,054	2,466,476	6
	11,893	29,566,998	74
Leverhulme Trust	2	2,195,410	6
Individuals	53,529	7,755,932	20
	65,424	39,518,340	100

Source: *Unilever Annual Report and Salient Figures 1985*

There are two ways of making money on the Stock Exchange. One is by buying shares and making a profit by selling them at a higher price. The second way is to hold shares that give a good annual dividend. Institutions will normally have a balance between shares whose prices tend to fluctuate and shares which yield a steady income but whose prices tend to remain fairly stable.

Banks

For a firm to operate successfully and expand, it will normally have to look to outside agencies for funds. The main sources of external finance for business are the clearing banks and the merchant banks.

Commercial banks

These are large, well-known organisations with branches in the high streets of most major towns. Their names will be familiar and include Barclays, Lloyds, Midland and National West-minster (The Big Four). The Scottish clearing banks are the Bank of Scotland, the Royal Bank of Scotland and Clydesdale Bank.

The term 'clearing' bank is also used because of the way in which most of these banks handle the exchange and settlement of cheques through the clearing house system. Cheques are not money. They are a kind of letter which requests money to be transferred from one bank account into another. A cheque will be drawn on a particular branch of a certain bank but it may well be paid into a different bank.

If, for example, June Smith receives a £100 cheque written out by Jack Jones, then Jack's account at his bank will need to be reduced by £100 and June's account increased by £100. If they both bank at the same branch then this is no problem. If they have accounts at different branches of the same bank or with different banks, then it is necessary for Jack's bank to be notified of the transaction so that the necessary funds can be transferred.

The clearing scheme has developed to provide a system for notifying banks of all the trans-actions undertaken by their customers. All cheques written out on a particular day are sent to the **central clearing house** in London where they are exchanged. Jack's bank will therefore receive his cheque and can then reduce his account by £100. June's account will have been credited with £100 when she originally deposited the cheque.

Two main financial services provided by banks are overdrafts and loans. **Overdrafts** are a short-term source of finance to a business, whereby a firm is allowed to overdraw on its account by up to a certain amount agreed with the bank manager. This allows a firm to finance the gap between payments and receipts. Even when a firm is trading profitably, it is unlikely that it will receive payments from customers which match the payments it must make to suppliers on a day to day basis. An overdraft facility allows a firm to pay out more than it has in its account on any one day. Interest is only charged on the amount actually overdrawn, which makes this an ideal form of finance when the firm does not know exactly how much it will need at any particular time.

Strictly speaking, overdrafts are repayable on demand and a bank manager can cancel an overdraft at any time if the company is seen to be getting into permanent difficulties. It must therefore be viewed as a short-term source of finance.

Banks can also make medium-term **loans** available to firms. These are for a fixed amount borrowed for a fixed period of time. Interest is calculated on the full amount of the loan. This form of finance is usually used for specific projects such as the purchase of a new piece of machinery. Normally some form of security is required. This could take the form of a claim on the company's assets or, in the case of the smaller firm, a personal guarantee usually backed by a claim on the proprietor's own assets such as a mortgage on his house.

The commercial banks offer a wide range of services to their customers who include businesses as well as members of the public.

The acceptance of deposits

Banks safeguard money deposited with them. These deposits may be in either **current accounts** or **deposit accounts**. Current accounts do not earn interest, but no prior notice is required for withdrawal and the cheque system operates through these accounts. Over 90% of debts (by value) are settled through the cheque system.

Interest is paid on money in deposit accounts, but a period of notice is normally required before money can be withdrawn.

The making of regular payments

A system of standing orders or direct debits is available whereby the bank arranges for the making of regular payments such as mortgages and insurance premiums.

The aiding of foreign business and travel

Banks are able, given notice, to exchange currencies and issue travellers cheques to customers. They may also provide help and advice on foreign business transactions, eg Barclays Bank publish an *Export Opportunities Review*.

Credit cards

Most bank customers now have credit card facilities available to them, eg Barclaycard and Access. Most banks also issue cards which can be used as identification and to guarantee cheques up to a certain amount.

A cheque guarantee card.

"....and does Sir have a bankers card?"

Other services

Banks provide a large number of other services including the provision of night safes, safe deposit boxes, financial advice and help with tax problems.

> Complete the following sentences:
>
> Commercial banks such as Barclays and Midland are also known as _____ banks. Cheques are sent to the _____ _____ in London where they are exchanged and returned to the bank on which they are drawn.
>
> There are two types of bank account. These are known as _____ accounts and _____ accounts. _____ accounts do not earn interest. The cheque system operates through these accounts. Other services which are offered by banks include the making of regular payments by _____ _____ or _____ _____ and the use of _____ _____ to enable deposits to be made after closing hours.

The Bank of England

The Bank of England is the country's central bank and is at the centre of the banking system. It was originally a private bank set up in 1694 and granted a Royal Charter in exchange for funds by William III who was fighting a war against Louis XIV of France. The Bank was nationalised in 1946.

Over the years, the Bank of England has taken on a number of important functions.

The note issue

The Bank of England is responsible for the running of the printing works where millions of notes are printed each week and distributed to the public through the commercial banks.

The government's bank

The Bank of England offers a range of services to the government. It keeps the government's accounts into which all central government receipts are paid and from which all payments are made. It also manages government borrowing and the **national debt**. This involves the weekly issue of treasury bills to meet the government's need for short-term finance and the issue of government stock which represents longer-term borrowing.

In addition, the Bank advises the government on financial matters and manages the UK monetary system. This includes control over the commercial banks in order to influence the availability of credit and the money supply.

The banker's bank

The commercial banks are the second most important customers of the Bank of England. They must all keep accounts at the Bank and it is through these accounts that the clearing system operates. Debits and credits are made to these accounts at the end of each day's business to reflect the movement of money from one clearing bank to another. Through these accounts, it is possible to make one adjustment at the end of the day to cover the millions of individual transactions which have taken place.

The old lady of Threadneedle Street

Private customers

The Bank still has a small number of private customers. These are mostly City of London firms and Bank employees.

International financial responsibility

The Bank of England is in contact with the central banks of other countries and it participates in the work of international monetary organisations such as the World Bank and the International Monetary Fund.

The Bank also operates in the foreign exchange market, buying and selling currency in order to influence the value of the pound.

Merchant banks

Merchant banks do not provide banking services to the general public, but rather offer specialised services to their business customers.

The name merchant bank comes from the fact that these institutions were originally merchants. These merchants often dealt with IOUs, known as trade bills, which were used to finance international trade. The more established traders were often prepared to guarantee the bills of lesser known merchants and they charged a fee for this service. In addition to this 'acceptance' business, the merchants also helped foreign governments to raise money on the London market and soon their banking activities became more profitable than their traditional trading activities.

Famous names in the field of merchant banking include Barings, Hambros and Rothschilds.

Merchant banks specialise in making their financial expertise available to their customers on matters such as the issue of shares, takeovers and mergers. They play a major part in the capital market by **underwriting** new share issues. This involves buying up any shares which are not bought by the general public or the other financial institutions.

Foreign banks

Over 400 foreign banks from more than 50 countries are directly represented in the City of London. Many of these are American and European banks but most major countries are represented. Their original purpose was to serve the needs of foreign residents and visitors to the UK, but many of them now deal with British companies and even private customers.

State run banks

The combination of the National Savings Bank and the National Girobank offers a full range of banking services.

The National Savings bank operates through the Post Office and allows customers to deposit and withdraw money. Interest is paid on National Savings deposits and the money is invested in government securities.

The National Girobank also operates through Post Office branches. It offers a wide range of banking services including loans and overdrafts, cheque books and cheque guarantee cards, current and deposit accounts, foreign currency and travellers cheques.

Building societies

Although they do not offer a full range of banking services, building societies are competing more and more with the commercial banks.

They receive deposits from customers and loan this money for house purchase. To attract deposits they offer a number of services, such as cheque books and cash machines, which compete directly with those provided by banks for private customers.

Form a number of small groups (three or four in each) and each choose a financial institution. This could be a clearing bank, eg Barclays, Lloyds or Midland, the National Girobank or a Building Society.

Collect leaflets describing the services offered by the institution you have chosen.

Making use of these leaflets, produce a poster advertising the benefits to be gained from opening an account with your chosen bank or building society.

Other sources of finance

Although the issue of shares, re-invested profits and bank lending provide the bulk of business finance, there are a wide range of alternative sources of finance available to firms.

Debentures

A debenture is a loan for a fixed period with a fixed rate of return. The holder is paid out first if the company goes into liquidation. As with shares, debentures can be bought and sold on the Stock Exchange. Unlike shareholders, however, debenture holders are simply creditors of the company and not owners.

Hire purchase

Hire purchase (HP) is a familiar form of finance which is available to a firm as well as to consumers. HP involves an initial down-payment with the remainder of the cost of the item, together with interest payments, being spread over a period of time. The item purchased in this way remains the property of the **finance house**, which provides the finance until the last payment has been made. HP is not a popular source of finance for business but may be used to purchase assets such as machinery or vehicles.

Leasing

An alternative to hire purchase is the leasing of equipment. Here a leasing company buys an asset and then hires or leases it to the firm for a fixed period of time – usually up to five years. A leasing agreement could include maintenance, but this often remains the responsibility of the firm leasing the equipment. At the end of the period of the lease, the equipment remains the property of the leasing company, who will either extend the lease at a small rental or will sell the asset, possibly handing over part of the income from the sale.

If a company leases equipment it will never own it and there are severe penalties for breaking the terms of a lease. It has the advantage, however, that a firm can replace equipment that becomes out of date at the end of the period of the lease and there are certain tax advantages to be gained.

Trade credit

Trade credit is an important source of short-term finance for a firm. If a firm's suppliers are prepared to give a period of credit before payment needs to be made, then this helps to bridge the gap between paying for materials and receiving payment from customers. Trade credit is, however, partly offset by the need for a firm to offer credit to its own customers.

Finance corporations

There are a number of specialist organisations offering finance to industry. These include the Finance Corporation for Industry (FCI) which borrows from the commercial banks, and lends to large companies, and the Industrial and Commercial Finance Corporation (ICFC). The ICFC is owned by the English and Scottish commercial banks and lends to smaller businesses.

Government finance

There are a wide, and constantly changing, range of grants and incentives offered to firms by the government. These include tax allowances, investment grants, research and development grants and business expansion schemes.

The government also runs a **loan guarantee scheme** which guarantees up to 80% of a loan made by a commercial bank to a small firm. This makes it easier for smaller firms to get finance from banks that might not otherwise be prepared to take the risk.

Fill in the blank spaces in the following sentences with words from the list below. No word may be used more than once.

Debentures	Overdraft
Broker	Preference
Ordinary	Hire purchase

When buying shares, the general public usually deals with a _____.

A finance house offers _____ facilities to consumers and to industry.

The two main types of share are _____ shares and _____ shares.

The holders of _____ are creditors of the company and not owners.

A firm has an _____ at the bank when more has been drawn out of an account than was credited to it.

Part 2 Uses of finance

We have seen where a company can get money from, but how is this money used? Whenever money comes into the business, it will be spent on those things which are needed to make the business work.

Business transactions

Let us consider in more detail the case of John Knight and his company 'Chess Mate'. He started his business with £2000 in cash. He used £1500 to buy a second-hand lathe. Items such as equipment and buildings, which a firm intends to keep to help with production, are known as **fixed assets**. John now has £500 in cash and a fixed asset worth £1500.

Sources of funds	Use of funds	
Owner's funds £2,000	Fixed assets (Lathe)	£1,500
	Cash	£ 500
		£2,000

He now needs to buy wood and other materials which will be used to produce the chess pieces. These cost £30, leaving £470 in cash. Items such as raw materials which are eventually to be sold are called **current assets**.

Sources of funds	Use of funds	
Owner's funds £2,000	Fixed assets (Lathe)	£1,500
	Current assets	
	Stocks of raw materials	£ 30
	Cash	£ 470
		£2,000

He now starts to produce his chess pieces and has to pay extra costs.

He pays himself a wage of £70. There is also the cost of electricity for lighting, heating his garage and running the lathe which amounts to £10. By the end of the first week he has produced ten sets. The cost of raw materials is £2 per set. £100 has therefore been spent on producing these ten chess sets.

Raw materials	$10 \times £2$	= £ 20
Wages		= £ 70
Power		= £ 10
Total cost of ten chess sets		= £100

He now has a stock of finished products which have cost £100. These are also current assets as they will eventually be sold. His stock of raw materials has now been reduced to £10 as he has used £20 worth in producing the chess sets. His cash has been reduced by £80 to £390. (£70 for his wages and £10 for power).

Sources of funds	Use of funds	
Owners funds £2,000	Fixed assets	£1,500
	Current assets	
	Stocks of raw materials	£ 10
	Stocks of finished goods	£ 100
	Cash	£ 390
		£2,000

On the Saturday he sells seven chess sets, charging £12 for each set. This gives him an extra £84 in cash which he can now spend on the things he needs to build up his stocks again ready for next week's market. His cash has therefore increased by £84 but his stocks of finished goods have fallen by £70, representing the cost of the seven chess sets sold. A profit of £14 has been made on the sales (£84 – £70).

Sources of funds	Use of funds	
Owners funds £2,000	Fixed assets	£1,500
Profit from sales £14	Current assets	
	Stock of raw materials	£ 10
	Stocks of finished goods	£ 30
	Cash	£ 474
£2,014		£2,014

So the cycle continues with money being used to finance fixed assets and current assets.

Recording transactions

John Knight has asked you to set up a system to help him to keep a record of all his payments and receipts.

What information should this system provide?

For a business to run successfully, all its transactions, whether it is buying or selling and whether it is for cash or on credit, must be recorded.

Business documents

These are a series of documents which pass between buyer and seller during the course of a transaction. These documents provide information and act as a record of the transaction for use at a later date:

- **An estimate or quotation** – This may be provided by the seller of a good or service and provides information to a possible customer on price, delivery date, special discounts etc.
- **An order** – If the quotation is acceptable, a customer will place an order. This will contain details of the number of items required, the agreed price and the address for delivery.
- **An advice note** – This is to advise the customer that the goods ordered have been dispatched and should soon be received.
- **A delivery note** – This is sent with the goods and the customer will normally sign one copy as confirmation that the goods have been received.
- **An invoice** – This is sent by the buyer to the seller after delivery and is a request for payment. The invoice will state the amount due and the date by which payment must be made.
- **A statement** – This is a summary of all transactions between a firm and a particular customer since the last statement was issued, usually the previous month. It records all payments made and money still outstanding. It also acts as a reminder to the customer.
- **A credit note** – This is issued if there has been a mistake on an invoice such as overcharging the customer, or if goods are returned because they are unsatisfactory.

An example of an order.

Payment terms

We have so far assumed that a customer will pay for goods after he has received them. This may not always be the case, however. There are three ways in which a customer can pay:

● **Payment in advance** – An invoice will usually be sent in advance of delivery.
● **Cash on delivery** – Here the payment will be made to the carrier.
● **Credit terms** – Payment will be made some time after delivery. Often up to 30 days is allowed before payment needs to be made.

The actual terms offered to a particular customer will depend on how well the supplier knows the customer and how confident the supplier is that payment will be made. A supplier may check on a customer's credit worthiness before offering credit terms.

Keeping the books

A firm must keep a record of all its transactions, both for tax purposes and also to enable the company to see how well it is doing. These records can be used by the management and by accountants who must check or **audit** the company's accounts.

Most large firms and many small firms now use computers to keep a record of transactions. Inexpensive computer software is now available which will automatically print out delivery notes, invoices and statements and will also keep a record of all sales and purchases.

A simple record of receipts and payments made by John Knight in his first week of trading is set out in Figure 3.

Figure 3: Receipts and payments for 'Chess Mate'					
Receipts			**Payments**		
		£			£
1.6.86	Owner's funds	2,000.00	1.6.86	Fixed assets (Lathe)	1,500.00
8.6.86	Sales	84.00	2.6.86	Purchases (raw materials)	30.00
			8.6.86	Electricity	10.00
			8.6.86	Wages	70.00

Part 3   Published accounts

Even when all John's transactions for the first week have been recorded, we still don't know how well (or badly) he has done. It is obviously not meaningful to draw any real conclusions from one week's trading, but we can still use the information recorded to calculate John's profit. We do this by producing a profit and loss account.

Profit and loss account

A profit and loss account is a calculation of the profit (or loss) that has been earned by a business over a particular period. For most firms this is a period of one year. The profit and loss account shows the difference between sales revenue and costs.

In our example, John Knight's **turnover**, that is his revenue from sales, is £84. His expenses in the first week are:

Raw materials	£ 30
Electricity	£ 10
Wages	£ 70
Total expenses	£110

This gives a total cost of £110. This cost is greater than the revenue of £84 and seems to indicate that John has made a loss of £26. We must remember, however, that he still has three chess sets in stock together with £10 worth of raw materials. The value of his stock therefore amounts to:

3 chess sets at	£10	= £30
Raw materials		= £10
		£40

The cost of the chess sets actually sold is therefore £70 (£110–£40). This gives a profit of £14. A simple profit and loss account for the first week's trading would therefore look like this:

Sales	£84
Cost of sales	£70
Trading profit	£14

In practice, for a larger company, the profit and loss account is broken down into three parts. The first part is the **trading account** which involves taking the cost of the goods sold away from the revenue gained from selling them.

Any revenue received from other activities such as interest earned on money deposited in the bank is then added. Similarly, any other costs such as electricity are taken away to give the overall profit or loss. This is the **profit and loss account**.

Finally, a breakdown is given of what is to be done with these profits, ie how much is to be paid to shareholders, how much retained in the business and how much is to be paid in tax. This is the **appropriation account**.

Figure 4: Simplified profit and loss account

		(£000)
Trading account	Sales (turnover)	200
	Cost of sales	– 155
Profit and loss account	Operating profit	45
	Interest received	+ 20
	Overheads	– 20
	Profit before tax	45
Appropriation account	Corporation tax	– 10
	Profit after tax	35
	Dividend paid	– 15
	Profit retained	20

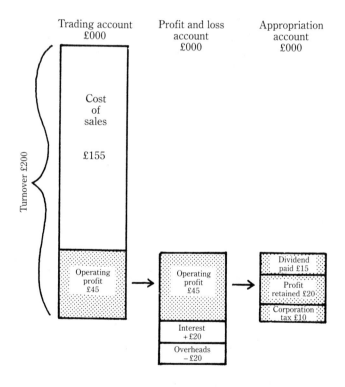

The published version of a company's profit and loss account contains very little information. It is only necessary to provide details of total sales, profit (only certain costs need to be identified) and what has been done with the profit. An example of a published profit and loss account is given in Figure 5.

Figure 5: British Telecom group profit and loss account (1986)

	£m
Turnover	8,387
Operating costs	6,292
Operating profit	2,095
Net interest payable	267
Profit before employee profit sharing and taxation	1,828
Employee profit sharing	18
Profit on ordinary activities before taxation	1,810
Tax on profit on ordinary activities	743
Profit on ordinary activities after taxation	1,067
Preference dividends	63
Profit attributable to ordinary shareholders	1,004
Ordinary dividends	450
Retained profit for the financial year	554
Earnings per ordinary share	16.7p

The balance sheet

Another important statement that can be produced using the accounting information is the **balance sheet**. This is a statement of the company's position at a point in time. It shows how much the company is owed by other people (assets), balanced against what the business owes to others (liabilities).

The liabilities side of the balance sheet shows where the business has got its money from. As we have seen there are three main sources of funds:

● The owners of the business.
● Other people who lend money to the business.
● Profits from trading.

When a firm borrows other people's money it is obviously a liability, as the firm owes that money. In the case of the owners own money, we must remember that a company is separate from its owners and can therefore owe money to them. In the same way, the profits that are retained within the business still really belong to the owners and therefore they too are owed.

The other side of the balance sheet shows where the money has gone to. It could have been used to buy things the company intends to keep (fixed assets) or things it means to sell, such as raw materials and stocks of finished goods (current assets). It could still be held in the form of cash or investments outside the company.

If John Knight produced a balance sheet after his first week of trading it would look like Figure 6.

Figure 6: Chess Mate balance sheet 8.6.86.

Liabilities	£	Assets	£
Owner's capital	2,000	Fixed assets	1,500
Profit	14	Current assets (stock)	40
		(cash)	474
	2,014		2,014

A balance sheet produced by an accountant will use accounting terms such as **reserves** and **current liabilities** but the nature of the balance sheet remains the same. One one side we have liabilities (where the money has come from), on the other side assets (where the money has gone to), and the two sides will balance.

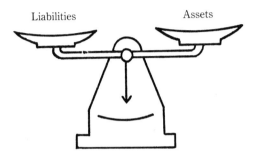

When looking at a balance sheet, you need to understand some of the words that accountants use to describe the various assets and liabilities.

Study the balance sheet for British Telecom (Figure 5) and list the terms used by the accountants that you don't yet understand. Try to provide a definition of each of these terms as you read through the next section.

Types of asset

We can divide up assets into three main types:

● **Fixed assets** – These are assets such as land and machinery which are not for resale, but are used to produce goods or provide services.
● **Current assets** – Current assets are those which can easily be changed into cash. These include stocks of raw materials and stocks of unfinished and finished goods. Any holdings of cash are also included as are debtors. Debtors are people who owe the company money.
● **Other assets** – A company may earn income from holding assets which are not part of their normal trading. They may, for example, have shareholdings in other firms or have money invested on the international money markets. These assets provide a separate source of income and allow firms to make use of any spare funds.

Types of liability

In the same way we can break down the liabilities side of the balance sheet:

- **Shareholders' funds** – In the case of joint-stock companies, the money that owners put into the company is known as **share capital**. In addition, some profits may be kept in the business rather than being paid out to shareholders. It is still their money but is normally shown as **reserves** on the balance sheet.
- **Long-term liabilities** – This is borrowing from people outside the business for periods of more than a year, eg debentures, H P loans and bank loans.
- **Current liabilities** – When money is borrowed for short periods it is known as a current liability. This includes bank overdrafts and creditors. Creditors are people that the firm owes money to – usually suppliers.

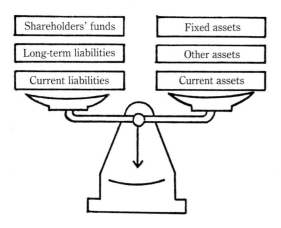

Presenting the balance sheet

Whilst it is possible to present the balance sheet in the way it has so far been shown, with assets on one side and liabilities on the other, a more modern method of presentation involves some rearrangement of the six elements as can be seen from Figure 7.

Depreciation

As fixed assets such as machinery and vehicles are used over a period of time, their value to the company will tend to fall. This decline is due to wear and tear and to obsolescence, as more modern plant and equipment become available. The value of an asset of this type should therefore be reduced over time and this will be shown on the balance sheet.

Figure 7: British Telecom group balance sheet (1985)

	£m
ASSETS EMPLOYED	
Fixed assets	
Tangible assets	10,603
Investments	134
Total fixed assets	10,737
Current assets	
Stocks	303
Debtors	2,490
Investments	1,014
Cash at bank and in hand	91
	3,898
Creditors: amounts falling due within one year	
Loans and other borrowings	465
Other creditors	3,188
	3,653
Net current assets	245
Total assets less current liabilities	10,982
FINANCED BY	
Creditors: amounts falling due after more than one year	
Loans and other borrowings	3,098
Provisions for liabilities and charges	659
Minority interests in subsidiary companies	112
Capital and reserves	
Called up share capital:	
Preference shares	750
Ordinary shares	1,500
	2,250
Profit and loss account	4,863
	7,113
	10,982

Choose a popular car such as the Ford Escort which has been available for at least five years.

Using a local newspaper or a magazine, such as *What Car*, compare the price of the car when new to models which are one, two, three, four and five years old. Plot your findings on a graph.

You will need to use an average price because prices will vary due to the month of registration, the mileage and condition of the car.

The amount by which the value of an asset is reduced is known as the **depreciation**. This represents the cost of using the asset. The cost is therefore spread over the life of the asset.

In order to calculate depreciation we need to know:

● The original cost of the asset.
● Its useful life.
● Its value at the end of its useful life (This may only be scrap value).

There are two methods of calculating depreciation. The **straight line** method involves reducing the value of the asset by a fixed amount each year over its life, eg

Original cost of asset   £10,000
Useful life   8 years
Scrap value   £ 2000

Depreciation $= \dfrac{\text{Total loss of value}}{\text{Useful life}}$

$= \dfrac{\pounds10,000 - \pounds2,000}{8}$

$= \dfrac{\pounds8,000}{8}$

$= \pounds1,000 \text{ per year}$

We can show this in the form of a graph.

Figure 8: Straight line depreciation

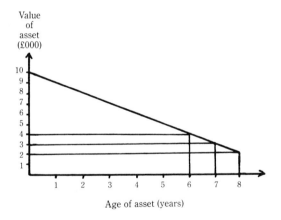

Age of asset (years)

Year	Depreciation	Value of asset (£)
—	—	10,000
1	1,000	9,000
2	1,000	8,000
3	1,000	7,000
4	1,000	6,000
5	1,000	5,000
6	1,000	4,000
7	1,000	3,000
8	1,000	2,000

Your earlier study of the market for used cars may well have shown a rather different picture to this. Assets tend to lose more of their value in the early years and this is shown by the **declining balance** method of calculating depreciation.

Using this method, depreciation is calculatd as a fixed percentage of the **book value** of the asset. Book value means the value shown on the balance sheet which will of course be less each year. Because the depreciation is calculated as a fixed percentage of a value which is getting smaller, the figure for depreciation will also get smaller from year to year.

Figure 9: Declining balance depreciation

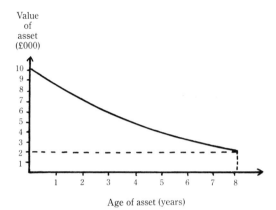

Age of asset (years)

Year	Depreciation (18%)	Value of asset (£)
—	—	10,000
1	1,800	8,200
2	1,476	6,724
3	1,210	5,514
4	993	4,521
5	814	3,707
6	667	3,040
7	547	2,493
8	449	2,044

The annual report

We have seen that an important role for the accountant in business is the recording of financial information. This involves recording all transactions and, at regular intervals, adding them up under certain headings to see where the company stands and how well it is doing. Having recorded these transactions, it is necessary to report on them so that the information can be used to help decision making and keep shareholders informed.

The amount of information the general public will have about a firm depends very much on its legal form. At one extreme, the accounts of the sole trader are not available to the general public. They need to be able to produce accounts which will satisfy VAT and Inland Revenue Inspectors but, other than this, there are no legal requirements.

At the other extreme, public joint-stock companies are required to disclose a great deal more information. Shareholders will receive copies of the **annual report and accounts** which may well be distributed more widely to employees, the press and other interested parties. Some companies even produce separate reports for employees and publish summaries of the accounts in the financial press to inform the general public as part of their public relations policy.

> Study a number of annual reports of large companies and compile a list of the things that they have in common. You can get hold of copies of these reports from libraries or by writing direct to the companies themselves.

The annual report and accounts of a large company is likely to contain the following:

● **Chairman's report** – It allows the company to set out its plans for the future and to explain particular features of its performance over the past year. There may also be some comment on the state of the economy and how it is likely to affect the company.

● **Directors' report** – This is a rather more formal statement setting out the present state of the company's affairs, recommending the dividends to be paid and indicating any changes in the nature of the company's business. An example is given in Figure 10.

● **Auditor's report** – This is a statement that the company's accounts have been properly prepared. Auditors are accountants who are independent of the company and who check on the company's accounts. A typical auditor's report is reproduced in Figure 11.

● **Profit and loss account** – As we saw earlier, this is a brief summary of the outcome of the company's activities over the past year showing receipts from sales, profits and what has been done with this profit.

● **The balance sheet** – This summarises the company's financial affairs at a point in time. It shows where the money to finance the business has come from and what it has been used for.

● **The source and application of funds statement** – This explains differences between this year's balance sheet and last year's. It shows where any extra finance has come from over the past year and what it has been used for.

● **Notes on the accounts** – Most firms try to keep the accounts as simple as possible. Any detail which would make the profit and loss account or the balance sheet more complicated are included in a set of notes at the end of the accounts. There may also be a statistical appendix at the end, providing further information which might be of interest to shareholders.

Figure 10:   Ford Motor Company: Directors' report

Fifty-seventh annual report of the directors of Ford Motor Company Limited.

The directors submit the annual report and accounts for the year ended 31 December 1985 for Ford Motor Company Limited and the group, which comprises Ford Motor Company Limited and its consolidated subsidiaries as detailed on page 31.

Statutory information including that concerning directors, auditors, dividends and donations is given below. Other statutory information is included in the Review of the Year.

Directors
The names of the present directors are given on the inside front cover.

As recorded in the last annual report, Mr AJ Trotman was appointed a director of the Company on 3 April 1985.

Mr RA Lutz, who was also a director during the whole of the year under review, resigned on 31 March 1986. The directors record their sincere appreciation for the help and guidance given to the Company during his period of office.

The director retiring by rotation under the provisions of Articles 106 and 108 is Mr WJ Hayden who, being eligible, offers himself for reappointment.

Auditors
In accordance with Section 384 of the Companies Act 1985, a resolution proposing the reappointment of Coopers & Lybrand as auditors to the Company will be put to the Annual General Meeting.

Dividend
The directors have resolved that an interim dividend of £2.56 per share (1984 nil) be paid on 7 April 1986 and recommend that this interim dividend be considered as final for 1985.

Transfer to general reserve
An amount of £25 million (1984 £50 m) has been transferred from retained profits to the general reserve.

Donations
Money given by the group for charitable purposes in the UK during the year amounted to £161,500 (1984 £138,400) which includes £62,500 paid under convenant to Ford of Britain Trust, a charitable organisation wholly supported by Company contributions. The covenanted income, together with other funding arrangements made by the Company, provided the Trust with an approximate total income for the year of £125,000.

Principal activity
The principal activity in which the group is engaged is the manufacture and sale of motor vehicles, together with associated finance operations.

By order of the Board

BW Parkes Secretary

1 April 1986

Figure 11: Ford Motor Company: Auditors' report

Report of the auditors to the members of Ford Motor Company Limited

We have audited the accounts on pages 16 to 31 in accordance with approved Auditing Standards. The accounts have been prepared under the historical cost convention and include additional information based on current cost accounting principles as set out in the Accounting Policies on pages 16 and 17.

In our opinion the accounts give a true and fair view of the state of affairs of the company and the group at 31 December 1985 and of the results of the company and the group and source and application of funds of the group for the year then ended and comply with the Companies Act 1985.

Coopers & Lybrand

Chartered Accountants

London, 1 April 1986

Information users

So far we have identified a number of sources of financial information. These include published accounts issued to shareholders, internal accounts produced to help managers make decisions, employee accounts containing information of interest to workers and financial information published in newspapers as part of a company's corporate advertising.

This information will be used by different groups of people. These include shareholders, creditors, the general public, employees, customers, managers and the government.

The shareholders have a legal right to certain information and they need to assess the security and profitability of their investment. Creditors need to be able to predict the possibility of further orders and the risk of the firm being unable to pay its bills. Lenders are equally concerned with the firm's ability to pay its debts.

The general public has an interest in the prospects of all large firms. A firm's employees are specifically concerned with the security of their own jobs and trade unions are interested in a firm's ability to meet their pay demands.

Customers will be interested in the future prospects of the firm and the profits it is earning, whilst management will be interested in how efficiently the firm is operating. Finally, the government will be concerned with VAT and corporation tax returns and also financial statistics which help them to see how well the economy is doing.

The three main types of information which are therefore required about a company are its ability to pay its debts, its efficiency and the rate of return paid to investors in the business. The method most often used to obtain this information is by means of **financial ratios**.

Financial ratios

A ratio shows the size of one factor in relation to another. Imagine two companies, the first makes a profit of £1,000 a year and the second £2,000. What does this tell us? It might indicate that the second firm is twice as efficient as the first, or it may just be that the second is twice as big. The figures are only useful if they are compared to other figures, such as the total value of sales. This gives a ratio of profit to sales.

A ratio itself is only meaningful if you have something to compare it with. Is a 1:10 (10%) ratio of profit to sales good or bad? There are three ways to find this out:

- **Trend analysis** – This involves looking at what happens over time. Is the ratio higher or lower than in other years?
- **Inter-firm comparisons** – This involves a firm comparing its own figures with another firm in the same industry.
- **Budget standards** – A firm can compare its actual performance with the targets it has set.

A company needs to know whether it can pay its debts, if it is efficient and the return to its investors. Financial ratios can help a company find this out.

Liquidity ratios

Liquidity is a measure of how easily a company can change its assets into cash and **liquidity ratios** measure the ability of a company to pay its debts.

The **current ratio** is the ratio of current assets to current liabilities. Current assets can be easily changed to cash and current liabilities are those that need to be repaid over a short period, such as overdrafts. The current ratio measures the ease with which a firm can pay its bills on time.

If a business is unable to pay its bills it could result in bankruptcy (in the case of a sole trader), or go into liquidation (if it is a limited company).

An individual who is declared bankrupt is unable to become an MP or a company director. The Romans dealt with bankrupts by cutting them into pieces and dividing them amongst their creditors. Today they are treated more leniently! An official receiver is brought in to sell off the

Figure 12: Bankrupt

WHO GOES BANKRUPT –
The High Risk Trades

Industry	% of total, 1984
Builders	11.6
Shops	10.5
Hotels and Catering	7.7
Restaurants, cafe and snack bars	6.4
Transport and communication	6.1
Manufacturing	5.0
Business Services	2.9
Motor Traders and petrol stations	2.5
Wholesaling	2.3
Farming and gardening	2.0
Financial Institutions	0.4
Other Industries and businesses	18.7
Employees, company promoters, unemployed, and unknown occupation	23.9

Source: DTI

1 What is the difference between 'liquidation' and 'bankruptcy'?
2 Describe and comment on the pattern of liquidations and bankruptcies illustrated in Figures 12 and 13 above.

Figure 13: Going broke

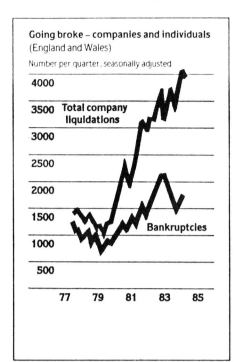

Source: DTI

3 Why do you think there is a greater risk of bankruptcy in some trades than in others?

---

debtor's assets in order to repay debts. The number of bankrupts has increased over the years to over 8,000 in 1984. Self-employed businessmen make up much of this total, but even the rich and famous can find themselves in financial difficulty. One recent bankrupt owed debts of £250m.

The equivalent of bankruptcy when applied to a company is liquidation. If a company goes into liquidation, the assets are sold off by a liquidator who is appointed by the courts or major creditors. As shareholders have limited liability, they are not personally liable for all of the debts. Shareholders are usually the last to be paid from revenue earned by the sale of assets. Before them will come debenture holders, holders of preferential debts such as the Inland Revenue and trade creditors.

Efficiency ratios

The efficiency of a firm is usually judged by the profits it makes. We saw earlier, however, that profits alone are misleading. We need to know how efficiently a firm uses its assets to earn this profit.

The most important of the efficiency ratios is the **return on capital employed** (ROCE) which measures how much profit results from the use of a firm's fixed and working capital.

$$\text{Return on capital employed} = \frac{\text{Profit (before tax and interest)}}{\text{Net assets employed (fixed and working capital)}}$$

The average figure for British industry as a whole is around 17%, although there are marked differences between industries as Figure 14 illustrates.

Figure 14: Rates of return on capital employed at historic costs (%)

Food retailing	25
Health & household products	25
Tobacco	22
Electronics	19
Other consumer goods	18
Newspapers & publishing	18
Electricals	18
Food manufacturing	17
Textiles	16
Stores	16
Brewers & distillers	15
Leisure	14
Building materials	14
Chemicals	13
Office equipment	12
Contracting & constructions	12
Mechanical engineering	11
Packaging & paper	11
Shipping & transport	11
Motors	7

Source: *Bank of England Quarterly Bulletin* September 1984.

Investment ratios

These measure the return which can be expected by investors and include the **dividend yield ratio** which measures the rate of return on the current market price of a share, ie If you bought a share now, what rate of return could you expect?

$$\text{Dividend yield} = \frac{\text{Dividend per share}}{\text{Share price}} \times 100\%$$

eg If a company declares a dividend of 15p per share and the current share price is £1.50 then:

$$\text{Dividend yield} = \frac{15}{100} \times 100\% = 10\%$$

Limitations of ratios

However useful ratios may be, they do not tell the whole story. Low profits may simply mean that a company has not set profitability as its most important objective. Alternatively, change in a particular ratio may be the result of changes in the firm's circumstances and nothing to do with management decisions.

In the same way, if you want to assess the future prospects of a company you will need to know about the state of the economy, what is happening in industry as a whole, how competitors are going to behave and what technological developments can be foreseen. All this requires information far in excess of that which is contained in a company's published accounts.

Part 4   Management accounting

We have so far concentrated on the role of the **financial accountant**, who is responsible for record keeping and the presentation of the company's accounts. Alongside the financial accountant in a large organisation will be the **management accountant** whose job is to provide information to help with management decision making. He or she will collect and interpret information about such things as costs and profitability and will make forecasts about the future. These will include calculating future needs for cash and assessing new investment.

The role of the management accountant is to help managers make decisions on what to produce, how much to produce and what prices to charge. They help by providing information which reduces the risk of making the wrong decisions.

Budgeting

An important task for the management accountant is to produce a **budget**. We are familiar with the idea of a household budget or the government's annual budget and a company budget is very similar. It is simply a forecast or estimate of future income and expenditure. A company will base its forecasts on some combination of experience, figures from previous years and research.

Even relatively small firms need to carry out some form of forecasting even if it is only to predict their needs for cash. If a firm has a bank overdraft, the bank manager may insist on the production of a **cash flow forecast**. This is an attempt to predict the likely income and expenditure for a firm each month. Even if a firm is trading profitably, it could still find itself in difficulties if there is a long time between paying for raw materials etc. and being paid by customers. It is sometimes even necessary to turn down profitable orders if it would have a bad effect on the firm's cash flow.

Financial Accountant

Management Accountant

The need to achieve a satisfactory cash flow makes it very important to make sure that customers pay their bills on time. This is known as **debtor control** and may involve giving discounts for prompt payment, following up invoices with reminders and telephone calls to late payers, checking credit worthiness before credit is given to customers and possibly the employment of **commercial collection agencies** who will attempt to collect money from late payers for a commission. At the same time, the business should take full advantage of any credit facilities which are available from their suppliers.

Most large firms take budgeting a lot further than simply producing cash flows. A firm can forecast future levels of sales, stocks, costs, capital expenditure and production. By comparing actual levels with those that have been predicted, the firm is able to spot possible problems such as low stock levels and take action to deal with them.

Costs of production

Businesses require information on costs in order

to work out the profitability of the goods they produce. Profits can be increased by controlling costs as well as increasing revenue from sales.

One distinction that businesses make is between **fixed costs** and **variable costs**. Fixed costs are those which do not vary with output. Examples would include the rent on factory premises or the costs of heating and lighting the factory. However much is produced in the factory, these costs remain the same. Other costs, such as raw materials costs and labour costs, will increase as output increases and these are known as variable costs.

> The costs of owning and running a car can be divided into fixed costs (not linked with the number of miles travelled) and variable costs (which increase as the car is used). List the costs of owning and running a car under the two headings 'fixed costs' and 'variable costs'.

A distinction is often made between **direct** (or prime) costs and **indirect** (or overhead) costs. Direct costs are those which are a direct result of producing a particular product. If no product is produced then there are no direct costs. Indirect costs, on the other hand, are not directly linked to the production of a particular product but include costs such as insurance and secretarial costs. These costs will be shared between the various products that a firm produces.

Figure 15 shows a possible cost breakdown for a product selling at £100.

Costing methods

It is not always possible to calculate the individual cost of each unit of output in the way we have so far described. The output of some firms does not consist of standardised units which are all identical and which all have the same costs. A system of **job costing** or **contract costing** may have to be used where each 'job' is costed separately. An example would be in the printing trade where the costs of printing individual books, magazines, leaflets etc. will have to be worked out separately.

In other firms, items are not produced singly but in batches and so **batch costing** will be used. Here the cost of producing a number of items will be calculated rather than the cost of individual items. An engineering firm producing castings, for example, may produce ten at a time.

In many firms, a range of products share a common production process and can only be distinguished from one another at the end of the production chain. In these cases it is common to use **process costing**. A cost is calculated for each process carried out in the factory. By dividing this by the number of units passing through the process, we obtain the cost per unit. Adding together the unit costs for each process that a product passes through gives the final production costs. This method is often found in the chemical and food processing industries.

In the case of service industries, it is common to use **operating costing**. Rather than calculating the cost of individual jobs, an average cost is calculated. An example would be the cost per tonne mile for transport. By multiplying this by the number of miles a load is to be carried, an estimate of the cost is obtained and this can form the basis of the price to be charged.

> What is the most appropriate method of costing in each of the cases a–d?
>
> **a** A builder carrying out maintenance work and building house extensions.
> **b** A confectionery manufacturer producing a range of boxes of chocolates.
> **c** A local bus service.
> **d** A baker producing bread and cakes.

Figure 15: Cost breakdown		£
Direct costs	Material	12.50
	Labour	25.00
	Expenses	17.50
	Prime cost	55.00
Indirect costs	Works or factory expenses (production overheads)	10.50
	Office and administrative expenses (establishment overheads)	14.50
	Cost of production	80.00
Direct selling costs	Selling expenses	2.00
	Distribution expenses	2.00
	Cost of sales	84.00
	Net operating profit	16.00
	Selling price	100.00

Dealing with overheads

Trident Timber Limited is a firm producing two products, packing cases and pallets. These are sold to industry for the storage and handling of goods. The direct cost of wages and raw materials for packing cases is £15 and for pallets is £10. The firm produces 100 packing cases and 200 pallets per month.

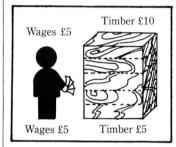 

In addition there are overhead costs of £1,200 per month including the salary of the managing director, the wages of his secretary and the accounts clerk and other expenses such as heating, lighting and insurance.

£1,200 per month

The packing cases sell for £25 each and the pallets for £16. Sales exactly match production with 100 packing cases and 200 pallets being sold each month.

1 How much profit does Trident Timber Limited make each month?
2 Which is the most profitable product – packing cases or pallets?
3. If the direct cost of packing cases was £25 per month, would it be worth continuing to produce them?

The first question should have presented few problems. You simply need to calculate the total revenue from selling each month's output and then subtract the total direct and indirect costs. The second question is rather more difficult and the answer depends on what you decided to do about overheads.

If we concentrate on direct costs alone we can calculate the following:

	Packing cases	Pallets
Sales revenue	2,500	3,200
Direct costs	1,500	2,000
Contribution to overheads/profit	1,000	1,200

It could be argued that because the production of pallets is making the biggest contribution towards overheads and profits, that this is the most profitable product. The third question in the activity deals with a situation where a product is making no contribution to overheads. It may seem that this product is not worth producing but there are certain circumstances where a product will be produced even if only the direct costs are being covered.

It may be, for example, that the firm has spare capacity which would simply stand idle if this good was not produced. The firm may feel that the industry is experiencing a temporary recession and that prices will pick up in the future. In the meantime, they will continue to produce in order to maintain the goodwill of customers and to keep their labour force employed. In the case of new products, it may be necessary to sell them at a price that does not cover the full cost in order to break into the market.

Break-even charts

The point at which sales revenue just covers direct costs and overheads (total costs) is known as the **break-even point**. Assume that Trident Timber Limited only produced packing cases with the same direct and overhead costs as before. How many would it have to sell before it would break even?

We can work this out mathematically or by using a **break-even chart**. Remember that the direct cost of each case is £15 and each one sells for £25. Each case therefore makes a £10 contribution towards overheads and profit. The break-even point is where overheads are just covered.

How many contributions of £10 are needed to cover overheads of £1,200? The answer is 120 (£1,200 ÷ £10). If the firm produces 120 packing

Imagine now that Trident Timber Limited produces only pallets. Remember that pallets are sold for £16, direct costs are £10 per pallet and overheads are £1,200 per month.

1 Draw a chart similar to the one below to show the break-even point.
2 What is the profit when 250 pallets are produced and sold?
3 What would be the effect on the break-even point of a 20% increase in direct costs? Illustrate this on your diagram.

The basis of investment appraisal is to compare the amount of cash needed to purchase a new item of capital equipment with the amount of extra cash which the firm receives as a result of that investment. Unfortunately, this is not quite as simple as it seems because of the uncertainty of future sales.

Other factors which should be taken into account include the risk of obsolescence, interest rates on borrowed money, government taxation policy and the availability of government grants. The impact of investment on the workforce must also be considered.

cases it will therefore break even. We can check that calculation:

Total cost of producing 120 packing cases:
Direct cost (120 × £15)	£1,800
Overheads	£1,200
Total cost	£3,000

Total revenue from selling 120 packing cases:
Total revenue (120 × £25)	£3,000

We can also illustrate the break-even point graphically as in Figure 16.

Investment appraisal
A further job for the management accountant is to advise on investment decisions. A wrong decision could lead to the firm making losses or at best being less efficient than it could be.

"PERSONALLY, I ALWAYS USE THE EENY-MEENY-MINEY-MO METHOD TO DECIDE ON INVESTMENT PROJECTS."

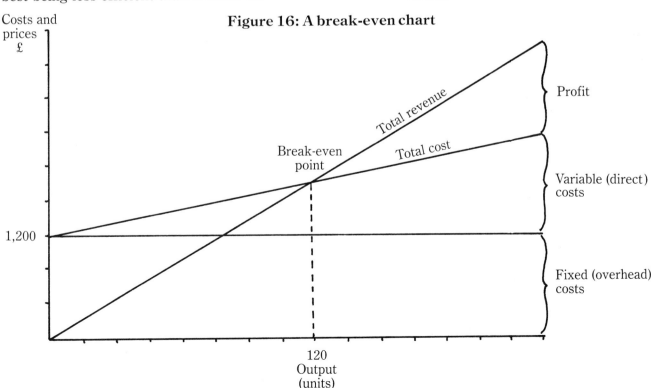

Figure 16: A break-even chart

QUICK QUIZ

1. Distinguish between:

   a ordinary shares
   b preference shares
   c debentures.

2. A share has a face value of £1. A company declares a dividend of 15%. If the market price of the share is £1.50, what is the yield?

3. List three factors influencing the price of shares quoted on the Stock Exchange.

4. Outline three ways in which the government can assist in providing finance for industry.

5. List three advantages claimed for leasing.

6. What are the main differences between a bank loan and an overdraft?

7. List three of the services offered by commercial banks to their business customers.

8. Explain what is meant by a profit and loss account.

9. Distinguish between an asset and a liability.

10. What information is needed to calculate depreciation?

11. Describe briefly the two main methods of calculating depreciation.

12. Why does a company need to measure its cash flow?

13. How are each of the following ratios measured:

    a The current ratio?
    b The return on capital employed?

14. Distinguish between:

    a fixed and variable costs
    b direct and indirect costs.

15. What is meant by the break-even point?

Case Study: The UK tobacco industry

Cigarette consumption in the UK has fallen from over 123 bn cigarettes in 1979, to less than 95 bn by 1986. Numerous factors have led to this decline.

Although there are still many people who are addicted to tobacco, the threat to health and social pressures have led many to give up. In April 1986 the Sports Council announced plans to ban the advertising of tobacco from sports. In June the Protection of Children (tobacco) Bill reached the House of Lords.

The Chancellor of the Exchequer continues to raise taxes on tobacco. Taxation on a packet of cigarettes already represents around 75% of its retail price, providing the government with over £5 bn a year in revenue.

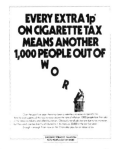 

In recent years, lobbying to reduce tax has increased. In 1986, tobacco retailers collected signatures on a petition for 'fair play' on tobacco taxation. They say that falling sales and consumption may result in a cutback of production, and unemployment in the industry.

Figure 1: The external influences on a firm

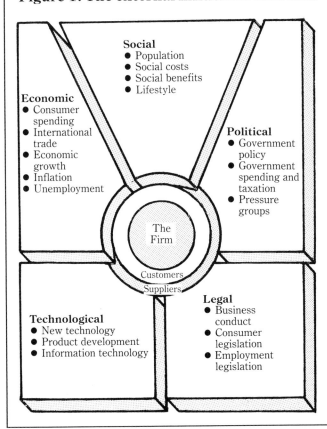

Figure 2: UK cigarette consumption

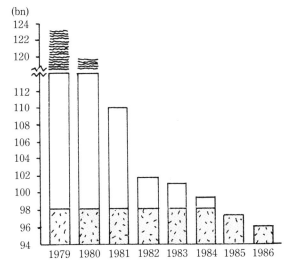

The case of the UK tobacco industry illustrates how many different external influences can affect the profit, output and sales of an industry.

1 Having read the case study, select as many external influences as you can find. Place each in one of the five categories illustrated in Figure 1.

Part 1   Economic considerations

Firms act as a link between resources and consumers. They buy the resources that they need in factor markets and change these into goods and services which are sold to their customers both at home and overseas.

Consumer spending

Comment on the changing pattern of expenditure illustrated in Figure 3.

Figure 3: UK household expenditure

| | Percentage of total expenditure | |
	1960	1983
Housing	9.3	16.8
Fuel, light and power	5.9	6.5
Food	30.5	20.7
Alcoholic drink	3.2	4.9
Tobacco	5.9	3.0
Clothing and footwear	10.3	7.0
Durable household goods	6.4	7.2
Other goods	7.5	8.0
Transport and vehicles	12.2	14.7
Services	8.9	11.3

Source: Family Expenditure Surveys

However large a company is, it will still be dependent on demand for its products. Demand will obviously be influenced by price, but other factors such as changing tastes and changes in national income will also cause changes in the pattern of consumer expenditure.

We can see from Figure 3 how the pattern of consumer spending has changed. The greatest increases have been in the proportion spent on housing, transport and services. Over the same period there has been a reduction in the proportion of income spent on food, drink, tobacco and clothing.

Expenditure on household durables continues to rise steadily. Around 98% of households now have television sets, 95% have vacuum cleaners and 94% have refrigerators. New products such as video recorders and micro-wave ovens have helped to boost sales of household durable goods.

Expenditure on services is another major growth area, although within the service sector there have been some areas of decline. In the field of transport, for example, air travel has increased rapidly whilst there has been a relative decline in expenditure on rail and bus services.

Similarly, in declining sectors such as food, there have been some areas of growth, notably in health food, reflecting the trend towards healthier eating.

Figure 4 shows some of the major areas of growth and decline.

Figure 4: UK consumers' expenditure 1973–83

Annual average percentage volume change

Major areas of growth

Radio, television and other durable goods	+9.6
Telecommunications	+6.8
Other services[1]	+6.6
Television and videohire charges, licence fees and repairs	+6.0
Gas	+5.7
Air travel	+5.5
Household expenditure abroad	+5.5
Women's, girls' and infants' wear	+4.7
Footwear	+4.4
Wine, cider and perry	+4.3
National Health Service payments and other medical expenses	+4.1

[1] 'Other services' includes types of casualty insurance, bank charges, stockbrokers' charges, stamp duties and funeral expenses.

Major areas of decline

Other fuel and power	−6.0
Coal and coke	−5.4
Buses and coaches	−3.5
Sugar	−3.1
Postal services	−3.1
Household and domestic services[2]	−2.6
Tobacco (inc. cigarettes)	−2.6
Betting and gaming	−2.6
Newspapers and magazines	−2.2

[2] Includes laundry and dry-cleaning, window cleaning, chimney sweeping, house contents insurance and domestic service.

Source: National Income and Expenditure HMSO 1984

International trade

The UK has traditionally been thought of as a country that imports food and raw materials and exports manufactured goods and services. At the beginning of the century our major exports were coal, textiles and metal manufactures. By the 1980s, this had changed with machinery, tran-

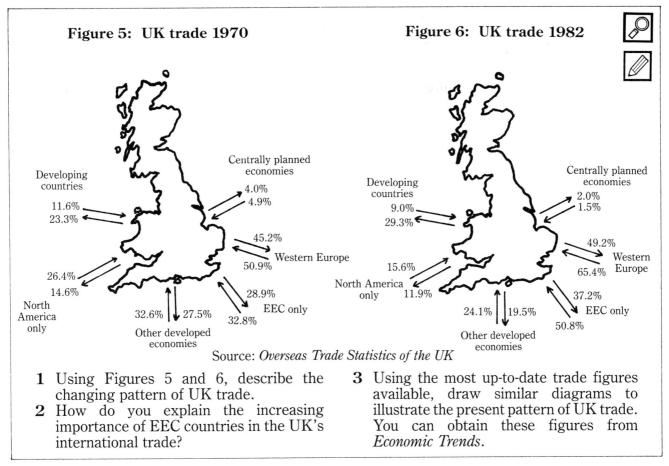

Figure 5: UK trade 1970

Developing countries
11.6%
23.3%

Centrally planned economies
4.0%
4.9%

45.2%
50.9%
Western Europe

26.4%
14.6%
North America only

32.6% 27.5%
32.8%
Other developed economies

28.9%
32.8%
EEC only

Figure 6: UK trade 1982

Developing countries
9.0%
29.3%

Centrally planned economies
2.0%
1.5%

49.2%
65.4%
Western Europe

15.6%
North America only 11.9%

24.1% 19.5%
Other developed economies

37.2%
50.8%
EEC only

Source: *Overseas Trade Statistics of the UK*

1 Using Figures 5 and 6, describe the changing pattern of UK trade.
2 How do you explain the increasing importance of EEC countries in the UK's international trade?

3 Using the most up-to-date trade figures available, draw similar diagrams to illustrate the present pattern of UK trade. You can obtain these figures from *Economic Trends*.

sport equipment and oil forming the bulk of our exports. This reflects the changes that have taken place in the pattern of world demand with new products becoming available and increased affluence amongst our major trading partners.

Another important change has been the emergence of the newly industrialised countries of Asia and S. America. These countries, such as Hong Kong and Taiwan, have entered the market for manufactured goods in competition with the UK. As a result, the pattern of UK imports has changed even more than the pattern of exports. We now import a large proportion of the manufactured goods bought in this country. In 1983, for the first time, our imports of manufactured goods exceeded our exports.

As well as changes in the composition of international trade, there have also been changes in the countries that we trade with.

The balance of payments

The record of the UK's trade with other countries is known as the **balance of payments account**. This shows all of the UK's imports (for which we pay other countries) and exports (for which we are paid by other countries).

The balance of payments accounts are divided up into a number of sections. The **current account** records the value of exports and imports of goods (known as **visible trade**) and services (known as **invisible trade**). Visible trade consists of trade in goods such as machinery, raw materials and food. Invisible trade includes services such as shipping, banking and tourism.

The value of the UK's exports is recorded **f o b** (free on board), which means that their value is taken at the port they leave from in this country and transport costs are excluded. The value of imports is measured **c i f** (cost, insurance and freight), which means that their value is taken at the port of landing with all transport costs included. This causes a slight problem in making comparision between imports and exports from published figures.

The **capital account** of the balance of payments records overseas investment by UK residents and investment by non-residents in the UK. The flow of money out of the UK on the capital account always exceeds the inflow as UK investment overseas is greater than overseas investment in this country.

The final part of the balance of payments is the **balance of official financing**. If the flow of money out of the UK on the current and capital accounts exceeds the inflow then the extra money must come from somewhere. If the inflow exceeds the outflow then the extra money must go somewhere. We either borrow from overseas or run down our reserves of foreign currency if we have a balance of payments deficit (outflow greater than inflow). We can repay loans or build up our reserves if we have a surplus (inflow greater than outflow).

Figure 7: The balance of payments accounts

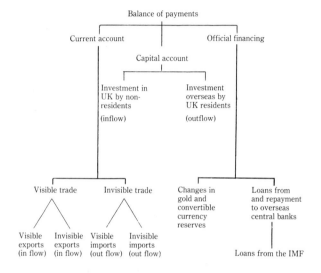

Figure 8: The UK balance of payments 1985 (£m)

Current account	
Visible trade	
Exports (f.o.b.)	78,702
Imports (f.o.b.)	80,140
Visible balance	−2,068
Invisible trade	
Government services and transfers	−4,612
Private services and transfers	7,338
Interest, profit and dividends	2,294
Invisible balance	5,020
Current balance	2,952
Total currency flow	
Current balance	2,952
Investment and other capital flows	−2,860
Balancing item	835
Total currency flow	+927
Official financing	−927

Source: *Economic Trends Annual Supplement* CSO 1986

The effect of international trade on the firm

International trade has a direct effect on UK firms. The most obvious effect is that all firms are exposed to foreign competition. Those firms which cannot compete with foreign producers will go out of business. This has led to the decline of whole industries such as textiles, where over-

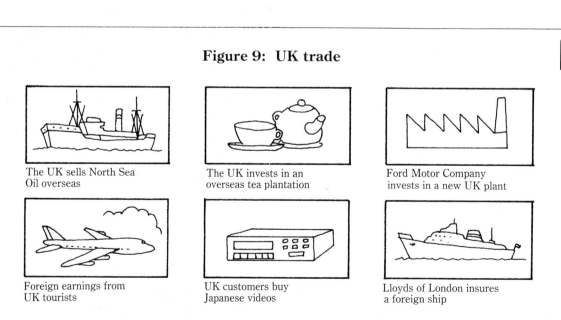

Figure 9: UK trade

The UK sells North Sea Oil overseas

The UK invests in an overseas tea plantation

Ford Motor Company invests in a new UK plant

Foreign earnings from UK tourists

UK customers buy Japanese videos

Lloyds of London insures a foreign ship

1 From Figure 9 find two examples of:

  a visible trade
  b invisible trade
  c capital movements.

seas manufacturers have been able to produce much cheaper products.

Those firms which do trade overseas have the advantage of a larger market. This allows them to obtain the benefits of economies of large-scale production and to spread their risk. If the home market is declining, they may be able to sell more of their goods in foreign markets.

One benefit of trade for the consumer is that goods will be available that could not be produced in the UK, eg tropical fruit. Overseas competition also means that consumers have a greater choice of goods, eg foreign cars as well as British ones.

A disadvantage of foreign trade to a firm is the extra cost involved in selling abroad. Not only are there extra transport costs, but firms may also have to set up overseas depots and employ agents to sell their products. Set against this, however, is the fact that overseas orders tend to be for larger quantities and this reduces packaging, handling and administrative costs.

A further problem is that it is more difficult to arrange credit for overseas sales. Customers may not be known to the firm and the problem is made worse by having to use an unfamiliar legal system to attempt to recover bad debts.

To help overcome this problem and to encourage overseas trade, the government's **Export Credit Guarantee Department** (ECGD) is often prepared to insure export orders in case the importers are unable to meet their obligations. The government also supports trade by offering information and advice to potential exporters and sponsoring trade exhibitions.

Import controls

Despite the benefits to be gained from international trade, many people argue that there should be some control over trade. Recent examples include calls for the control over the import of foreign cars, notably from Japan.

The need for import controls

A number of arguments have been put forward in support of import controls:

● If people buy foreign goods rather than those produced by British firms, this could lead to a fall in output and employment.
● Control of imports will protect new industries from competition.
● Controls are needed to protect industries of national importance, such as shipbuilding.

The methods used to control imports could include:

● **Quotas** – This sets a limit on the amount of foreign goods allowed into a country.
● **Tariffs** – These are a tax making foreign imports more expensive. Tariffs are effective in preventing **dumping**, when one country may sell a good at below cost price in another country in order to gain a foothold in that market.
● **Embargo** – A complete ban on trade with a particular country or in a particular good, eg drugs or arms. This could be used for political reasons, such as the recent call for an embargo on South African goods.
● **Administrative barriers** – This could be the use of safety standards to prevent imports, or more extreme barriers such as the insistence by the French that imported snails have health checks before being allowed to enter a country.

Import controls can lead to problems for businesses and consumers. Other countries may retaliate, which reduces the exports of British businesses and consumers will not be able to benefit from a wider choice of cheap foreign goods.

 Organise a debate with speakers for and against the motion:

'Britain should ban the import of cheap denim jeans from Taiwan.'

International finance

As different countries use different currencies, firms that deal with overseas suppliers or customers have to be able to buy the currency of the country they are dealing with. A French manufacturer, for example, would expect to be paid in francs and not in pounds.

The foreign exchange market

As with other prices, the price of a currency is determined by supply and demand. Firms and individuals demand foreign currencies in order to trade, for foreign holidays or simply in the hope that the currency price will rise and they will be able to sell later at a profit. In exchange they will have to sell their own currency.

If a lot of people want to sell pounds in exchange for say francs, the number of francs that you get for a pound will go down, ie the price of francs will increase and the price of pounds will fall. This is known as **depreciation** of the pound.

In practice, the government may buy and sell pounds through the Bank of England in order to influence the price. This is because of the effect that changes in the value of the pound will have on exporters and importers.

The effect on imports and exports

Imagine a fall in the value of the pound from £1 = $2 to £1 = $1. Before the depreciation of the pound, a good costing $2 to produce in the USA would cost £1 in the UK. After the fall in the value of the pound, $2 worth of goods would cost £2, ie the cost of imports rises.

Taking the same change in the value of the pound, ie from £1 = $2 to £1 = $1, we can look at the effect on UK exports. Before depreciation, a good which cost £1 to produce in the UK would sell for $2. After the fall in the value of the pound the producer can sell the same good for $1, ie the cost of exports fall, or they can keep the price at $2 and make a bigger profit.

Economic growth

In simple terms, growth means an increase in output and demand in the economy. The effects on the firm are obvious. High levels of economic growth mean increasing sales and increasing profits. Low rates of growth or no growth at all, mean static markets and increased competition for customers.

Firms themselves are the key to achieving high growth rates, as it is their output and the incomes they pay to their factors of production which will determine demand.

From the economy as a whole, there are three main factors which will increase the rate of growth:

- An increase in the country's stock of factors of production, eg population (labour supply).
- An increase in the amount that can be produced with a given amount of factors (productivity).
- Technological advances in production techniques.

It is sometimes argued that slow rates of economic growth may result from trade union activity leading to strikes and preventing the introduction of new technology. Others would blame the government for imposing high rates of tax and introducing controls on the building of new factories. Management has also been criticised for a lack of investment and inefficiency in organising resources.

Inflation

Inflation is defined as a persistent rise in the general level of prices. Some prices will be rising and others falling at any one time, but when there is a general upward trend in the level of most prices then this is inflation.

Inflation is usually measured using the **Retail Price Index** (RPI). This involves measuring the prices of a selection of goods and services which a typical household would spend their money on over a period of a month. Each month researchers compare the prices of these goods in a range of retail outlets to see how they have changed. There are around 600 items included in the RPI.

If, on average, the price is 1% higher one month than it was the month before, then it means that prices are increasing at a rate of around 12% per year. (Inflation is usually measured at an annual rate.)

Inflation and the business

Low rates of inflation do not present a real problem for a firm, but when prices are going up rapidly it can lead to problems. One problem is that those people on fixed incomes such as pensioners and students find that their money buys less than it used to. The balance of payments also tends to get worse as the rising prices of home produced goods make our exports more expensive to overseas customers, and our imports relatively cheap.

Very high rates of inflation can lead to panic buying as people stockpile goods before they increase even more in price. This leads to shortages and prices rise further because of the increased demand.

Figure 10: A guide to the Retail Price Index (1987)

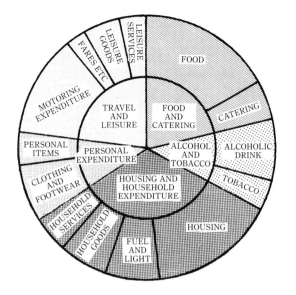

1 From Figure 10, estimate the percentage a typical household might spend on each of the main categories of goods and services.
2 Carry out a survey in your own home to determine the approximate breakdown of monthly spending. Compare your results with those obtained by other members of the class.
3 As a group exercise, decide on a typical selection of goods and monitor price changes over a one month period. Calculate your own inflation index.

There is a general uncertainty in the market during times of inflation which discourages investment, as firms don't know what is going to happen in the future. Wage demands by workers attempting to get pay increases to keep pace with inflation can also cause industrial unrest with lost output because of strikes.

In extreme cases (known as hyper-inflation), there may be a complete breakdown in the economic system. People will refuse to accept money and there may be a return to a barter system with people preferring to accept goods, whose prices are going up, rather than money.

Causes of inflation

There are two main causes of inflation:

● **Demand pull inflation** – This is where demand in the economy is rising faster than supply and, as a result, prices are forced up as people compete for the available goods. On a small-scale, we can see how the excess demand for tickets to a pop concert can lead to a black market with high prices being charged by 'ticket touts'.
● **Cost push inflation** – This is where the increase in price is due to increases in any of the costs of production. This could include an increase in wages or the price of imported raw materials.

Figure 11: Average weekly pocket money 1975–87

Year	Amount	% Change	Annual inflation rate
1975	33p	–	–
1976	36p	+9%	16.5%
1977	45p	+25%	15.8%
1978	62p	+38%	8.3%
1979	78p	+26%	13.4%
1980	99p	+27%	18.0%
1981	113p	+14%	11.9%
1982	95p	–16%	8.6%
1983	122p	+29%	4.6%
1984	105p	–14%	5.0%
1985	109p	+4%	5.0%
1986	117p	+7%	6.1%
1987	116p	–1%	3.9%

1 Describe the changes in average weekly pocket money illustrated in Figure 11.
2 a Using Figure 11, pick out those years when the increase in average pocket money was greater than the rate of inflation.

   b How are you affected when your pocket money does not increase in line with rising prices?

3 Class activity. Carry out a survey of pocket money in your class. Use the information you collect to illustrate:

   a the average level of pocket money
   b any difference between pocket money for girls and boys
   c changes in pocket money since last year.

Unemployment

It could be argued that unemployment is of benefit to a firm. They should find it easier to find the workers they need and wages will tend to be lower as the unemployed will be prepared to accept low wages in order to get a job. Wage demands and strikes will also be reduced as those in employment do not want to risk losing their jobs.

There is, of course, another side to the coin. Despite high levels of unemployment, it is still often difficult to fill vacancies where certain skills are required. A great deal of effort on the part of the Manpower Services Commission goes into filling this 'skills gap' through training schemes. When people are unemployed for a long time, they may begin to lose the skills that they have and find it difficult to adjust to working again if a job becomes available.

Unemployment also means low income which, as well as being a serious social cost, reduces the level of demand in the economy. If demand is low, firms cannot sell their goods. This leads to further redundancies and a vicious circle of falling demand and rising unemployment will result.

Causes of unemployment

Unemployment can be caused by a number of factors:

● **Frictional unemployment** – This is where there is a short break in moving from one job to another. The period of unemployment is usually less than four weeks and does not represent a serious problem.

● **Casual unemployment** – This is where labour is employed on a short-term basis. In a number of industries, such as construction, jobs are not permanent and employees are hired only when there is work available.

●**Seasonal unemployment** – This is similar to casual unemployment but is influenced by seasonal patterns of demand or weather conditions. In agriculture or tourism, for example, there will be a higher level of demand for staff in the summer than in the winter.

● **Structural unemployment** – The demand for labour depends on the demand for goods and the demand for goods is continually changing. This will affect the labour market and the structure of industry will constantly be changing with some firms contracting and others expanding.

In theory, workers should move from contracting firms and industries into expanding ones, but this does not always happen. The number of jobs being lost in contracting industries may not be matched by the number of new jobs being created in expanding industries.

Workers may not have the skills required to be employed in the jobs created in expanding industries. Even if a hundred job losses at a coalmine were to be matched by a hundred new jobs at a local supermarket, the unemployed workers are unlikely to take up all of these vacancies.

The new jobs being created may not be in the geographical areas where unemployment is particularly high. As a result people will have to move if they are to find work. They may be unwilling to make this move, however, because of family and social ties. High house prices in the more prosperous areas of the country will also discourage movement.

● **Technological unemployment** – Over the years there have been continuous improvements in methods of production. This has mainly taken the form of labour-saving technology. Investment does not always result in a loss of jobs as new methods of production often reduce costs and increase demand. Recent advances in automation and robot technology have tended to result in unemployment despite increasing demand. Those jobs that remain are often highly specialised, involving the repair, maintenance and operation of the new equipment.

SEASONAL UNEMPLOYMENT   THE 'UNEMPLOYABLE'   STRUCTURAL UNEMPLOYMENT

● **Cyclical unemployment** – If we study the pattern of demand in an economy over a number of years, it is possile to trace a regular pattern or cycle. During a period of slump with low levels of demand, there will be high levels of unemployment. During a 'boom', with high levels of demand, unemployment will be much lower.

● **Residual unemployment** – There will always be some people who are either voluntarily unemployed, making no attempt to find work, or are unemployable because of serious mental or physical disability.

● **Hidden unemployment** – If we use official unemployment statistics to measure the extent of unemployment, we must recognise that the figures may be misleading. They exclude, for example, housewives who may be seeking work but do not register as unemployed. Also excluded are people on government training schemes such as YTS who are not in permanent, full time employment.

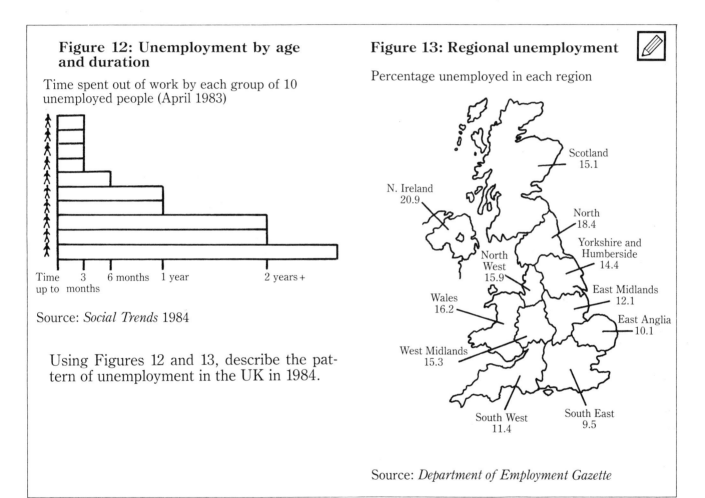

Figure 12: Unemployment by age and duration

Time spent out of work by each group of 10 unemployed people (April 1983)

Time up to | 3 months | 6 months | 1 year | 2 years +

Source: *Social Trends* 1984

Using Figures 12 and 13, describe the pattern of unemployment in the UK in 1984.

Figure 13: Regional unemployment

Percentage unemployed in each region

Scotland 15.1
N. Ireland 20.9
North 18.4
Yorkshire and Humberside 14.4
North West 15.9
East Midlands 12.1
Wales 16.2
East Anglia 10.1
West Midlands 15.3
South West 11.4
South East 9.5

Source: *Department of Employment Gazette*

Part 2   Political considerations

At one time, government activity was limited to financing defence spending. Gradually, however, it has been recognised that the government needs to play a much more active role in the economy. The main aims of government policy are:

● To provide goods and services, such as defence and law and order, which it would be difficult to provide on an individual basis.

● To provide a range of services where it is thought that individuals may not make decisions that are in their own best interests, eg education and health.

● To protect the rights of the individual, eg freedom of speech.

● To reduce the social costs of economic activity such as pollution and congestion.

● To regulate the economy to ensure :

a   high levels of employment
b   stable prices, ie no inflation
c   a sound balance of payments
d   steady economic growth and increasing living standards
e   a more equal distribution of income.

Government objectives are not always compatible. Should, for example, people be free not to wear a seat belt if the result is that society has to pay the cost of hospital bills for people injured in car accidents? Should the government introduce policies to increase employment if the result is rising prices?

Government economic policy

There are a number of different ways in which the government can influence the economy. We normally place these policies into three categories.

Monetary policy

This involves control of the monetary system by the government and includes control of the banking system. This control is intended to influence the amount of money that banks lend, who they lend to and the price they charge (interest rates).

The term **monetarist** has been used to describe those economists who emphasise the need to deal with inflation as the government's first priority and who recommend monetary policy to achieve this. They argue that inflation is caused by too much money and therefore too much demand in the economy. If bank credit is reduced, then this will reduce demand and hence inflation.

Fiscal policy

This involves attempts to control demand by adjustments in government spending and taxation. The government is able to spend more than it raises in taxes by borrowing from the public or from financial institutions. As govern-

ment spending is a major part of demand in the economy, if they increase their spending then this will increase demand. People will need to be employed to produce the extra goods demanded and thus unemployment is reduced.

Changes in taxation will have an effect on the amount of money people have to spend. Low levels of tax leave people with more money to spend. Demand increases and unemployment falls.

Direct policy

Both monetary and fiscal policy are aimed at regulating the economy through their effect on demand. The government can, however, act directly to influence the economy. It can impose controls on rent, prices and wages for example. Regional policy and incomes policy are the best post-war examples of direct controls.

> Government policies are constantly changing. You should, however, make a point of keeping up to date with changes in policy. One way is to keep a 'scrap book' of newspaper articles or to organise a weekly debate, where one member of the class reports on news items which would be of interest to the businessman (and the student of business studies).

Government spending and taxation

We saw earlier that fiscal policy is one way in which the government can influence the economy. This involves adjustments to government spending and taxation.

The Budget

The government's plans for expenditure and taxation are set out each year in the **Budget**. In his Budget speech in the House of Commons in March or April of each year, the Chancellor of the Exchequer gives a statement of government income and spending for the previous financial year and gives estimates for the year ahead. He or she will also review the progress of the economy and explain the policies which the government intends to use to overcome economic problems.

Figure 14: Public money 1987–88

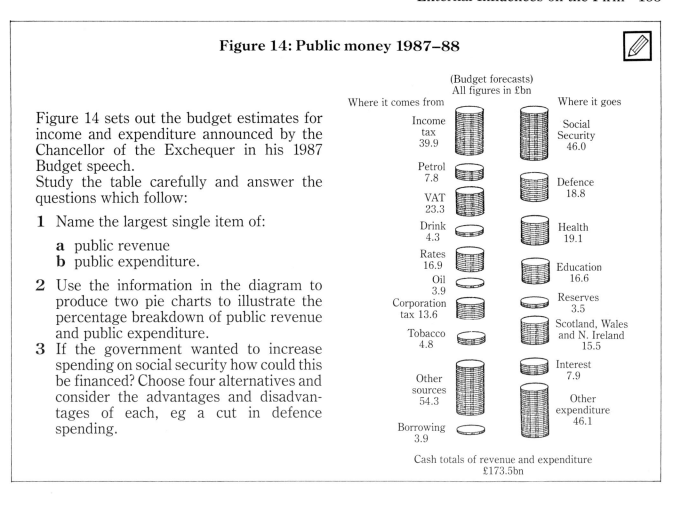

(Budget forecasts)
All figures in £bn

Where it comes from

Income tax	39.9
Petrol	7.8
VAT	23.3
Drink	4.3
Rates	16.9
Oil	3.9
Corporation tax	13.6
Tobacco	4.8
Other sources	54.3
Borrowing	3.9

Where it goes

Social Security	46.0
Defence	18.8
Health	19.1
Education	16.6
Reserves	3.5
Scotland, Wales and N. Ireland	15.5
Interest	7.9
Other expenditure	46.1

Cash totals of revenue and expenditure
£173.5bn

Figure 14 sets out the budget estimates for income and expenditure announced by the Chancellor of the Exchequer in his 1987 Budget speech.

Study the table carefully and answer the questions which follow:

1 Name the largest single item of:

a public revenue
b public expenditure.

2 Use the information in the diagram to produce two pie charts to illustrate the percentage breakdown of public revenue and public expenditure.

3 If the government wanted to increase spending on social security how could this be financed? Choose four alternatives and consider the advantages and disadvantages of each, eg a cut in defence spending.

Taxation

Taxation finances over 80% of government expenditure. The rest comes from sources such as rent, interest and borrowing. There are many different taxes. Some are levied on the income of an individual or a firm, some on expenditure and others on capital or wealth.

Taxes can be described as direct taxes or indirect taxes. **Direct taxes** are those that cannot be passed on. The person handing over the tax cannot pass the cost on to somebody else. A good example would be income tax.

Indirect taxes can be passed on. VAT, for example, is paid by manufacturers and retailers, but is passed on to customers in the form of higher prices.

Most taxes are paid to one of two collecting authorities. These are the **Inland Revenue** which collects income tax and corporation tax, and the **Customs and Excise Department** which collects VAT and taxes on petrol, alcohol and tobacco.

Some taxes are described as **progressive**, that is they take into account a person's ability to pay and are linked to income. A progressive tax will take a larger proportion of a rich person's income than a poorer person's income. Income tax, with its different rates for higher income groups, is one example of a progressive tax.

A **regressive** tax, on the other hand, is one which takes no account of ability to pay. It takes a larger proportion of a poor person's income than it does of a rich person's income. A TV license would be an example of a regressive tax.

The main taxes on business are as follows:

● **Corporation tax** – This is a tax paid by companies on their profits.
● **Income tax** – Although income tax is mainly paid by private individuals, sole traders and partnerships are taxed at income tax rates rather than at corporation tax rates.
● **Value added tax** – This is payable at each stage of production on the value added by the business. The tax is normally passed on to customers in the form of higher prices.
● **Capital gains tax** – This is a tax on gains made through the sale of assets, eg if a company sells land for a higher price than it was bought for, then capital gains tax is payable on the profit earned.

● **Excise duties** – These are additional taxes on top of VAT placed on certain goods, eg alcoholic drink, tobacco and petrol.

● **Custom duties** – These are additional taxes on imported goods.

● **Employer's national insurance contributions** – These have been described as a 'tax on employment'. They are a contribution made by employers towards the National Insurance system.

Find out the current rates for the following taxes:

a Corporation tax.
b Income tax.
c Value added tax.

Pressure groups

We mentioned earlier how the number of groups representing interests of consumers has grown in recent years. Any group of people who get together to promote a particular interest is known as a **pressure group**. Many of us are members of pressure groups of one form or another or we at least sympathise with their aims.

They include the following:

● **Trade unions** – They represent the interests of workers within a particular industry or with a particular skill.
● **R A C** – This is an association representing the interests of motorists.
● **Friends of the Earth** – Representing those who care about the environment.

The main aim of pressure groups is to influence government policy by making the public and politicians aware of their views. This can be done in many ways including marches and petitions, 'lobbying' individual MPs, publicity stunts and the use of public relations firms to obtain press coverage of their activities. Some, notably animal welfare groups, may resort to illegal activities to make their point.

Pressure groups often resort to extreme measures to obtain publicity.

As well as attempting to influence governments, pressure groups may also try to influence businesses. The three types of pressure group likely to exert the greatest influence are trade unions, consumer groups and environmental groups.

Business can itself lobby the government to promote its interests. This has increasingly been the case as more and more legislation affecting industry passes through Parliament. Large multinational companies may have their own units with the tasks of keeping in touch with proposed legislation in both the British and European parliaments and building up good relationships with MPs and civil servants.

Other large companies may have an MP on their board of directors or retain an MP as an advisor. Another alternative is for a company to employ outside consultants who specialise in parliamentary lobbying. Smaller firms tend to rely on the CBI or on the many trade associations that exist to promote their interests.

> Divide into two groups. The first, representing the anti-smoking group ASH, should devise a newspaper campaign to demand a total ban on tobacco advertising. The second group, representing the Tobacco Advisory Council, should devise a campaign to prevent any further restriction on the industry.

Part 3   Technological considerations

Every aspect of industry and commerce is affected by technological change. It leads to new and improved products and new production methods. It also plays a major part in improving the efficiency of administration and management.

Technological progress is moving faster today than at any time in history. The main advances have come in the area of micro-processors, but major developments have also taken place in nuclear technology and fibre optics.

Microprocessors have become increasingly minaturised and cheaper to produce. As an example, the equivalent of today's pocket calculator would have been the size of a suitcase 20 years ago and would have cost over one hundred times the price.

Figure 15: The size of a computer with the same power as a human brain

1950	London
1960	The Albert Hall
1970	A double decker bus
1980	A taxi
1990	A television set

Source: *The Sunday Times*

A range of new products and production techniques have been developed as a result of these improvements. They include calculators and digital watches. New techniques include robots and automated production lines. In addition, there have been new methods of information storage, retrieval and communication.

> **Technological change – Some key issues**
>
> **Favourable**
>
> - New products, eg digital watches.
> - Improvement to existing products, eg micro-processors in cars.
> - Better management information, eg micro-computers in the office.
> - Better customer service, eg stock control.
> - Better quality control, eg automated inspection.
> - New methods of production, eg robots.
> - Greater job satisfaction, eg routine office filing is computerised.
> - Increased international competitiveness, eg lower production costs.
>
> **Unfavourable**
>
> - Expense – a high turnover is needed to justify the cost of development.
> - Risk – products quickly become obsolete.
> - Skills become redundant – machines may take over some skilled jobs, eg newspaper typesetting.
> - Health and safety, eg visual display units (VDU screens) have been criticised as being bad for the eyesight.
> - Training – this has not always kept pace with change.
> - Alienation – the workplace is even more de-humanised.

The commercial implications of new technology are great and firms need to exploit the new technologies to ensure that they do not lose out to foreign competitors. They need to develop and produce new products to meet rapidly changing demand. In addition, existing products have to be modified to take advantage of new technology and production methods need to be changed to increase productivity and to remain competitive.

There are problems attached to new technology, however. The pace of change means that risks are high. Products can quickly become out of date (obsolete) as new, more sophisticated ones take their place. The cost of the research and development needed to keep pace with advances in technology is also high. In addition, there are social problems with rapid technological change. Whilst society benefits from new, better and cheaper products, there may be a cost in terms of employment.

Technology and employment

The effect of new technology on employment can be both favourable and unfavourable.

There will obviously be job losses as many products such as clockwork watches become obsolete. New products will also be more simpli-fied than the ones they replace, requiring fewer components and less labour. This simplification can be seen in household items such as TV sets, where printed circuits have replaced valves. To give one example, Singer makes a sewing machine in which one micro-processor has replaced 350 mechanical parts.

New production techniques also cut down on manpower and this can be seen in both manual and white collar employment. Automation has replaced shop floor workers and electronic office equipment has reduced the need for clerks and typists.

Set against this, however, is the fact that new products create new demand. This can clearly be seen with pocket calculators, video recorders and computer equipment.

Better quality products will lead to increased sales as will lower production costs. A whole new industry has also been created in the design, manufacture and maintenance of new technology equipment.

It is debateable if these will balance each other out. Previous predictions of mass unemployment as a result of mechanisation have proved groundless. It has been argued that micro-computers had the effect of creating more jobs than they replaced for the first 15 years. The balance would now seem to have moved towards job losses, but it must be remembered that the cost of not introducing new technology may have been even

Access to sales and records

Portable and fixed terminals

Telephone links to all departments

Up-to-date information from Prestel

Technology in the office

greater. If we cannot compete with overseas producers on price and quality, then UK producers will lose their markets and their employees will lose their jobs.

Production technology

As well as its role in the office, new technology can improve production on the shop floor. There are a number of benefits to be gained:

● Control over the movement of materials to make sure that they are available at the right place and at the right time.
● Accurate control over variable processes such as temperature, which has to be altered at certain critical times during production.
● Simple processes such as shaping, cutting and moulding can be automated.

● The assembly of components can be carried out by robots.
● Quality control processes such as inspection and testing can be carried out quickly and accurately.
● Production can be organised more efficiently. This includes better stock control, better design etc.

The management of technological change

New technology may be seen as a threat by the workforce and its introduction must be carefully managed. Employees may fear the loss of their jobs or being moved to a new job. Their skills and

---

Study the two photographs and answer the questions which follow:

1 Describe briefly the two scenes illustrated.

2 In which factory would you prefer to work? Explain your answer.

experience may become worthless and their status lowered. This anxiety may result in a resistance to change.

Managers will need to overcome this resistance. One way will be to involve the workers from the beginning in planning the introduction of new technology. As much information as possible should be provided, as rumours quickly spread when insufficient information is available.

Reassurance needs to be offered about the future. If the nature of employment is going to change then workers will need to be told about what they are going to be required to do and the training and support they are going to be given.

Where job losses are inevitable redundancies should be on the basis of 'last in first out'. Compensation will need to be paid to those who are made redundant.

Part 4 Social considerations

Business is an important part of modern society. It influences individuals and groups within society and at the same time it is influenced by them.

Population

People are both workers and consumers. A study of the size and structure of the population is therefore essential in understanding the factors which influence business activity.

The supply of labour is determined by the size of the population and by its age structure, occupational distribution and geographical distribution.

The total population
The total size of the population in a country is determined by three main factors.

- **The birth rate** – This is usually measured as the number of live births per thousand population. The birth rate has tended to fall because of later marriages, smaller family sizes and an increase in birth control.
- **The death rate** – This is measured as the number of deaths per thousand population. The death rate has also tended to fall due to improvements in health, nutrition and working conditions, which increase life expectancy.
- **Net migration** – This is the difference between the number of foreign nationals entering the country (immigrants) and the number of UK nationals leaving the country (emigrants).

The working population

We can see from Figure 16 that, of a total population of 33.5m of working age, ie between 16 and 65 for men and between 16 and 60 for women, 26.5m are in the working population.

The unemployed are included in the working population, as they are available for employment and would work if there were suitable vacancies available. The percentage of the population who are working or seeking work is known as the **activity rate**. Factors which account for the difference between those of working age and those who are in the working population include:

- Those in full-time education.
- Housepersons or those with other domestic commitments, such as caring for dependants.
- The severely handicapped.
- Those who retire early (occupational pensioners).
- Those who have no need to work.

Implications of an increasing population

- An increase in the labour force.
- Increased demand for food, shelter, clothing etc.
- Increased imports if demand is not met by home produced goods.
- Increased investment as a result of the increased demand for goods and services.
- The pattern of demand changes, eg a rising birth rate leads to more demand for goods used by children.
- Social costs of population growth, including congestion and pollution.

Implications of a declining population

- A falling labour supply.
- A fall in demand.
- If caused by a fall in the birth rate, the average age of the population will change.

Figure 16: Labour force numbers

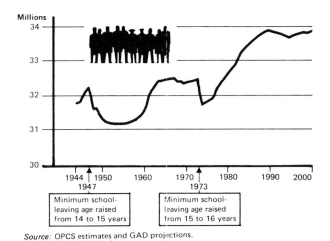

Millions

- 34
- 33
- 32
- 31
- 30

1944 | 1950   1960   1970 | 1980   1990   2000
1947   1973

Minimum school-leaving age raised from 14 to 15 years

Minimum school-leaving age raised from 15 to 16 years

Source: OPCS estimates and GAD projections.

Labour Force numbers

THERE are 33½ million people in Great Britain of working age. 26½ million are in a paid job or seeking one — four million more than in 1951, and one million more than in 1975.

In 1976 the population of working age was almost the same as in 1944 (31.9 million) although it had varied substantially meanwhile. In the late 1970s and early 1980s the combined effects of the 1960s' baby boom and the drop in retirements caused by low birth rates during the First World War led to a marked increase. There were annual rises of 0.2 million or more in 1978, 1979, 1983 and 1984. By 1984 the population of working age had risen 1.6 million above the 1976 total.

To add to the problems of finding employment for the extra people of working age is the fact that a higher proportion of them are nowadays in the labour force — that is, in work or actively seeking it.

Between 1951 and 1984 the number of men remained around 15-16 million but the number of women in, or looking for, work increased from seven million to nearly 11 million.

Over the next few years the numbers reaching school-leaving age will decline, but so will retirements and other exits from the labour force. The combined effect is that the population of working age will rise by around 0.5 million to a little over 33.9 million in 1989, and will then remain broadly unchanged until at least the year 2000.

Source: *Employment News* March 1985

1   What has happened to the size of the working population since 1951?

2   Explain the effect of the following on the size of the working population:

   a   The 1960's baby boom.
   b   The drop in retirements.
   c   The increase in the number of women seeking work.

3   What is expected to happen to the working population up to the year 2000?

4   Why do you think that the number of women in work or looking for work, from 1951 to 1984, increased from 7 m to nearly 11 m?

The growth in the UK labour force over the past century has, in part, been due to an increase in the overall size of the population. The most important factor, however, has been increased activity rates. The reason for this has been the increase in the number of women working.

The geographical distribution of the population

Looking at total population alone can be misleading. The population is not evenly spread throughout the whole country. There are some areas which are far more densely populated than others. There have also been marked shifts in the population between different areas in recent years. These changes have great significance when considering the unemployment and social implications of population changes.

The bulk of the country's population still live in urban areas with the greatest concentrations in Greater London, the West Midlands, West Yorkshire, South East Lancashire, Merseyside, Tyneside and Clydeside.

Despite this concentration of population in the urban areas and the continuing drift from North to South, reflecting the decline in the traditional industries, there has been a trend for a movement away from the cities towards the areas surrounding the towns (the suburbs) and the country.

As Figure 17 illustrates, the faster growing areas include East Anglia and the South-West.

Figure 17: Population by type of area – Great Britain

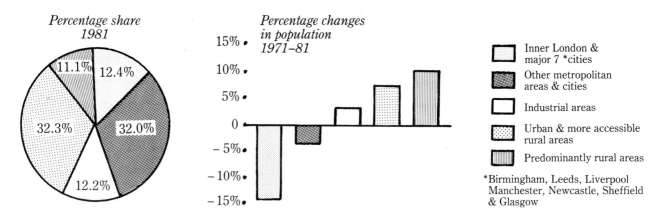

Source: *Regional Trends* 1984

The occupational distribution of the population

We saw earlier how the distribution of the working population has changed over the years. The primary industries have declined to the point where only about 3% of the working population are employed in this sector. The decline in employment in manufacturing and construction (the secondary sector) has not been quite so marked, but the pace of change has increased in recent years, as the UK imports more and more of its manufactured goods. Technological advance has also led to falling employment in manufacturing industry.

The main increases in employment have been in the tertiary or service sector. The most rapidly expanding service industries include financial services, public administration, education and distribution.

Population and demand

Although only a portion of the population are producers, the whole population are consumers. The ratio of the working population (the producers) to the total population (the consumers) is known as the **dependency ratio**. The old and the young are obviously dependent on the working population to provide them with the goods and services they need. The larger the number of people in the dependent age ranges, (below 16 and over 65), the greater the burden on the working population.

Figure 18: The welfare burden

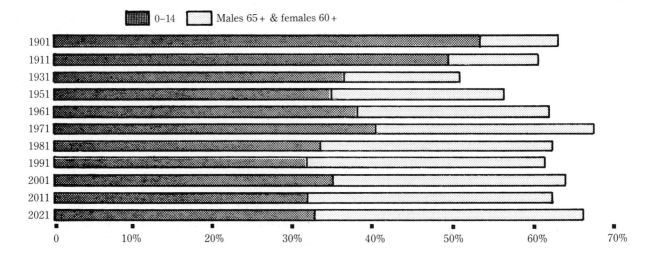

As consumers, the population demand the output of goods and services from both the public and private sector. The size and composition of the population will therefore determine the pattern of demand.

The government needs information about the population and future trends in population growth if it is to plan for the provision of such services as health and education as well as planning output in the energy, housing and transport industries.

Taking education as an example, the government, together with the local authorities, will need to know the birth rate in order to be able to predict the need for places in primary schools and later for secondary schools and further education.

> Describe the type of information about the size and structure of the population which would be of interest to:
>
> **a** The National Health Service.
> **b** The housebuilding industry.
> **c** A record company.
> **d** The Department of Education and Science.

The age distribution of the population

Apart from the total size of the population, the most important factor influencing demand will be the age distribution of the population. The decline in the birth rate and the death rate over time has led to an ageing population. In 1901, the under 15 age group made up one third of the population. By 1981, this proportion had fallen to a fifth. In contrast, the proportion of the population over retirement age had risen from 6% to 20% over the same period.

Figure 19: UK population pyramid (1981)

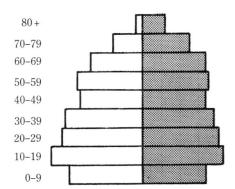

The age distribution of the population is usually illustrated by means of **population pyramids** such as those below. These show the proportion of the population in each age group and clearly illustrate an ageing population.

> **Compact Discs**
>
> Major changes are taking place in the music industry. The compact disc is creating a new boom in sales with record companies re-releasing many records using this new medium. The policy of the music industry is being influenced by factors other than new technology, however.
>
> It is estimated that by 1996 the UK will have the smallest teenage population since 1961. This has led the industry to shift its focus to an older audience. The biggest market is now the so called 'baby boomers' or Beatles generation. Those who were part of the post war baby boom and who where the teenage market of the 1960s.
>
> This shift in the market can be seen in the popularity of artists whose music is clearly aimed at the 'older market'.
>
> **1** How is the music industry affected by the age distribution of the population?
> **2** Taking the current top ten records in the charts, carry out a survey amongst friends, relatives and neighbours noting their age group and preferences.
>
> Do any patterns emerge linking age with the type of music preferred?

Lifestyle

Changes in the way people live will have an effect on business. Improved education is one change which has influenced firms. Improved education increases productivity, but also tends to result in more school leavers wanting to take up white-collar jobs rather than manual work. The government is actively trying to encourage more school leavers to enter manufacturing industry and is placing greater emphasis on technology training in schools.

Improved standards of education have also meant that the public are more likely to question the claims of advertisers and demand value for money. More and more consumer groups have emerged to protect the interests of the public against the power of 'big business'.

Increased living standards have resulted in changing patterns of demand, with goods which would have been considered as luxuries to one generation, being seen as necessities to the next. This is clearly illustrated in Figure 20. Increased access to television, the cinema and foreign travel have also changed people's tastes. Fashions and eating habits have become more 'cosmopolitan' with overseas influences, particularly from Europe, becoming stronger.

Figure 20: UK lifestyle by ownership (%)

	1957	1987
House	33	63
Car	24	61
Television set	66	97
Washing machine	34	85
Fridge	15	98
Vacuum cleaner	65	96

Source: *Industry sources*

The social costs and benefits of industry

Business activity imposes costs on the community but also creates benefits.

The main costs that result from business activity are pollution and congestion. An extreme case of pollution can be seen in Japan before anti-pollution legislation, where Tokyo pedestrians had to wear masks over their noses to protect them from pollution in the air.

In recent years, international pollution issues have become increasingly important. Acid rain is said to have destroyed 30% of West Germany's forests. The ozone layer, which protects the earth from the harmful rays of the sun, has become eroded by the constant use of aerosol sprays. Tests have shown that heart and kidney complaints result from the high level of lead in petrol used in cars. Some modern cars are now designed to run on lead-free petrol and the government has taken action to reduce the price of lead-free petrol through taxation.

Congestion is an added problem. Much of our road system was built at a time when car ownership was limited and there were no heavy lorries. Even the relatively modern motorway network has problems coping with today's volume of traffic. Ring roads have to be built to reduce damage to buildings where major roads pass through small towns and villages. Major bottlenecks occur when roads are too narrow to handle the volume of peak hour traffic or where road repairs result in holdups.

The results of the greater volume of traffic are higher pollution, longer travelling times and increased risk of accidents as tempers get frayed and motorists take unnecessary risks.

Because of the important role they play, firms have a responsibility to society and to the community in which they operate, as well as a responsibility to their shareholders and customers. Sometimes these responsibilities are enforced by

---

Back to the future as city traffic crawls along

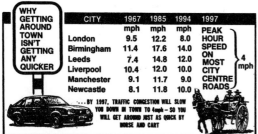

WHY GETTING AROUND TOWN ISN'T GETTING ANY QUICKER

CITY	1967 mph	1985 mph	1994 mph	1997
London	9.5	12.2	8.0	
Birmingham	11.4	17.6	14.0	PEAK HOUR SPEED ON MOST CITY CENTRE ROADS
Leeds	7.4	14.8	12.0	
Liverpool	10.4	12.0	10.0	
Manchester	9.1	11.7	9.0	
Newcastle	8.1	11.8	10.0	

4 mph

'...BY 1997, TRAFFIC CONGESTION WILL SLOW YOU DOWN IN TOWN TO 4mph — SO YOU WILL GET AROUND JUST AS QUICK BY HORSE AND CART'

By MICHAEL KEMP
Motoring Correspondent

RUSH HOUR drivers in Britain's cities may be forced down to the horse and cart speeds of 100 years ago.

And that could mean crawling along at 4 mph.

The warning comes from the British Road Federation, which says that today's speeds — ranging from 11.7 mph in Manchester to 17.6 in Birmingham — are the fastest possible on existing roads.

The future, it says in a report to the Government, looks decidedly slower.

'In London, the average rush

'HORSE AND CART' PACE IS LOOMING

hour speed will be down to 8 mph by 1994 and 5 mph in the inner-city boroughs — almost back to horse-cart speed,' the federation says.

'Britain cannot go on fiddling with existing road space, because capacity has been reached. Assuming normal traffic growth, there will be horrendous jams by the mid-90s unless there is action now.'

The pressure group says the Government, already committed

to reviving city centres, 'has got to develop new roads, or commercial centres will crawl to a near halt.

Rush hour speeds have been going up since 1967. But, the federation says, they are now set to drop again.

The figures are: London 9.5mph in 1967, 12.2 in 1985, 8 forecast for 1994; Birmingham 11.4, 17.6, 14; Leeds 7.4, 14.8, 12; Liverpool 10.4, 12, 10; Manchester 9.1, 11.7, 9; Newcastle 8.1, 11.8, 10.

Yesterday the BRF said: 'Leeds traffic has been speeded by easy reach to a motorway.

'All the fiddling with old roads, by introducing new restrictions, is not going to stave off falling commuter speeds.

'You must be able to drive through by car.'

Source: The *Daily Mail* June 29 1987

1   According to the writer, what is happening to traffic speeds on city centre roads?

2   How can the problem of rush hour congestion be eased?

3   What is the effect on business of increased congestion on the roads?

legislation such as the Health and Safety at Work Act, but many firms recognise their responsibilities without being forced to.

These responsibilities include:

- the payment of a fair wage
- adequate working conditions for employees
- welfare and recreational facilities for workers
- the minimising of noise and environmental pollution.

Pressure groups have made businesses even more aware of their public image and firms must increasingly take into account the effect that their decisions have on the workforce and on the community at large. There may appear to be a conflict between the desire to make profits for shareholders and the desire to provide good pay and working conditions. This may not always be the case, however. A concern for the environment is good for public relations and care for the firm's staff increases loyalty and productivity. Profits can therefore be increased by taking a socially responsible attitude.

Measuring costs and benefits

We have seen that the activities of firms produce both costs and benefits. The government attempts to reduce the costs by setting standards for pollution and by enforcing health regulations. **Cost benefit analysis** has also been used for major public sector projects, such as the siting of the third London airport, in order to make sure that social costs and benefits are taken into account in addition to financial costs and benefits.

Cost benefit analysis involves attempting to put a money value on social costs and benefits so that the true cost of a project can be calculated. A well known example is the building of the Victoria underground line in London. The cost of building this new line was much greater than the extra revenue which it was expected to produce. When the benefits, such as shorter journey times for commuters and reduced conjestion on the roads, were added to the revenue figure, however, the new line was seen as being worthwhile.

National Westminster Bank PLC
Statement by the Chairman Lord Boardman

We are very conscious of our social responsibilities. Each year, as part of our Community Service Programme, National Westminster Bank deploys around one per cent of profits before taxes to help a wide range of social causes and concerns to achieve their praiseworthy objectives. We also release selected members of staff to work for varying periods within a number of voluntary service agencies.

In 1984 we allocated £5.1 m to these activities.

As employers, our policy is to provide job opportunities regardless of race, creed, colour and sex. During 1984 over 3,000 new entrants joined us. Additionally, in support of the government's Youth Training Scheme, 500 young people are currently under training with us.

The strength and stability of the National Westminster Bank Group are considerable by any standards and it is in the national interest as much as our own that we should remain strong. We make a substantial contribution to the nation, not only in the form of overseas earnings, but also through the rates and taxes that the bank and its employees pay, and in the support we continue to give British business, in times both of recession and of growth.

Boardman

With the help of the extract above, discuss the ways in which a company, such as National Westminster Bank, can benefit the community.

Figure 21: Map of the A975 to Millhaven

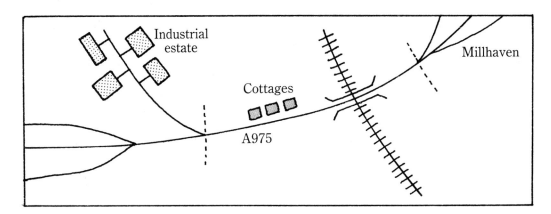

The A975 is a busy trunk road but one stretch, near the town of Millhaven, is a major bottleneck at peak travelling times. The government is considering proposals to make the busiest stretch of the road into a dual carriageway. A public enquiry is held at which the following information is presented:

● Average journey times would be reduced by 10 minutes.
● It is estimated that there would be 20 less accidents per year.
● The road widening scheme will cost £1.5m with an additional annual maintenance cost of £20,000.
● Fuel consumption would fall as a result of higher average speeds and pollution would be reduced.
● Compulsory purchase orders would have to be placed on three cottages which face onto the existing road and would have to be knocked down to make room for the road widening.
● Over the 12 months of the building project, there will be considerable delays on the road.
● Industry may be attracted to the recently completed industrial estate if the traffic problems can be eased.

In the light of this evidence, and any other factors which you feel are important, discuss whether you would support the proposal or not? Explain your answer.

Part 5   Legal considerations

There are many laws which govern the relationship between people and organisations. The main areas which concern us in studying business are as follows:

● Laws relating to the setting up and conduct of organisations.
● Laws relating to the organisation's relationships with customers.
● Laws relating to the organisation's relationship with employees.

Setting up an organisation

There is little legislation relating to the activities of sole traders and partnerships as these organisations do not have a separate legal identity. Most legislation relates to the formation and conduct of limited companies.

Much of this legislation is contained in the 1948 Companies Act but this Act has been revised on a number of occasions. We have already dealt with most of the issues relating to the setting up of a company in unit 2.

The conduct of the organisation

The main legislation influencing the conduct of firms is **competition policy**. This policy deals with monopolies, mergers and restrictive practices.

A **monopoly** is a situation where there are no close substitutes for the goods which a firm produces. This could allow the firm to exploit the consumer by charging high prices or offering a poor service to customers who cannot go to another supplier. Electricity supply can be seen as one example, although there is still some competition from other fuels such as gas.

Some of the 'natural monopolies', such as electricity supply, are in the public sector, but the policy of privatisation is designed to transfer more of these businesses into the private sector. Safeguards therefore have to be provided to protect the interests of consumers.

Increased competition is one safeguard and this has been achieved in the case of British Telecom, for example, by removing their monopoly in supplying telephone equipment. An organisation has also been set up to monitor complaints from Telecom customers (OFTEL).

Other checks on both private and public sector firms are the **Office of Fair Trading** and the **Monopolies and Mergers Commission**. Their job is to ensure that firms with a large share of the market do not exploit their position and act against the public interest.

The Office of Fair Trading was set up in 1973 and its role includes looking into proposed mergers and investigating industry and the professions, with the aim of encouraging competition and attempting to break down restrictive practices. 300 investigations were carried out in 1986 alone.

A **restrictive practice** is any activity by a firm which has the effect of reducing competition. Such activities include price fixing and the formation of cartels, (groups of firms who get together to fix output or other conditions of sale).

Major legislation on restrictive practices was passed in 1956 and the **Restrictive Practices Court** was set up. Any restrictive practice is seen as being against the public interest and therefore illegal unless the Restrictive Practices Court can be convinced that the benefits from a particular practice outweigh the costs. If, for example, it could be shown that safety standards would suffer as the results of price competition then a price fixing agreement may be allowed to continue.

Further legislation in 1964 dealt specifically with **resale price maintenance**. This was the practice whereby manufactures fixed the price at which their products could be sold. This practice was made illegal with the exceptions of books and pharmaceuticals. For all other products, manufacturers can recommend a price but cannot enforce it.

The following arguments were put forward by Cadbury Bros. Limited in an attempt to justify to the Restrictive Practices Court a policy of fixing the resale price of chocolate and sugar confectionery.

● Supermarkets will only cut prices on a small number of selected lines.
● Smaller retailers will not be able to compete and will go out of business.
● Specialist sweet shops will be hardest hit and the number of outlets offering a wide range of confectionery will therefore fall.
● Closures will reduce overall sales as the industry relies heavily on 'impulse' buying.

Do you think that Cadbury Bros. should have been allowed to continue fixing resale prices? Explain your answer.

(This exercise could be organised as a role play with Cadbury's case being presented to the Restrictive Practices Court who then present their verdict.)

The Monopolies and Merger Commission can be traced back to 1948. One of its tasks is to investigate certain mergers. These are mergers involving large firms or where a monopoly would be created. As with restrictive practices, a merger will be investigated to see if it is in the public interest.

Figure 22: Major MMC reports into take-overs and mergers (1980–1986)

Companies involved	Decision
1980 Blue Circle/Armitage Shanks	For
1981 Lonrho/House of Fraser	Against
1982 Nabisco Brands/Huntley and Palmer	For
1983 GUS/Empire Stores	Against
1984 P&O/Trafalgar House	For
1983 Lonrho/House of Fraser	For
1986 British Telecom/Mitel	For
1986 GEC/Plessey	Against

Role play

A merger is proposed between two major high street banks and the proposal has been referred to the Monopolies and Mergers Commission.

Divide into three groups:
● **Group 1** – This group represents the Office of Fair Trading and should prepare a report demonstrating how the proposed merger could be against the public interest.
● **Group 2** – This group represents the banks and should prepare a report demonstrating the benefits of the merger.
These reports will then be presented to:
● **Group 3** – This group represents the Monopolies and Mergers Commission, who will consider the reports and make a decision on the proposal, setting out their reasons for reaching their decision.

Consumer Law

As well as its responsibility for encouraging competition, the Office of Fair Trading (OFT) also has the task of collecting information on all consumer problems and trading matters.

The Director General of Fair Trading presides over the OFT and has the following duties:

● To publish information for the guidance of shoppers and traders.
● To encourage trade organisations to prepare codes of practice.
● To propose new laws to help fair trading.
● To prosecute those who break consumer legislation.

Amongst the OFT publications available free from your local trading standards department, consumer advice centre or citizen's advice bureau are the following:

● *Fair Deal* – a comprehensive shoppers' guide to consumer rights.
● *How to put things right* – a guide to your legal rights and where to get help and advice.

It would be useful to obtain copies of these publications to include in your files.

Sale of Goods Act 1893

Most of our consumer rights are set out in the Sale of Goods Act 1893, amended by the Supply of Goods (Implied Terms) Act 1973. When you buy a good, you enter into a legal contract with the seller. As soon as your offer to buy a good is accepted then the seller and not the manufacturer must deal with any complaints you have to make. The seller must ensure that the goods that are sold are satisfactory:

● They must be of merchantable quality, ie fit for their normal purpose. A new item must not be damaged or broken and it must work properly.
● They must be fit for any particular purpose, ie if you have specifically asked for a tube of glue which will mend china, then the glue must do this.
● They must be as described by the manufacturer or seller, eg a pair of shoes described on the box as 'real leather' should not be made of plastic.

The 1973 Act ensured that these rights are not removed by getting customers to sign guarantees offering less protection than was already available under the 1893 legislation.

The legislation does not cover goods which are sold privately or where defects are pointed out to you. Particular care should therefore be taken in buying second-hand goods which, although still covered by the Act, would not reasonably be expected to be of the same quality.

Food and Drugs Act 1955

This makes it a criminal offence to undertake any of the following:

● Sell food or drink which is unfit for consumption.
● Wrongly describe the contents of any food.
● Mislead people about the nature, quality or nutritional value of food.

Consumer Protection Act 1961 (Amended and replaced by Consumer Safety Act 1978)

Under this Act the government has the power to control the safety of particular types of goods to reduce the risk of death or personal injury. (This includes the composition, labelling and packaging of goods.)

Regulations cover products such as oil heaters, night dresses, toys, electric blankets, pencils and crayons, baby's dummies, prams and pushchairs. It is a criminal offence to sell goods which do not comply with these regulations.

Weights and Measures Act 1963

This Act makes it a criminal offence to give short weight or short measure. The weight and/or volume of most prepacked goods must be accurately marked on the packet. This Act also states that certain products can only be sold in specific quantities, eg milk.

Trade Descriptions Act 1968 and 1972

It is a criminal offence to give a false or misleading description of a good or service. A claim that a watch is 'Swiss' or 'waterproof' must therefore be true. This legislation resulted in a significant change in advertising with 'shock proof' watches becoming 'shock resistant' and 'waterproof' raincoats becoming 'shower resistant'.

This Act also covers bogus sales. If a price is shown as being marked down from say £5 to £3.50 in a sale, then it must have been on sale at the higher price for at least 28 consecutive days over the previous six months. If this is not the case then it should be clearly indicated.

Since 1982 it has also been required that 'country of origin' labels should appear on all foreign produced clothes, textiles, footwear, electrical equipment and cutlery.

Unsolicited Goods and Services Act 1971

This makes it a criminal offence to demand payment for goods which were not ordered. This relates particularly to goods which are sent through the post.

Fair Trading Act 1973

It was this Act which established the Office of Fair Trading. The Consumer Affairs Division of the OFT looks after the interests of consumers and has had a great deal of success in investigating and preventing unfair trade practices.

Consumer Credit Act 1974

This deals with credit transactions and states:

● All businesses connected with the granting of credit must be licenced, eg banks, moneylenders and retailers.
● Those providing credit are jointly liable with the businesses selling the goods for any which are faulty.
● There should be a 'cooling off' period during which goods bought on credit in your name can be returned if you change your mind.
● When buying on credit, you must be told the full cash price so that you can see how much extra you are paying.

Local government services to the consumer

In addition to national legislation, local bodies are also concerned with consumer protection. Amongst the first consumer protection bodies were the local authority **weights and measures departments** who had the job of checking measuring instruments such as shop scales and petrol pumps. These departments have been replaced by local **trading standards departments** which have a much wider role in consumer protection as the extract below demonstrates.

Figure 23: Work of a trading standards officer

A DAY IN THE LIFE OF A BUSY TRADING STANDARDS OFFICE

Department store
9.30 Mr Robinson and I leave the office for a major department store in Bromley High Street. The store is visited every three months or so. A thorough inspection of the store, which is carried out less often, can take 2½ days, much of the time being spent in examining labels that describe the fibre content of garments ('85% cotton' etc.).

Garage
2.05 Second-hand cars. We arrive at the garage and head for the used car depot. This garage sells a high proportion of ex-company cars which are often more vulnerable to such practices as altering the mileage.

After meeting the manager we start to look at the cars on sale, most of which cost upwards of £2,000. All have a disclaimer 'Trade Descriptions Act 1968 – This mileage is not guaranteed'. We also look for evidence of high mileage such as different tyres to the originals fitted, worn upholstery, touched-up paintwork and overlooked service invoices left in the glove compartment.

Supermarket
3.25 We visit a supermarket in a town within the Borough of Bromley. Mr. Nelson spends about a day a week in supermarkets. He always carries with him the latest edition of the monthly publication Shaw's Guide to Fair Retail Prices. This gives the recommended prices of all brand name products to be found in supermarkets and is used mainly to check that bargain offers really are the bargains they are said to be.

Source: *Consumer News*

Another local authority department which deals with consumer issues is the **environmental health department**. Their role is one of protecting the public health but this includes checking on the standards of cleanliness and hygiene on premises selling food.

Some local authorities also run **consumer advice centres** which provide information and advice to shoppers. A similar function could be provided by a local **citizen's advice bureau** who advise on a range of issues including consumers legal rights. These can be found in most towns and are staffed partly by full-time employees but mainly by trained volunteers. It is estimated that they deal with 3.25 m enquiries a year.

Other services to consumers

There are a wide range of other services available to help the consumer.

Codes of Practice

Many trade associations draw up codes of practice for their members. A code of practice is a set of rules which they voluntarily agree to abide by.

We have already seen how the Advertising Standards Authority has drawn up a code of practice for its members. Similar codes exist in trades such as travel agents and motor traders. Complaints against members may be investigated by the association and those who ignore the codes of practice may be excluded from membership.

Figure 24: Examples of trade associations

Association of British Travel Agents

Motor Agents Association

Product labelling

Many manufacturers have responded to pressure from the government and consumer groups to provide better information on product labels.

Independent associations

In addition to trade associations, there are a number of independent associations offering advice to consumers. Amongst the better known of these are the AA and RAC offering advice to motorists, and the Consumers Association which offers general advice through its monthly publication *'Which'?*

The National Consumer Council

This was set up by the government in 1975 to carry out research into consumer problems. It acts as a pressure group and has strong links with other consumer organisations.

Employment legislation

Over the years, a great deal of legislation has been passed to protect the interests of employers.

Contracts of employment

The basis of employment is a legally binding contract between employers and employees.

In the case of a contract of employment, a written document is drawn up. All employees working more than 16 hours per week must be given a contract by their employer within 13 weeks of starting work. This contract will contain the following details:

● The names of the employer and the employee.
● The date on which employment started.
● The title of the job the employee is to do.
● The hours of work.
● The rate, timing and method of calculation of wage payments.
● The entitlement to holiday and sick pay.
● Pension rights.
● The length of notice required to terminate employment.

The employee should also be provided with details of disciplinary rules and what to do in the event of a grievance against the employer.

Dismissal of employees

Employees must be given a minimum of one week's notice of dismissal once they have been employed for four weeks. After two years this increases to a period of one week for each year's service up to a maximum of 12 weeks.

'Fair' dismissal can come about for a number of reasons:

● An employee's performance or conduct is inadequate and does not improve after formal warnings have been given.
● A post becomes redundant, ie the job is no longer required.

● It would be illegal to continue the employment.

There are usually strict procedures laid down for dismissal. Dismissal without notice is rarely justified. It is normal for an employee to be given a verbal warning of unsatisfactory conduct or performance, followed by a written warning if there is no improvement. If the problem remains, there may be a right to a formal hearing, often with the employee being represented by his or her trade union.

Putting an employee in a position where he or she is forced to resign may be regarded as constructive dismissal. It may therefore be seen as unfair and in breach of the contract of employment.

Circumstances in which dismissal without notice may be considered fair include:

● Stealing from the employer.
● Fighting on the employer's premises.
● Repeated absenteeism.
● Refusal to obey reasonable instructions.
● Gross misconduct such as persistent drunkenness.
● Breach of safety rules.

In the case of redundancy, an employee working more than 21 hours per week, and with at least two years service, is entitled to redundancy pay

---

Unfair dismissal

Mrs Fielding has been employed by a large retailer for the past six years. She is unhappy with the pay and conditions at her place of employment and has been active in encouraging her colleagues to join a trade union.

In June 1987, the store manager announces that the turnover of the store has fallen and head office have decided that two of the fifteen full-time staff will have to be made redundant. A week later, Mrs Fielding and another female colleague are told verbally by the manager that their employment is to be terminated at the end of the week. No redundancy payment is offered and no further information is provided.

1 Has the management acted correctly? Explain your answer, referring to the relevant legislation.
2 If Mrs Fielding considers that she has been unfairly dismissed, what can she do about it?

based on age and number of years of employment.

If the rules for fair dismissal are not observed, the dismissal is said to be 'unfair' and employees can complain to an **industrial tribunal**. When dismissal is judged to be unfair the employee is entitled to be given his job back and can also claim compensation.

Industrial relations legislation

It is only since 1971, with the passing of the Industrial Relations Act, that the government has attempted to influence negotiations between employers and workers. Since then, further legislation has been passed dealing with such issues as:

● Limits on picketing of the workplace, eg only a reasonable number of pickets on each factory gate.
● Restrictions on 'secondary picketing', ie picketing a work place other than that which is the subject of the dispute, such as coalminers picketing a power station.
● Public money being made available for secret ballots on strikes and on the appointment of union officials.

Health and safety legislation

The main pieces of legislation dealing with health and safety are the 1961 Factories Act and the 1963 Shop and Railway Premises Act. These Acts have been updated and revised by the 1974 Health and Safety at Work Act. The main objectives of this legislation are:

● To ensure the health, safety and welfare of employees.
● To protect the health and safety of visitors to business premises.
● To control the storage and handling of dangerous substances.
● To establish a **health and safety officer** in every place of work.

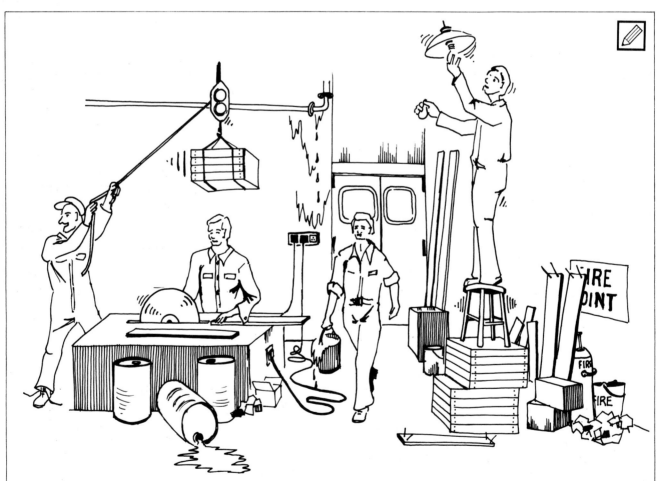

The cartoon illustrates a number of situations which could prove dangerous to workers. How many can you identify?

Explain exactly why each might prove dangerous.

The Act places a number of duties on both employers and employees. The duties of the employer include:

● To maintain plant and systems of work which are safe and without risk to health.
● To ensure safety in the use, handling, storage and transport of articles and substances.
● To provide training and supervision in health and safety matters for employees.
● To ensure that the workplace is maintained in a safe condition.
● To provide adequate facilities for the welfare of employees.
● To ensure that people not in direct employment are not exposed to risk.

The duties of employees include:

● Taking reasonable care for their own health and safety and for other workers.
● Co-operating with employers in meeting health and safety requirements.
● Not misusing or interfering with safety equipment.

Other protection at work

There are several other pieces of legislation which protect the interests of employees at work.

Wage payments

The Truck Acts (1831–1941) were designed to safeguard manual and shop workers against the payment of wages in kind, rather than in cash. The legislation also limited the ability of an employer to make deductions from wages, other than statutory deductions, eg income tax and National Insurance. This automatic right of manual workers to insist on being paid in cash has now been removed by the 1986 Wages Act, which should result in an increase in non-cash systems of wage payment such as cheques and bankers orders.

Sex discrimination

The Sex Discrimination Act (1975) makes discrimination on grounds of sex unlawful in employment and education. A body called the **Equal Opportunities Commission** has been set up to enforce the legislation and disputes concerning discrimination in employment can be taken to an industrial tribunal.

The legislation states that there should be equal treatment of the sexes and that there should be no discrimination on the basis of sex or marital status.

This legislation supports the Equal Pay Act which came into force at the same time and is designed to ensure that there is no discrimination between men and women in terms of conditions of employment. A woman employed in the same job as a man must have the same conditions of employment and rate of pay.

This legislation is strengthened by European Laws. The Treaty of Rome states that men and women must receive equal pay for doing equal work. What is meant by 'equal work' is still open to dispute however.

Jean Taylor is a secretary with the Shirebrook Building Society. She has worked as a cashier with the society for five years and has just had an unsuccessful interview for the post of senior cashier.

The job has been given to John Ellis, a recent recruit who has been with the society for two years since leaving school.

A couple of days after the interview, a friend overhears a conversation in the staff canteen where the personnel officer who conducted the interview is heard to say:

'It makes no sense to give senior posts to women as they leave after a few years to have a family. Women are always off work with minor ailments or for domestic reasons. The senior cashier post is a stepping stone to further promotion and only men go on to management posts. The female cashiers would not be prepared to work for another woman and prefer a male supervisor.'

1   Draft a letter from Jean to the personnel manager setting out her argument against these comments.
2   What legal action could Jean take if she feels she is being unfairly discriminated against?

Racial discrimination

The Race Relations Act (1976) forbids discrimination on racial grounds.

The **Commission for Racial Equality** was set up under the Act to enforce the legislation and to promote racial equality. Disputes over discrimination in employment can be referred to an industrial tribunal.

The terms of the Act cover nationality, colour and ethnic origin. As with sex discrimination, it is unlawful to discriminate on racial grounds in offering employment or in the conditions of employment, including training opportunities or promotion prospects.

In all cases of discrimination, be it sex or racial, care must be taken to avoid indirect as well as direct discrimination. Indirect discrimination is where it appears that opportunities are equal but one group is still favoured. Adverts such as the one below could be seen to favour one sex over the other, although direct discrimination has been avoided.

WANTED

Personal Assistant

Must be attractive with pleasant manner

Males or females may apply

Write to: J. Hermitage, 15–18 Moor Street, London, SW1

QUICK QUIZ

1. List the five main external factors affecting a business.
2. Distinguish between the current account and the capital account on the balance of payments.
3. List the benefits of international trade to:

   a a firm
   b consumers.

4. How does the Export Credit Guarantee Department help to encourage international trade?
5. Briefly explain four motives for controlling the import of goods.
6. List three methods of controlling the import of goods.
7. What is meant by the 'depreciation' of a currency?
8. a Briefly explain what is meant by economic growth.
   b How can the rate of growth be increased?
9. Give a brief definition of:

   a inflation
   b hyper-inflation
   c demand pull inflation
   d cost push inflation.

10. How may firms benefit from high levels of unemployment in the economy?

11. Briefly describe the main causes of unemployment.
12. What is the difference between 'monetary policy' and 'fiscal policy'?
13. List three forms of action which a pressure group can take.
14. List three favourable and three unfavourable results of rapid technological change.
15. What are the three main factors influencing the size of the total population?
16. Why is the age distribution of the population important to business?
17. List three social costs which result from business activity.
18. Name two Acts of Parliament which relate to:

   a the setting up and conduct of an organisation
   b the organisation's relationship with employees
   c the organisation's relationship with customers.

19. Name five of the pieces of information contained in a contract of employment.
20. Under what circumstances could an employee be dismissed without notice?

Index

above the line 47
ACAS 114–115
account group 49
activity rates 158
administrative barriers 147
administrative economies 75
advertising
    – agency 48–49
    – benefits 51–52
    – control 49–51
    – criticisms 51
    – definition 45
    – media 46–48
    – types 46
Advertising Standards Authority (ASA) 49
advice note 128
agencies 48
agents 57
air transport 62
annual report 133–134
answering machines 107
application forms 89
appointment 90
appropriation account 130
arbitration 115
articles of association 17
assets 131
assisted areas 81
audit 129
auditor's report 134, 135
authorised share capital 119
authority 23
autocratic leadership 29

balanced portfolio 123
balance of official financing 145
balance of payments 145–146
balance sheet 131–133
banded offers 52
bank notes 7
Bank of England 125
bankruptcy 135
bar codes 60
barter 6
batch costing 139
batch production 68
bear market 121
below the line 47
benchmark jobs 98
Big Bang 122
birth rate 158
board of directors 27
Bolton Committee 78
book value 133
branding 32

brand names 41–42
break even 140–141
British Code of Advertising Practice 49–50
British Standards Institute (BSI) 72
brokers 122
Budget 152
budgeting 137
budget standards 135
building societies 126
bull market 121
business documents 128
buying economies 75

capacity 71
capital 2
capital
    – account 145
    – gains tax 153
    – goods 10
    – intensive 71
cash flow forecast 137
casual unemployment 150
CBI 114
certificate of incorporation 17
chairman 27
chairman's report 134
channel of distribution 56–61
charity promotions 52
cheques 123
cif 145
citizen's advice bureau 168
clearing banks 123–125
closed shop 112
cluster sample 35
Code of Advertising Practice 49
Code of Sales Promotion Practice 52
codes of practice 168
coins 7
collection agencies 138
collective bargaining 110–115
combative advertising 46
commercial banks 123–125
commercial services 11
Commission for Racial Equality 171
communication 102–108
communication technology 106–108
competition policy 165
competitive pricing 66
components 69
conciliation 115
conditions of demand 64
conditions of supply 64
confravision 107
conglomerate merger 76
consultative leadership 29

consultation 103
consumer advice centres 168
Consumer Credit Act 167
consumer demand 63
consumer goods 10
consumer law 166–169
consumer panels 37
Consumer Protection Act 166
consumer spending 144
consumer trials 73
containers 62
contract costing 139
contract of employment 90, 169
controlling 28
convenor 114
co-operatives 19–20, 58
co-ownership 110
corporate advertising 46
corporate image 54
corporation tax 153
cost benefit analysis 163
costing methods 139–140
cost plus pricing 65
cost push inflation 149
costs of production 138–141
coupons 52
craft unions 111
credit card 124
credit note 128
cumulative preference shares 119
current account 124, 145
current assets 128, 131
current liabilities 132
current ratio 135
customer relations 54
customs duties 154
cyclical unemployment 151

databases 108
day release 92
death rates 158
debentures 126
debtor control 138
decentralisation 24
declining balance 133
de-industrialisation 9
delegates 114
delegation 23
delivery notes 128
demand 63
demand curve 63
demand pull inflation 149
democratic leadership 29
departments 24
department stores 58
dependency ratio 60
deposit account 124
depreciation 132–133, 148
design 71
desk research 36
development areas 81
differential pricing 66

direct costs 139
direct debit 124
direct labour 71
directors 17
director's report 134
direct policy 152
direct selling 57
direct services 11
direct taxes 153
discipline 28
discount stores 58
dismissal 164
distribution 55–63
diversification 77
dividend 119–120
dividend yield ratio 137
division of labour 7–8
door-to-door sales 59
dumping 147
durable goods 10

economic growth 148
economies of scale 75
efficiency ratios 136
electronic point of sale (EPOS) 60
embargo 147
employee co-operatives 20
employer's associations 114
employment agencies 89
employment legislation 169
enterprise 2
enterprise zones 81
environmental health department 168
Equal Opportunities Commission 171
Equal Pay Act 171
equilibrium price 65
equities 119
estimate 128
excise duties 154
executive directors 27
executive search 89
Export Credit Guarantee Department 147
exports 145
extension strategies 41
external advertising 88
external communication 106
extractive industries 10

facsimilie transmission (FAX) 107
factors of production 2
factory shop 57
Fair Trading Act 167
field research 36
finance corporation 127
finance department 118
finance house 126
financial accountant 137
financial economies 75
financial ratios 135–137
fiscal policies 152
fixed assets 127, 131
fixed costs 138–139

flow production   68
fob   145
Food and Drugs Act   166
foreign banks   126
foreign exchange markets   148
formal communication   105
formal consultation   109
formal organisation   25
franchising   60–61
free enterprise   4–5
freefone   107
free offers   52
free samples   52
frictional unemployment   150
FT 30 Index   121
functional relationships   25

general partners   16
general unions   111
generic advertising   46
gossip   106
government finance   127
grapevine   26, 106
gross pay   96
group PBR   96

head hunting   89
Health and Safety at Work Act   170
Herzberg   101
hidden unemployment   151
hierarchy of needs   101
hire purchase   126
holding company   17
horizontal communication   105–106
horizontal merger   75
hygiene factors   101
hyperinflation   149
hypermarkets   58

import controls   147
imports   145
income tax   96, 153
incorporation   14
Independent Broadcasting Authority (IBA)   50
independent trader   57–58
indirect costs   139
indirect labour   71
indirect taxes   153
induction   90–91
industrial concentration   74–78
industrial inertia   80
Industrial Relations Act   170
industrial tribunals   115
industrial union   111
inflation   148–149
informal communication   106
informal organisation   26
informative advertising   46
infrastructure   10
initiation rites   26
institutional investors   123
interest   118
inter-firm comparisons   135

internal candidates   87–88
internal communication   105–106
internal organisation   22–29
international finance   147–148
international trade   144–147
interviews   36, 90
investment appraisal   141
investment ratios   137
invisible trade   145
invoice   128
issued share capital   119
issuing house   123

jobbers   122
job
   – centres   89
   – costing   139
   – descriptions   86
   – enlargement   100
   – enrichment   99
   – evaluation   98
   – grading   98
   – production   68
   – ranking   98
   – rotation   99
   – specification   86
joint-stock company   119

labour   2, 71
labour
   – direct   71
   – indirect   71
   – intensive   70
   – needs   85–86
   – quality   71
   – turnover   85–86
land   2, 69
lateral merger   75
leadership   28–29
lease   69
leasing   127
legal personality   14
liability   131
lifestyle   161–162
limited company   16
limited liability   14
limited partnership   16
line management   25
line relationships   25
liquidation   14, 135–136
liquidity ratios   135–136
loan guarantee scheme   127
loans   124
location   79–82
logos   54
loss leaders   54

mail order   58
maintenance   72
management
   – accountant   137
   – process   27–29
   – role   26–27

managerial economies 75
managing director 27
managing technology 157
market
    – definition 4
    – prices 63–66
    – research 33–38, 73
    – segmentation 34
    – stages 34
marketing
    – definition 32
    – department 32
    – economies 75
    – history 32
    – mix 31
markets 4
mark-up 65
Maslow 101
McGregor 101
mediation 115
medium of exchange 6
memoranda 104
memorandum of association 17
merchant banks 126
mergers 75–76
migration 158
minutes 104
mixed economy 6
mobile outlets 59
monetarists 152
monetary policy 152
money
    – attributes 7
    – functions 7
    – shops 59
monopoly 165
Monopoly and Mergers Commission 165
motivation 101–102
motivational research 38
multinational company 19
multiple stores 58

National Consumer Council 169
national debt 125
national executive 114
National Girobank 126
national insurance 96, 154
National Savings Bank 126
nationalised industries 6, 20–21
natural wastage 85
negotiation 103
net pay 96
non-executive directors 27
non-financial rewards 99
notice 90

objectives 27
observation 38
obsolescence 39
offer for sale 122
Office of Fair Trading 163
official strike 112
off-the-job training 92

OFTEL 165
on-the-job training 92
operating costs 139
opportunity costs 4
oral communication 104
orders 128
ordinary partnership 16
ordinary shares 119
organisation charts 23–24
organising 28
overdrafts 124
overheads 139
own label products 60

packaging 42–43
parent company 17
participating preference shares 119
partnership 15
partnership agreement 15
party plans 59
patenting 73
pay as you earn (PAYE) 96
payment by results 95
payment systems 94–96
payment terms 129
pay slip 97
penetration pricing 65
perks 99
personality promotions 52
personnel specifications 86
persuasive advertising 46
persuasive leadership 29
physical distribution 61–63
picketing 170
piece work 95
placing 122
planned economy 6
planning 22
point of sale promotion 53
points rating 98
pollution 162
population
    – age distribution 161
    – geographical distribution 159
    – occupational distribution 160
    – pyramids 161
postal questionnaire 36
preference shares 119
premium offers 52
pressure groups 154–155
Prestel 108
prices 63–66
primary data 36
primary production 10
prime costs 139
private limited company 17
private sector 14–20
privatisation 20–22
prize promotion 52
process costing 139
product brief 73
product development 39, 73

production
- batch 68
- flow 68
- job 68
- line 99–100
- personnel 68
- process 68
- scale 74
- services 71
- technology 157
product launch 74
product life cycle 39–41
Professional and Executive Recruitment 89
profit 118
profit and loss account 130
profit sharing 96, 110
progressive taxes 153
promotional pricing 66
prospectus issue 122
prototype 73
psychological pricing 66
public
- corporations 20
- limited company 17
- relations 54–55
- sector 20–22
- services 11
prospectus issue 122
published accounts 130–137
purposive sample 35

quality control 43, 72
quality inspectors 72
quotas 147
quota sample 35
quotation 128

racial discrimination 171
radiopaging 107
radiophones 107
rail transport 62
random sampling 35
recruitment 86–91
redundancy 85, 169
references 89
regional development grants 81
regional policy 80–82
regressive tax 153
rent 2
reports 133–134
resale price maintenance 165
research agencies 38
research and development (R & R) 39, 72–74
research methods 36
reserves 132
residual unemployment 151
responsibility 23
restrictive practices 165
Restrictive Practices Court 165
retail audit 37
retail branding 42
retail co-operatives 19

retail outlet 57–61
retail price index (RPI) 148
return on capital employed (ROCE) 136
rights issue 122
risk-bearing economies 75
road transport 61–62
rumour 106

salaries 94
Sale of Goods Act 166
sales promotion 52–54
samples 35
sampling methods 35
scale of production 74–79
seasonal unemployment 150
sea transport 62
secondary data 36
secondary production 10
selection 89–90
self-service 59
selling economies 75
sex discrimination 171
share capital 132
shareholders 16
shares – types 119
shareholders' funds 132
shift work 70
shop stewards 114
shortlists 89
single use goods 10
skimming 65
sleeping partners 16
small firms 78–79
social benefits 162–163
social capital 10
social costs 162–163
sole trader 15
sources and application of funds 134
sources of finance 118–127
span of control 24
specialisation 7
staff appraisal 93
staff colleges 93
staff relationships 25
stages of production 10–11
standing order 124
statements 128
state run banks 126
stock control 69
Stock Exchange 120–123
straight line depreciation 133
stratified sample 35
structural unemployment 150
subsistence economy 6
supermarkets 58
supply 63–64
supply curve 63

take-home pay 96–97
takeover 75
tariffs 147
taxation 153–154

technical economies   75
technological change   155–158
technological unemployment   150
telecommunications   107–108
teleconferencing   107
telephone communications   104
telephone surveys   36
telex   108
tertiary production   11
test marketing   37
theory x   101
theory y   101
time rates   94–95
token stoppage   112
trade credit   127
Trade Descriptions Act   167
trade directories   107
Trade Union Congress (TUC)   114
trade unions   105, 110–115
trading account   130
trading standards department   168
training   91–94
transport   61–63
trend analysis   135
turnover   130
two-tier boards   109

underwriters   122, 123
unemployment   149–151
unfair dismissal   169
Unsolicited Goods and Services Act   167

value added   3
value added tax   153
variable costs   139
variety chains   58
vending machines   59
vertical communication   105
vertical merger   75
viewdata   107
visible trade   145
voluntary chains   58
vouchers   52

wages   94, 97–99
wealth   2
Weights and Measures Act   166
weights and measures department   168
Welfare State   9
white collar unions   111
wholesalers   56–57
word processors   107
worker directors   109
worker participation   109
working population   158
work study   71
work to rule   112
written communication   104

yield   120
YTS   92–93